THE GREAT GUNNERY SCANDAL

Arthur Pollen

THE
GREAT GUNNERY
SCANDAL

The Mystery of Jutland

ANTHONY POLLEN

COLLINS
St James's Place, London
1980

William Collins Sons & Co Ltd
London · Glasgow · Sydney · Auckland
Toronto · Johannesburg

First published 1980
© Anthony Pollen 1980

ISBN 0 00 216298 9

Set in Garamond
Made and Printed in Great Britain by
T. J. Press (Padstow) Ltd, Padstow, Cornwall
for William Collins Sons & Co Ltd, Glasgow

CONTENTS

DIAGRAMS OF
THE BATTLE OF JUTLAND

EPIGRAPH

The mystery of Jutland is not that
there was an unforeseen factor
that robbed us of victory.
It was simply that a factor that
was foreseen and provided for
was not understood by those to whom
the nation had entrusted its security.

A. H. Pollen. *The XIX*th *Century*. August 1927

AUTHOR'S PREFACE

I well remember the day when my father's name first appeared on the cover page of *Land and Water*. I had grown accustomed to reading occasional articles in the *Westminster Gazette* or the *Sunday Times* by 'our Naval correspondent, A. H. Pollen', but it was obvious even to my untutored eye, that to be rated on a par with the celebrated Hilaire Belloc, in the leading war weekly of the day, was something rather different.

To his two schoolboy sons it was a constant embarrassment to be asked how it was that, without having served in the Navy, he had become a recognized authority on naval affairs. For what could be more improbable than that a young barrister of thirty-four years of age should suddenly have decided to devote himself to the study of naval gunnery, a subject for which he had no possible qualification except the imagination to see that here was a matter of vital importance to the country, to which no attempt had yet been made to apply scientific principle. Then again, who would have believed that having embarked on this ambitious venture, he would, within five years, have become accepted as 'the pioneer of naval gunnery'? Not that either my brother or myself, at that time, had any but the vaguest idea of what he had done for the Navy, or what that phrase, beloved by his publicists, really meant.

For he was a man of wide interests, an amateur par excellence, capable of tremendous enthusiasms, intellectual, aesthetic or sporting. At home there was always something new and exciting to talk about and it was not in his nature to

9

dwell on past misfortune or injustices. In 1912 I had been too young to know what was happening when the Admiralty suddenly abandoned their right to the monopoly of his inventions and decided to make do with an inferior imitation. By the time I was fourteen he had become a personality, lionised by Society hostesses, with the Duke of Norfolk and other celebrities taking the chair for his lectures in aid of the Red Cross.

Nevertheless it was a revelation to read two years later an article in *Land and Water* by Admiral Sir Reginald Custance, the former Director of Naval Intelligence, eulogising his work and emphasising his standing and repute in professional circles. 'Seamen know him' wrote the Admiral 'as a creative and original thinker on naval war, whose investigations into the subject of fire control have revolutionised the art of naval fighting the world over, and should have revolutionised it altogether in our favour'. We longed to know more, but the article had appeared at a most critical moment of the war and life was far too exciting to get him to look back into the past and talk about his work with the Navy; and no sooner was the crisis over than he was off to America on an important mission of propaganda for the Navy. And so it went on, with always something new in the air and no time to waste on vain regrets over the past.

Thus it came about that it was not until my own retirement from business, in 1965, that I had the time or the energy to attempt a serious study of his contribution to naval thought. The papers had come to me three years earlier on my mother's death and my interest had been further stimulated by the fact that the operation of the fifty year rule (now thirty years) had led to the release of the official papers of the period and to the consequent production of a series of histories and biographies by the new generation of historians.

To them, my father's long years of close co-operation with the best brains in the Service were clearly a closed book. They knew him only as a severe critic of the tactics of Jutland and of the subsequent mishandling of the battle against the German submarine guerrillas: and they tended to write him off as a disappointed and disgruntled inventor with a grudge against Admiral Jellicoe, 'the man who turned him down before the war'.

Yet I soon found among the papers thick files of correspondence with such men as Sir Herbert Richmond, Sir Reginald Custance, Sir William Henderson and Sir Reginald Plunkett (later Ernle-Erle-Drax), which established beyond any possibility of doubt that over a long term of years, both before and after the war, he had been accepted as an equal by these leaders of thought.

As regards his relations with Admiral Jellicoe, there survives among my father's papers a file of forty of his handwritten letters mostly written during his time as Director of Naval Ordnance, which leave no doubt as to the sincerity of their early friendship. For example, in a letter dated 25th August 1907, on giving up his appointment as D.N.O., Jellicoe writes 'I have never received a more kindly expressed letter, and it has given me the greatest possible pleasure to know that you harbour no resentment against me for sundry "ten minutes" which have occurred' – and the three page letter ends, 'Anyhow my dear Pollen I have derived much pleasure from our acquaintance, official and social, and I hope very sincerely that the acquaintance, and if I may say so, friendship will continue, and needless to say I wish you every success both for the sake of the Service and for your own sake.'

Their friendship survived the ups and downs of my father's later bad relations with the Admiralty to the extent that after the Battle of Jutland, despite all the anxieties of the moment, Jellicoe found time within ten days of getting back to Scapa to write him no less than three hand-written letters. It is significant, too, to find my father six months later figuring as the principal attraction at a party given by Jellicoe in December 1916, for the wives and families of all ranks of the *Iron Duke*, on giving up his command to go to Whitehall as First Sea Lord.

An essential feature of my father's approach to gunnery was

his insistence that all tactics, whether on land or sea, were dependent upon the nature and effectiveness of the weapons employed. On land, the pike, the bow, the horse, the musket had all in their turn revolutionised tactics.

At sea, the introduction of steam, by relieving the commander of his dependence on the elements, had revolutionised naval warfare. To Pollen it seemed self-evident that a further no less important emancipation of the tactician would follow from the introduction of a system of fire control, such as he had to offer, which would make it possible to keep on hitting while ships were changing course at high speed.

This approach led him to a study of the whole question of battle tactics at sea and the related problems of ship design. To the serious student of naval warfare his early writings on these subjects, often printed for private circulation, may well prove to be the most interesting aspect of his work. They cover a wide field, beyond the scope of this personal story, and will shortly form the subject of a further publication by the Navy Records Society.

My purpose in now writing this brief monograph is first to tell the strange story of his rivalry with Frederic Dreyer which began in 1907, when Dreyer first came to the Admiralty as a gunnery lieutenant, and ended dramatically nearly twenty years later when the Royal Commission on Awards to Inventors, with Admiral Sir Frederic Dreyer, CBE, KCB, a Lord of Admiralty, and Arthur Pollen, standing before them as rival claimants, found in favour of my father and made him a handsome award, not, as might be expected, in respect of the instruments supplied by him to the Admiralty, but in respect of one that bore his rival's name.

To the generation that remembers Winston Churchill as the architect of victory over Hitler, it will come as a surprise to find Churchill cast in the role of the Minister responsible for the failure to insist on my father's far-reaching claims being properly tested. For there is a close parallel between the remarkable achievements of Doctor R. V. Jones, in what came to be known as 'The Battle of the Beams', in the 1940s, and Arthur Pollen's contribution to naval gunnery, a generation earlier. In each case the man of genius had to face the opposition of less enlightened officials. In each the man responsible for the final decision was Winston Churchill. Jones, in his admirable story *Most Secret War — British Scientific Intelligence 1939-45*, makes no secret of what he owed to the personal support of Winston Churchill. It is surely no mere coincidence that having been bluffed by the officials into the wrong decision in 1912, Churchill did not hesitate to override their successors in 1940, and back the man of genius.

My second objective is to recall my father's rise to fame and influence in his wartime role of naval writer and critic. From the start it can have been no easy task to have to defend and justify a regime from whose false doctrines and follies he had suffered for so long. Yet by mid-1916 we find him firmly ensconced as chief confidant and spokesman for the Whitehall Establishment, and at the same time on good terms with both Admiral Jellicoe, the Commander-in-Chief and Admiral Beatty, the dashing leader of the fast Battle-Cruiser Squadrons.

The Battle of Jutland, fought on the 31st May of that year was a big disappointment in the sense that we failed to win the decisive victory the country expected and needed. Yet my father remained faithful to Jellicoe and to the Establishment until the following spring when the successes of the German submarines against our merchant fleet seemed about to bring us to our knees. The question 'Can the Army win the war before the Navy loses it?' had ceased to be just a cruel sarcasm and become a live issue. Desperate measures were called for and all of a sudden my father discovered that the life of a naval critic in wartime could be as full of adventure and acrimony as that of an inventor.

The storm that blew up in April 1917 is not to be confused with the great Jutland controversy that developed after the war and in which my father again took a leading part. It is beyond the scope of this personal biography to seek to revive that debate, other than to make it clear that while he was critical of the defensive tactics officially adopted by the Fisher clique before the war, and resolutely adhered to by Jellicoe at Jutland, it was his belief, convincingly expressed on a number of occasions that Jellicoe was the victim not the author of those policies.

In presenting my story, I have had the benefit of my father's correspondence with his many friends in the Service and, in addition, the complete files of his official correspondence with the Admiralty at all levels: First Lord, Secretary, Director of Naval Ordnance and Director of Contracts. A further important source is provided by the briefs prepared for Counsel in preparation for the hearings before the Royal Commission on Awards to Inventors in 1923 and 1925. Then again, in the final stages of the dispute with the Admiralty in 1912 and 1913, a great many letters were written and drafts prepared which entailed setting out the history of my father's relations with the Admiralty since the earliest days. Finally, recent research among official records has brought to light three official reports, of which one confirms my father's belief as to the support he enjoyed among experts in the Service and the two others, *per contra*, throw light on the nature of the opposition.

In my narrative I have relied very largely on my father's interpretation of events, first checking against the facts of which we have documentary proof. Yet working from such sources it has not always been practicable to offer a convincing 'source' reference such as is customary in historical works.

To give but one example, the bald statement in Chapter IV as to the total failure of the manual plotting system with which the Navy had been ordered to experiment in the summer of 1908, lacks any supporting reference. The facts are, first, that its failure was common knowledge in the Service throughout the late summer, secondly that its failure was referred to time and again in my father's later correspondence and briefs for Counsel; and finally, and most importantly, that its total inadequacy was implicitly (but not explicitly) admitted by the

Admiralty, early in the New Year, when they agreed to reopen negotiations with my father for a re-trial of his mechanical system.

In these unusual circumstances, I venture to hope that readers faced with other seemingly unsupported statements, will reserve judgement until they have the whole story before them. For the proof of such statements is sometimes to be found, not in documents, but in the subsequent course of events.

In conclusion I wish to thank all the kind friends who have helped me to piece together this story of my father's long association with the Navy. First Captain Stephen Roskill, CBE, DSC, RN, the historian, now a Fellow of Churchill College, for his constant kindness and encouragement.

More recently, when all seemed settled, I had the good fortune to discover in Jon Sumida, of the University of Chicago, a keen student of British history who, in his search for the reasons behind Admiral Lord Fisher's espousal of the concept of the big gun battle-cruiser in 1905, and quite independently of my own parallel studies, had alighted upon Arthur Pollen with his promise of accurate long-range gunnery, as the source of Fisher's inspiration.

His infectious belief in the quality and originality of my father's writings, and in his influence on contemporary thought, his understanding of the technique of the computer, and above all his ready and friendly co-operation, have been a tremendous help.

Finally, I wish to thank Mr J. D. Brown of the Naval Historical Branch, Mr A. W. H. Pearsall of the National Maritime Museum and Mr Rod Suddaby of the Imperial War Museum for their understanding and patience in tracing essential documents of the period.

Of the papers which I inherited in 1962, my father's wartime writings in *Land and Water* and elsewhere are now held by Churchill College, Cambridge and the remainder are still in my possession.

July, 1980   ANTHONY POLLEN

CHAPTER I

The Pioneer of Naval Gunnery

Of Arthur Pollen's early life, the best account is that given by his life-long friend Theo Mathew, the barrister. In a characteristically neat little sketch that appeared in *The Tablet* as an obituary in January 1937, he has left a vivid picture of the precocious and self-confident schoolboy. Obituaries are rightly suspect, but as a record of his early life the account is unique; moreover, we see him here through the eyes of a no less brilliant contemporary. They had been boys together at the Oratory and both went on to Trinity, Oxford, and were later called to the Bar, where Mathew won for himself a reputation as one of the wittiest men in his illustrious profession:

> As a boy he had all the qualities of his maturity – energetic, clever and versatile, he did everything with ease. Those of us who were shy and clumsy admired his self-possession, and the slow-witted envied his effortless acquisition of book-learning. Even in those days he was a good speaker; he played the piano well by ear; by heredity he was an artist; he could sing a song; he played in the eleven; he won the 'Norfolk' prize for classics; and he was one of the star performers in the Latin play.
>
> At Oxford he made a considerable figure as a speaker at the Union, eloquently advocating the then unfashionable causes of Liberalism and Home Rule; and when, in 1887, Lord Randolph Churchill and Mr John Morley were guests of the Society, he was chosen to open the debate.
>
> Always ready to undertake any kind of task, he accepted Raper's invitation to prepare a design for the new ironwork flanking panels of the old Trinity gate, and his drawing was at

17

once accepted; and when, as a member of a reading party he found himself in a German village on the anniversary of Sedan, he did not hesitate when called upon for a speech, to address the crowd assembled below the balcony in their own tongue.

After leaving Oxford he began his many-sided career; for a time was a tutor; travelled with Lady Henry Somerset's son in the United States and Canada; shot tigers in India; was called to the Bar; stood for Parliament; was on the editorial staff of the Daily Mail; and then became a business man, a director of companies and an inventor.

Many of his friends regretted that he did not follow the profession for which he was so well fitted. A natural gift of speech and a handsome presence are assets of great value to a barrister; but, like many others, he dreaded the prospect of idle years of waiting.

Of his travels with Somers Somerset there is an excellent account in *The Land of the Muskeg*, written by Somerset and rather charmingly illustrated with sketches from Arthur Pollen's notebook. It covers the expedition they made together through the Rocky Mountains of Canada, in 1893. Starting in June from 'the little town of Edmonton', in Alberta, they worked their way up to Dunvegan and from there out west, crossing the Rockies by the Pine River Pass and returning to civilisation via McLeod Lake and the Fraser River. Although fortunate enough to have enlisted the help of the most famous Indian hunter in the district, their expectations as to the game they would find were grievously disappointed and for the last three weeks they were desperately short of food and on the verge of starvation. In all, they covered some 750 miles, much of the journey through the swampy Muskeg country, and part of it above the snow line: a great adventure from which they were fortunate to return unscathed.

A trip to India with Harry Whitney, a year later, conducted in the greatest luxury, provided a welcome contrast and gave him a further opportunity to indulge his love of big game hunting.

On his return to England he dedicated himself once more to his profession but as Theo Mathew has indicated, progress was slow and he found it necessary to supplement his meagre earnings by writing. His first patron was J. A. Spender of the *Westminster Gazette*. When asked a few years later what his status had been as a writer on the Westminster, Pollen defined his position as 'critic on artistic, literary and dramatic subjects', and included within that definition, music: a range of subjects which today would raise a smile from the editor of a school magazine. Yet the Westminster was already recognised as the most intelligent and highbrow evening paper in the country. In addition, an amusing series of sketches of proceedings and personalities in the Law Courts suggests that he was also in demand as a writer in a lighter vein on other subjects.

Against such a background, the decision to devote himself to the problems of Naval gunnery seems strangely out of character. The explanation lies first in the fact that in 1898 he had married the daughter of Joseph Lawrence[1], who in addition to being a Member of Parliament and Sheriff of the City of London, had brought the Linotype to this country. Linotype, although well established as the leading manufacturer of newspaper printing machinery, and incidentally, therefore, a manufacturer of precision instruments of the highest quality, was not without its problems, and Lawrence was shrewd enough to realise that his versatile son-in-law would be a valuable acquisition if he could be induced to join the business. In particular, Pollen's experience of Fleet Street and his knowledge of America would be valuable assets. The Linotype was an American invention and Lawrence could see the time coming when fresh terms would have to be negotiated with the parent company in New York, and who better to handle so important a mission than this forceful and intelligent young barrister. The invitation to join the company was fortified with the usual parental argument that it was time to settle down to a more stable and remunerative way of life. To this there was no easy answer and before the end of the year Arthur Pollen was installed as Managing Director.

Two years later, in February 1900, a family visit took him to Malta where his uncle, Sir Clement La Primaudaye RN, had been in office for twenty years as Superintendent of Police. On arrival he learnt that some units of the fleet would be going out in two days on gunnery trials. His hunting expeditions in the Rockies and in India had made him something of a marksman and he had retained his interest in shooting of all kinds. His curiosity about Naval gunnery led to the suggestion that he should attend the trials and by a happy chance his cousin Bill Goodenough[2], who was later to distinguish himself as Commodore of the Second Cruiser Squadron at Jutland, was in a position to invite him to sail as his guest, in the cruiser *Dido*.

The South African war was then at its height, Ladysmith had just been relieved and, by a singular coincidence, *The Times*, the very day they sailed, carried a lengthy account of the part played by the Navy's 4.7″ guns in silencing the enemy's artillery at a range of 10,000 yards.

In the trials, he saw the Navy's largest guns, the 13.5″s of the *Empress of India*, being employed very ineffectively at a range of under 2000 yards.

To Pollen the contrast between what was being so unsuccessfully attempted at Target Practice and what had been achieved on land in South Africa made a deep impression.

As a sportsman with experience of shooting both big game and small, Pollen knew the difference between shooting with a rifle at Bisley and with a gun on the moor. On the one hand the painstaking accuracy of the marksman, achieved with the aid of a telescope and sights precisely calibrated for range: on the other, the quickness of hand and eye and the judgement of speed and distance required to bring down driven grouse in full flight.

Watching the Battle Practice he had at once perceived that the Navy were employing the technique of the sportsman on a task crying aloud for scientific aid. A simple calculation showed that at a range of ten miles, a range already within the capacity of the big guns of the day, the enemy ship would be capable of travelling nearly a quarter of a mile while the projectile was in flight and at least as far again while the sights were being set and the guns trained on the target. This meant that at long ranges the gunnery officer would have found himself faced with the impossible task not merely of correcting observed errors, but of guessing where to aim the next salvo.

Little wonder that, in 1900, gunnery practice even with the largest guns was limited to ranges of less than a mile, and little wonder, too, that Pollen at once declared that the system employed never could make long range gunnery a practical proposition.

To his surprise he found that the Navy was not even contemplating the application of mathematical science to the problem. Pollen returned from Malta with his mind in a turmoil at the discovery that Naval gunnery was still at so primitive a stage. Could it be that this was the great opportunity of his life – a new and unexplored science of vital importance to the country and a matter of the utmost urgency? All of a sudden the Managing Director's chair at Linotype, in which but two years before he had so reluctantly taken his place, had been transformed overnight from a place of confinement to an ideal base from which to embark on his great adventure. Bill Goodenough and the other young officers to whom he ventilated his ideas saw the point and welcomed his enterprise, but made no secret of the difficulties they foresaw, above all in handling Whitehall. There was nothing unusual about a layman inventing new weapons – indeed it was the normal pattern. But here he was concerned not with weapons or instruments but with the method of their use. How would the Admiralty react to a suggestion from a layman that their whole system of fire control should be mechanised – that instead of relying on the eye and judgement of the gunnery officer, elaborate instruments should be devised, first, to record the movements of the enemy ship and next to calculate the appropriate settings for the sights?

Undeterred by the obvious difficulties, Pollen had sufficient self-confidence, vision, sense of duty, call it what you will, to dedicate himself to the study of Naval gunnery. Within a year[3] he had addressed a letter to Lord Walter Kerr, the First Sea Lord, setting forth his ideas and offering to manufacture a set of instruments which would make it possible to find the speed and course of any ship that could be kept under observation, up to a range of 20,000 yards. He drew their Lordships' attention to the tactical advantage of having such information constantly before the commander, and went on to claim that with his instruments there would be a better chance of scoring hits on the enemy ship at 10,000 yards than hitherto at 5000 yards. In the light of later history, it is interesting to note that in this his first communication, the tactical importance of the information was put first, the aid to gunnery second. Lord Walter Kerr was a family friend, but the letter was written in formal style as from the Managing Director of the Linotype Company. Even so, for a young man of thirty-four, who had only once been to sea in a warship, to address himself direct to the First Sea Lord with the suggestion, however courteously expressed, that their Lordships' gunnery could be greatly improved by the adoption of scientific principles, was certainly courageous if not presumptuous, and it was no great surprise when he was informed that his proposals were of no interest to their Lordships.

However, he persevered with his investigations and two years later, paid a second visit to Malta. This time the atmosphere in naval circles was very different. Much had happened since his first visit. In particular, Captain (later Admiral Sir) Percy Scott on the China Station, had had a tremendous success with his new system of training naval gunners. Prior to his reform, the elevation of the gun was fixed and the art of the gunner lay in his ability to fire at the precise moment when the roll of the ship brought his gun on to the target. Scott, inspired perhaps by his experience of shooting game, introduced the practice known as 'continuous aim'. This was achieved by employing two competent men, one to control the elevation of the gun, the other, the lateral training. By this method Scott had virtually overcome the basic difficulties of pitch and roll, and thereby increased the effective range of his guns from 2000 yards to 3000. Up to 3000 yards or thereabouts, the big guns were firing 'point-blank', that is to say the trajectory of the projectile was virtually flat and no allowance had to be made for range. Beyond that figure the extra height required to get the distance and the consequent sharp angle of descent made knowledge of the range essential; and it was here that Pollen had to take over from Scott. The task before him was formidable and from the start he realised that no effective solution could ever be developed without experience at sea, which in effect meant without the co-operation of the Admiralty.

In these early days no question arose of competition. The young and intelligent school of gunnery men with whom he was in contact recognised the need for research, and welcomed his intervention: they knew that as a layman he could talk to Whitehall in a way that was denied to them and they gave him every assistance. Yet the opposition to his ideas was vocal, powerful and not always unintelligent. An influential body of opinion refused to believe that naval battles ever would be fought at long range, and deplored the time and thought that was being given to long range gunnery and the consequent neglect of the vital art of fighting at what was called decisive ranges. 'What will you do' they asked, 'if the enemy, having specialised in short range fighting are determined to close the range, and advance at full speed? Are you going to order the British ships to turn and run so as to maintain the long range at which you believe yourselves to be superior?' This was no idle question for the opinion was widely held, right up to the outbreak of war, that the Germans had no faith in long distance gunnery and if cornered would seek to close and fight at short range.

Finally they went so far as to claim that the success of the Japanese against the Russians at Tsushima was due in no small measure to their lack of system and the consequent spread of fire. The argument ran as follows:

> Had there been a well organised system by which all guns fired together any mistake made by the system would have been repeated by every gun. There being no system there were a great number of misses but so many shots were fired and with such a fine freedom of selection that there was inevitably a good proportion of hits.

Tsushima was virtually the only naval action fought under modern conditions from which to argue and the Japanese had scored a quick and decisive victory. Arthur Pollen's reply was that it reminded him of Charles Lamb's story of the Chinese burning down their houses in the hope that a pig would be roasted in the process.

Allied to these reasoned arguments and doubts, there were the prejudices of the old school against the introduction of machinery; the old sea dogs who thought it madness to make our gunnery dependent on delicate instruments that would inevitably be shot away or break down in action conditions. They preferred to rely on the fighting qualities of the British sailor who had never known defeat.

In the early years, these objections, coupled with a natural scepticism as to the possibility of devising the necessary instruments, threatened to prevent his ever getting started. Years later, after the break with the Admiralty in 1912, he was often accused of having been dictatorial and intolerant in his dealings with the Admiralty. Yet as we shall see, he had a great deal to put up with and for a man by nature so quick in repartee, it is remarkable how few mistakes he made; to this day, the long years of patient but lively propaganda make impressive reading. Among the papers that survive is a reprint, privately circulated in 1906, under the title *Jupiter Letters*, of extracts from six letters addressed personally to senior friends in the Service in an attempt to convince them of the importance of being the first power to develop an effective system of long-range gunnery. In contrast to the formal submissions to the specialist departments at Whitehall, these propaganda letters reveal an attractively light and imaginative touch. For example:

Am I guilty of lèse majesté in suggesting that there is not a little amateurishness in the kind of way 'engaging under battle conditions' is sometimes discussed? When you think of it, if we went to war tomorrow every gunnery lieutenant would be liable to be called upon to engage a fast moving target at a moment's notice, and this is a thing of which not a single one of them, nor any Captain, nor any Admiral has had any practical experience whatever. It took hours the other day to convince ——— and Admiral ——— that the problem was going to be so very different from battle practice. 'Oh!' they said, 'with very few shots we should certainly get the enemy's speed within a knot or so, his course within a point or so; we can always get his bearing approximately'. That is the kind of talk that I call amateurish. They do not know that they can do what they say, and, if they could do it, it would not take them very far.

These opinions are not popular. They do not sort with the kind of gush which brilliant journalists in and out of the Service supply to the technical and lay press about naval gunnery and gunnery progress. But I doubt if there are half-a-dozen Admirals or Captains who do not, in their heart of hearts, share them. Have you ever met one who did not hold that our proper tactics in action would be to close to decisive range as quickly as possible? I have heard the phrase a dozen times. It tells you a good deal. It means that we have a well-founded belief that at ranges where range finding and change of range are not problems – i.e., 4000 yards or under – our superior fire discipline and the excellence of our gun layers' training should give us a crushing advantage. But what a confession of impotence to solve the problem of using our artillery. It virtually admits that all our fire control is but an elaborate attempt to improve the chances for a few first hits only. It is not a method of gunnery complete and final in itself. Yet I have seen a 12in. gun placing shot after shot in a forty yards circle at 8000 yards. Why are we not to use them at these ranges, and at these ranges only? Merely because we have no means of making the hit – not want of skill in aiming – not want of brains in the officers – not want

of zeal, keenness, discipline – solely want of right method of getting the data for the proper elevation and deflection of the gun.

A striking feature of the letters is the elementary nature of
the arguments advanced. By the end of 1905 when they were
written, Pollen had been at work for four years, and for the last
six months engaged in trials at sea on one of His Majesty's
ships. Yet he has to keep reminding his correspondents, of
whom five were Admirals, that 'battle practice' as it was called,
bore no relation to true action conditions: that guesswork
could never be the equal of scientific calculation, and that
manual methods could never achieve the accuracy, rapidity or
reliability of machines.

He complains that what he calls the encyclicals of the so-
called naval experts and the pronouncements of the Navy
League were 'all in the same strain'. They thought and wrote
only in terms of statistics: they eulogised the speed, the weight
of broadside, and the rate of fire of our latest ships without ever
a thought for the real test of efficiency which was the ability of
the gun to hit. 'When will it finally be realised that it is hits and
hits only that count?' The old saying that 'only numbers can
annihilate' was still true, but only if related to the number of
hits – not the number of ships, tons or knots – just simply the
number of hits.

Even more striking is his insistence that by revolutionising
gunnery he would revolutionise naval warfare. 'I am not surprised at your scepticism of my claim that A.C.[4] will revolutionise naval warfare. It is one of those sweeping statements
that startles friends and delights enemies.' In his easy, casual
way he then proceeds to reel off his ideas as to how tactics and
ship design will have to be changed to conform to the requirements of long range hitting.

The new factors, Pollen wrote, would be the increased angle
of the projectile's descent and its decreased velocity. The increased angle would limit the positions that could safely be
taken relative to the enemy: the end-on position would become
barred and make new distribution of guns and armour

necessary. Guns all available broadside, armour, less vertical
(i.e. the walls of the ship) more horizontal (i.e. decks), and so
on.

He ends with the prophetic statement that 'if certain principles emerge there is no difficulty in showing how these principles will make new subdivisions of fleets possible and thus
multiply the means of bringing the enemy to battle.'

It is not contended that the ideas so lightly put forward in
these letters were incontrovertible; on the other hand the
range of subjects touched upon is remarkable as evidence of the
breadth of vision that inspired his approach to his subject.

The *Jupiter Letters* from which the above extracts are taken
were written in 1905-6, at a time when relations with the
Admiralty were still on a friendly and co-operative basis. It is
therefore gratifying to find a no less imaginative example of
Pollen's advocacy written two years later, to Reginald Bacon,
the rather hostile D.N.O. of the day, at a time when he was
smarting from the totally unjustified rejection of his system.
The letter dated 8 February 1908 runs as follows:

> You touch the heart of the matter when you say 'how far
> mechanisms should supersede the human brain involves serious
> practical considerations'. For the real issue as to the Admiralty
> taking or rejecting the A.C. system, turns on confidence or no
> confidence in machinery. The struggle is as old as the dawn of
> exact science. Galileo had far fiercer opponents in the
> astronomers than in the College of Cardinals. Harvey never got
> anyone over forty to believe in the circulation of the blood.
> Henry Bessemer's patents ran out before he could find an iron-
> master with intelligence enough to adopt his principles. The in-
> ventor of aniline dyes failed to find a capitalist to back him and
> so a British invention became the foundation of a vast German
> industry. Lord Kelvin could not be brought to believe in
> wireless telegraphy. Telephones were in use for twenty years
> before the London police heard of them. And the Navy has
> some odd records of its own.
>
> If you analyse it out, it is really the same spirit that kept
> masts and sails in ships for fifty years after steam was invented;

it is the spirit that inspired the remark that the screw propeller was an ingenious toy of no practical utility; exactly the same habit of mind that thought the monopoly of the Whitehead torpedo not worth buying – at a fraction of what was afterwards paid for it annually – because a well-handled spar torpedo was 'just as good' and the machinery of the fish torpedo could not be trusted to work.

The issue between A.C. and no A.C. is, I think exactly as you state in your letter, and I cannot help thinking that, in a matter of such crucial importance as getting hits in battle, the future must be with the machine.

The Pollen story inevitably highlights the lack of vision and the prejudices of the ruling clique at Whitehall in the decade that preceded the war of 1914. In fairness to the older generation, let us therefore look at what Admiral Sir William James has to say in their defence. In his delightful and illuminating life of Admiral Sir Reginald Hall, the famous war-time Director of Naval Intelligence, Sir William, himself one of the bright young gunnery men of his day, prefaces his story with a brief resumé of the role of the Royal Navy throughout the nineteenth century. He points out that after Trafalgar, the Navy was left for nearly a hundred years without a rival, before the Germans first appeared as challengers.

'During the intervening years, the main duty of the Navy had been to police the seas and show the flag, and as there was no prospect of a maritime war, little attention was given to fighting efficiency.' When Fisher came to power the senior officers in the Fleet were all men who had won their promotion in sailing ships. To them seamanship and discipline were still the basis of naval efficiency. They were suspicious of the new instruments and apprehensive lest the concentration on 'armament practices' should weaken the fundamental disciplines on which the supremacy of the Navy had hitherto rested. As they saw it, it was the duty of the gunnery schools to teach men to shoot and for the captains to teach them to fight.

Sir William's diplomatic and understanding analysis of the mentality and attitudes of the senior officers, during his early days in the service, will help us to understand the opposition provoked by Arthur Pollen's advanced thinking and mechanisms in the practice of fire control and gunnery.

CHAPTER II

The Requirements of Fire Control

Parallel with the imaginative and necessary propaganda exemplified in the *Jupiter Letters*, Pollen had for five years been conducting a scientific study of the problem of long range gunnery, or fire control, as it came to be known. Despite his lack of training in mathematics or mechanics he had by nature a scientific turn of mind and it is fascinating to see how, as a layman, he pioneered the way to an entirely new science.

When in February 1900, he was invited to witness a fleet target practice, he had been struck by the fact that even the largest guns, such as the $13\cdot5''$ of the *Empress of India*, were being practised at ranges under 1500 yards. He was told that longer ranges could not be usefully practised because the rangefinders were not reliable. He was further told that self-contained rangefinders could not be made with a longer base. With *The Times* account fresh in his mind, of the accuracy with which the naval $4\cdot7''$ guns had been used on land in South Africa, the 'discrepancy', as he put it, was indeed startling.

His first step was to have large scale plans made of two Drakes (then the fastest ships afloat) approaching each other at top speed, head-on, and assuming an opening range of 10,000 yards. At that time, he tells us, his solitary scrap of ballistic learning was that the time of flight of a $6''$ gun was somewhere in the neighbourhood of thirty seconds, at this range. He was amazed to find that had the first Drake shot at the second, the range would have altered nearly half a mile while the shell was in the air. From this it was at once evident that while it was essential to find a means of measuring ranges precisely, the major problem would be to ascertain the future position of the target.

Further reflection led him to the following conclusions:-

1. The only clue to the future position of the target must be found in its past movements. If it were to double like a hare after you had fired, no power on earth would enable you to hit it.

2. Of its past movements the only information that could be obtained must be a succession of synchronous ranges and bearings.

3. If these were plotted with due allowance for our own progress through the water, a plan of the paths of both ships would result.

4. From such a plan the forecasting of future ranges, and of the angle of deflection, must be a mere matter of calculation.

At this point it may be helpful to record that from first to last the instruments comprising the A.C. System fell into two groups; first those required to observe and plot the relative movements of the two ships, hereinafter referred to as the Plotting Unit or Plotter, and, secondly, the Computer or Clock, as it was then known, which integrated the information provided by the plotter and transferred the required data as to range and deflection direct to the guns. Furthermore it should be borne in mind that money was short and the success of the system regarded as problematical, and that in consequence the Admiralty were never willing to help to finance the development of the Clock until it had been proved that the plotter could produce information sufficiently accurate to make the system viable.

Thus it came about that although the first trial of the plotter took place in 1905, it was not until 1909 that a Clock was manufactured and formally submitted for trial.

To complete this brief outline of the instruments of which Pollen's A.C. System was composed we must revert to the basic problems of finding the range. (Incidentally, it should here be explained that the name A.C., given to the System, stood for 'Aim Correction', a perhaps deliberate understatement of its very wide objectives.)

'All rangefinding,' as he wrote 'is based on some form of triangulation which consists in ascertaining two angles of a triangle of which the base is known.' To simplify the calculation it was usual in self-contained rangefinders to set one lens at right angles so that only one angle had to be measured, as shown in figure II rather than as in figure I.

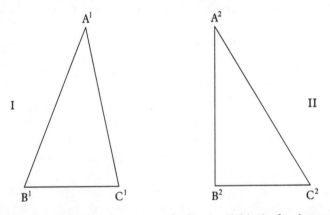

Prior to 1906 the best rangefinder available had a base of only 4′ 6″. To Pollen's lay mind it was astonishing to find that the angle at C remained measurable if, as happened at sea, the triangle was elongated to a point two or three miles away, while the base BC was only 4′ 6″. In practice 5000 yards (nearly three land miles) was the maximum at which ranges could be measured with even approximate accuracy.

To a perfectionist like Pollen, who was setting out to revolutionize[1] gunnery not just to improve it, this simply was not good enough. To him the only solution was to revert to the basic surveying practice of employing two observers and setting them as far apart as possible. 'The base,' he wrote, 'will be the longest base that can be got, e.g. from the extremities of the bridges; the port ends of the fore and aft bridges for the port-side, the starboard ends of the same bridges for the starboard side, the forward bridge from end to end being the base for straight ahead, and the aft bridge from end to end the base for straight astern.

That there would be difficulties in synchronising the observations of the two observers was self-evident but he refused to believe that they could prove insuperable.

By 1904 a scheme for the observing instruments had been evolved. In a pamphlet dated August 1904, entitled *Memorandum on a Proposed System of Finding Ranges at Sea and Ascertaining the Speed and Course of any vessel in Sight*, Pollen summarised his conclusions as follows:

> Rangefinding at sea differs essentially from rangefinding on land. On land it consists in ascertaining the distance between two fixed points. At sea, rangefinding, in the sense of giving the guns the distance at which they are to fire, is a forecast of what will be the distance between two moving objects at a future time. Hence an accurate knowledge of range at any one moment is no help to forecasting an accurate range at a future moment unless the rate of change (i.e. rate of approach) is known. To ascertain this rate of change it is necessary to know the course steered and the speed of both ships. This can be obtained by the proposed system and apparently in no other way with certainty.

This pamphlet of August 1904, the first technical memorandum on A.C. ever submitted, is historically of interest, first for the revolutionary assertion that the ability to hold the range was far more important than the relatively simple task of finding the range at any given moment: secondly, for the positive statement that to ascertain the rate of change it was necessary to know the speed and course of both ships. It would have been easy to fall into the trap of assuming that if neither ship changed course a plot of the ranges for, say, five minutes would enable you to forecast the range for the following two minutes. By August 1904 Pollen had long been aware that this was not so and that bearings were essential; yet, the fallacy was actively propagated by his chief rival no less than four years later.

Thirdly, the pamphlet is notable for the emphasis placed on the fact that the range used would be the mean of the observations, and that, for this reason 'the accuracy of the system is always greater than the accuracy of the observations.'

Finally it could be said that the most significant item in the whole memorandum was the allusion to 'a rate of approach of, say, twenty yards a second' for, twenty yards a second (more usually expressed as 1200 yards a minute) was in fact the rate of approach of two of the fastest cruisers of the day advancing head-on. The very casual nature of the mention of this extreme figure reflects Pollen's confident belief in his ability to provide what he called the 'complete solution', covering every movement and every situation that could arise in battle.

Admittedly such a rate of approach could not continue for more than a few minutes – but that very fact increased the complexity of the problem. In war, if two ships suddenly found themselves approaching head-on, the weaker would at once turn away. If neither was disposed to give way both would gradually swing round in the same direction until eventually they reached parallel courses at fighting range.

Pollen would not have spoken, in this formal submission, of this extreme change of range had he not already analysed the circumstances in which it could come about and its effect upon the rate of change to which he attached such paramount importance. His analysis would have revealed that, as they turned away, the rate of change, starting at 1200 yards a minute, would fall at first rapidly and then more slowly to zero. To anyone seeking a mechanical method of holding the range throughout the approach, such variations would clearly have presented complex mathematical and mechanical problems. Yet the whole tone of the pamphlet reflects his confidence at this early date in his ability to master the problem.

The secret of his confidence was revealed some years later in a pamphlet entitled *The Gun in Battle*, that was printed for private circulation early in 1913. Pollen there recalls that 'when I first began the design of the observing instruments in the spring of 1904 I submitted the whole scheme to Lord Kelvin who was my colleague on the Board of a company of which I was Managing Director. He was much interested, and, as always, extremely sympathetic with a new venture; and so exceedingly encouraging in urging me to go forward that I hardly recognised the significance of his warning when he added "It is a very big project. You have ten years hard work before you." ' For Kelvin, long recognised as the leading figure in the world of applied science, had a particular interest in Naval affairs and would have been delighted to find his young colleague at Linotype so deeply involved.

It so happened that one of Kelvin's many claims to distinction was the invention[2] some twenty-five years earlier of the tidal harmonic analyser and the tide predictor. Kelvin, in 1904, would at once have appreciated the similarity of the technical problem then facing Pollen, which was to find a means of predicting mechanically and instantaneously ranges developed by continuously changing Rates.

There can be little doubt that Kelvin then introduced Pollen to the theory of mechanical analogue computation and assured him that a proper application of the principle would solve his problem, as indeed it did some few years later.

Pollen's submission of August 1904 led to the appointment in October of a Commission[3] of Enquiry, under the Chairmanship of Admiral A. C. Parr to investigate Pollen's proposals. The Commission expressed interest in Pollen's ideas but called for a more complete and more specific statement of the scheme and of the instruments involved. This led in December to the production of *Fire Control and Long Range Firing* 'an essay to define certain principia of gunnery and to suggest means for their application.' In this he expanded the account of the mechanism of the plotter given in the August pamphlet and in addition spelt out, for the first time, the role and functions of the 'Change of Range Machine' subsequently known as the

Clock. The December memorandum was thus the first complete definition of the A.C. System as a whole.

Throughout 1904 and 1905, Pollen was working under the great handicap that the continuously running gyroscope, the need for which he had foreseen five years earlier, had not yet been produced.

Under the A.C. System the rangefinder was used as the basic instrument of observation, for both ranges and bearings. Every reading taken from the rangefinder automatically recorded time, range and bearing. Bearings could be measured by reference either to a compass or to keel-line. Compasses were ruled out in Pollen's judgement by their inability to function effectively while big guns were firing. Keel-line, on the other hand, was subject to the deviations introduced by yaw.

From time immemorial it had been known that at sea every vessel from the smallest rowing boat to the largest battleship, had a tendency to swing to right or left, a movement known as yaw, as distinct from roll or pitch. In his original letter of 26th January 1901, to Lord Walter Kerr, the First Sea Lord, Pollen had spoken of 'means for combining the telescope for observation with an arrangement of one or more gyrostats whereby very much more accurate observations could be taken on shipboard than had customarily been effected,' thus showing that from the start he had appreciated the importance of yaw and the fact that it could be counteracted by gyro. His faith in the gyro is the more remarkable when we recall that at this early date none ran[4] for more than a couple of minutes.

For his purpose Pollen needed one that would both run continuously and have sufficient power to control the transmission of the corrected bearings; and before the end of the year 1900 he had put his engineers to work on finding the solution.

With this brief outline of the A.C. System and its instruments in mind, we can now return to the story of Pollen's negotiations with the Admiralty. It so happened that in February 1905, shortly after the submission of his comprehensive December paper, Captain J. R. Jellicoe, the future

Commander-in-Chief, took over from Captain H. D. Barry as Director of Naval Ordnance (D.N.O.) and thus assumed responsibility for advising on A.C.

Pollen's objective at this time was to persuade the Admiralty to accept responsibility for the manufacture of the A.C. instruments. As Managing Director of Linotype he had developed his natural gift for analysis of novel problems and had learnt that the experts usually found the solution if his analysis was really complete. Hence his oft-repeated saying that 'a problem stated is a problem solved'. On the other hand, he was in no sense either a practical engineer, a theoretical mechanic or even a mathematician. In 1905 he would have been content, as in 1900, with the role of discoverer of the problem and originator of the theoretical solution. However, Jellicoe, although alive to the possibilities of the system was much too cautious to commit himself to any such arrangement. The most he would do was to make the small contribution of £4500 towards the cost of the instruments for trial. In point of fact a trial at this date was the last thing Pollen wanted. To his great disappointment the engineers had not yet solved the problem of the continuous running gyroscope and without it he saw no hope of success. Yet it was vital to keep the Admiralty interested. Furthermore, the Admiralty experts assured him that yaw would not be a material factor; so, against his better judgement, he agreed to submit his plotting scheme for trial. The £4500 contribution barely covered the cost of producing the plotting unit and left nothing for the production of the clock. The trial was therefore limited to the plotter.

In agreeing to go forward with the trial Pollen was much influenced by the sympathetic and interested attitude of the Parr Commission. Throughout the trials which took place in November in the *Jupiter*, Pollen lived on board on the best of terms with the Commission by whom he was accepted as a member of the team, participating freely in all their discussions.

Yet from the standpoint of results the trial was almost a total failure. For this there were two reasons; first that the plotting had been done manually, and not mechanically, and secondly, that the extent of the yaw was far greater than the Admiralty experts had foreseen. As to the first point, Pollen was fully prepared and designs for an automatic plotter were already far advanced. As regards yaw, the service gyros had been able to take advantage of a few quiet moments, and the results then obtained were sufficient to prove the value of a gyro and to confirm the need for further trials.

However, the month of January 1906 saw a dramatic change in the situation with the announcement that his engineers had found the solution to the problem of the continuous gyro. Pollen at once declared against wasting time on any further trials until the new gyro had been built, by which time he would also have his automatic plotter in working order.

Another welcome development at this time was the appearance of the much improved Barr & Stroud 9′ rangefinder. Pollen was still convinced, and rightly so, that his two-observer system would produce results infinitely more accurate than any self-contained instrument, however long. But the practical difficulties and objections were numerous, not least, at this moment, the expense and time involved in its development. Yet it is probable that Pollen would have held on patiently, as he had done in waiting for the gyro, had he not realised that his system of averaging the observations would result in the ranges used being far more accurate than the individual observations. Thus the year 1906 saw a double break-through first in the solution of the problem of the gyro and secondly in the production of a self-contained rangefinder of adequate accuracy.

The Commission thus had no difficulty in advising in favour of an agreement with Pollen that would preserve monopoly for the British Navy for a further term of years, on conditions to be agreed.

Having cleared the first hurdle Pollen now found himself

faced with the no less difficult task of persuading first Jellicoe, the D.N.O. and next Lord Tweedmouth, the First Lord, of the immense importance of his scheme, and of getting them to put their names to a contract which would reflect what he regarded as its true value. The Admiralty were accustomed to buying instruments at a price based on cost of production, plus a suitable profit, plus, perhaps, in the case of a new invention, some extra payment for monopoly.

Pollen's approach was that of the businessman. What was his invention worth to the buyer? If a battleship cost £2,000,000 and the Pollen system doubled or trebled the hitting power of twenty or thirty battleships what should they be prepared to pay for its monopoly? What would be a fair price? Here clearly there was scope for imaginative advocacy.

Officially Pollen corresponded with Jellicoe the D.N.O., but from time to time points would occur to him that would perhaps carry more weight with the First Lord, and in such cases, and almost certainly to the knowledge of Jellicoe, Pollen would write direct to Tweedmouth. One such letter was that of the 14th February 1906, from which the following is taken:

> Supposing we are the first power to develop long range hitting at a moving target we can then gradually reconstitute our Fleet in view of the knowledge we should have. We might well keep the secret for five or six years. In that time we should have constructed probably twenty armoured ships in the light of the tactical requirements of our new accomplishment. The revolution in naval fighting would then have cost us nothing.

He goes on to say that 'were other Powers to acquire the art' then the requirements of naval supremacy would make it necessary for us to build with far greater rapidity and in much greater numbers. So, too, with the cost of acquiring the patents. 'As long as you are dealing with a single individual who is more anxious that the Navy should have the monopoly than you are, it cannot be difficult to agree on terms.' On the other hand, were he told that the British Navy did not want it, he would be forced to develop it commercially. In the process, he would inevitably lose control to some international company which, in due course, would demand a full commercial price, simply for the right to use the patents without monopoly.

In principle the Admiralty was willing to come to terms, but the gap was wide and the end of July found the two sides no nearer agreement. Accordingly, on the 9th August a conference was called and attended by Jellicoe, Pollen, Black the Director of Contracts, and Captain E. W. Harding the D.N.O.'s assistant.

The discussion started favourably enough against the background that all parties recognised the great possibilities of the system and were united in wishing the Royal Navy to have the monopoly of its use should their hopes be justified. Next it was agreed that the need for absolute secrecy made it impossible for Pollen to finance development privately and that the money would have to be found by the Admiralty. More surprisingly the terms for the acquisition of monopoly, should the system prove its value, though closely argued, were settled. Where they were all defeated was in finding a way to overcome the Admiralty's apprehensions as to the situation that might develop should the system not come up to expectations. The Admiralty men expressed their anxieties very frankly. The Minute reads as follows: 'if the trial took place Mr Pollen could not fail to obtain further knowledge of rangefinding in general, and of British Naval methods in particular', and if the trials were unsuccessful 'we might in fact be almost obliged to accept his terms so as to keep that knowledge from others.'

Pollen, writing next day, to submit a revised summary of the terms he would accept, begged their Lordships to believe that it was his desire 'first that they should have the opportunity of ascertaining the value of his system at the smallest cost to the country', secondly to suggest terms for a monopoly 'which are demonstrably moderate', and finally 'to be strictly reasonable in the clauses proposed for his own protection'.

Pollen's protective clauses were prophetic in their foresight.

First 'that my invention shall not be pirated': secondly 'that, if found to be of so small value that the secret is not worth keeping, that I shall be free to develop it on my own account'.

'The first clause I fear must appear now as a bald request that the Admiralty shall undertake to treat my invention as mine: a mere matter of common honesty and therefore superfluous. But obviously in years to come the fact that the invention is mine may not seem so obvious – and the protection given by the clause may be advisable'.

The conference proved indecisive and negotiations dragged on without much sign of agreement. Fearing that the good understanding established with Jellicoe would be frustrated by the bureaucrats and lawyers Pollen decided the time had come to appeal once more to Lord Tweedmouth, the First Lord; in a letter dated the 27th August 1906 he summarized the history of his relations with the Admiralty as follows:

As stated in the official letter of the 21st, I am the inventor of a new system of gunnery, consisting briefly of semi-automatic means for reducing the difficulties in making hits on a fast moving target at long range to the simple proportions of hitting a stationary target with a stationary gun. I first brought this system to the notice of the Board of the Admiralty in the year 1900, and, during subsequent years, on various occasions, urged various considerations to show that it was worth examination and trial. For some time, however, the importance of hitting at long range at all was not easy to establish, and I was altogether unable to arouse sufficient interest in the subject to make an a priori case in its favour. The only response I received, consequently, was a repetition of the statement that my system would be of no value to the Service, and that I was at liberty to patent it abroad and develop it in any way that I saw fit. (I have received in all seven official intimations that my gunnery inventions were of no value and need not be kept secret). I held on, however, till 1904, when the great developments in the art of gunnery within the Service had given rise to new systems of fire control, and made the employment of artillery at long range seem, not only possible, but necessary. An enquiry was made into my system, and finally, in May 1905, an agreement was entered into by the Admiralty to pay me a sum of £4,500 to supply instruments for trial . . . What I have to sell is not instruments, but a system, the embodiment of certain laws of gunnery which I have been the first to codify. My instruments as at present designed will no doubt soon be superseded by others that embody the essential features of my system more completely. The monopoly of instruments is only incidental. It is the knowledge of the system which they make workable, and the exclusive knowledge of it, to which high, possibly supreme, value attaches.

On receipt of this letter Lord Tweedmouth at once consulted the First Sea Lord, Admiral Sir John Fisher, the great Jackie Fisher, later Lord Fisher of Kilverstone. Fisher, on holiday in Carlsbad, replied[5] (10th September) in characteristic style:

Pollen's invention is simply priceless and I do hope we may hesitate at nothing to get ITS SOLE USE. We shall NEVER be forgiven if we do not!

Four days later he wrote again to thank Tweedmouth for his support:

The case is marvellously like the introduction of the Whitehead torpedo (1866). We should have had the absolute monopoly of that marvellous weapon (and Mr Whitehead body and soul into the bargain!) but the Admiralty of that day haggled over £80,000. But thanks to you, I hope we shan't make such an idiotic mistake over Pollen.

From Pollen's standpoint, Fisher's backing in September 1906 was vital and decisive. Within a month a formal letter[6] was received from the Admiralty that established what Pollen had been seeking for five years, namely an agreement to go ahead together, virtually in partnership, to explore the possibilities of the system. The letter, a remarkable document, recognized him as the sole inventor of a System of Gunnery and agreed to a costly series of experiments and trials of his instruments. If the system proved successful the Admiralty would buy the monopoly for the sum of £140,000 plus a 25% royalty on the instruments, all of which, except for the rangefinders, must be bought through him. Most remarkable of all, it recognized that the instruments as first submitted would necessarily be modified but that the terms of the agreement would apply to all such modifications regardless of whether they had been patented or not and regardless of whether the modifications had been suggested by Pollen or from within the Service. It seems that both sides regarded it as in their own interest that the agreement should not be frustrated by minor modifications in the instruments.

Such terms were without precedent and an interesting early example of an attempt to devise something in the nature of a partnership between a private inventor and a government department. Yet the problem that had baffled them all from the start, as to the situation that would arise should the Admiralty not wish to acquire the system, remain unresolved. Pollen's bold insistence on protection against the eventual theft of his ideas had been met by the inclusion in the contract letter of a clause to the effect that, 'My Lords have no intention of questioning your claim to be regarded as the sole inventor and originator of the system for obtaining the data for gunnery by the use of ranges and bearings taken simultaneously and used in connection with a chart gyroscopically corrected.' Yet even this clear statement was destined to prove insufficient, and from the Admiralty side, the thought that they might eventually be blackmailed into buying something they did not want remained to haunt them for years to come.

The debate over the terms of the contract had been hard fought. Jellicoe, the Director of Naval Ordnance knew his subject; his principal assistant, Captain E. W. Harding of the Royal Marine Artillery was a keen student both of gunnery and of tactics and already well known in the Service as a writer[7] and authority on these subjects. It was to Harding that Jellicoe had entrusted the responsibility for investigating the A.C. System, and a copy of his final report on which the agreement was based fortunately still survives. Much of it is of necessity rather technical, but there are many points of interest to the layman, in particular his very practical approach to the uncertainties involved in paying a high price for a monopoly. What chance was there of simultaneous discovery by another inventor? Were the instruments so conspicuous in design or appearance that their secrets could not long be concealed? Ought the Admiralty to buy the inventions outright and develop them themselves or would it be better to allow Arthur Pollen to keep the sole right of manufacture and thus retain the benefits of his continued co-operation? To all these questions Harding was in no doubt as to the answers. There was nothing to suggest that any other inventor at home or abroad was alive to the nature of the problem. Pollen, it seemed was alone in understanding the factors involved and in attempting to solve them. As to the advisability of allowing Pollen to retain the sole right of manufacture, Harding was confident that Pollen would be more likely to effect improvements in the mechanisms than any outside firm whose interest in the matter would inevitably be limited.

On the tactical implications of the system there was again a complete meeting of minds. 'Tactical superiority depends eventually on Fire superiority'; and again, 'Moreover by its reaction on Tactical thought, to the extent that it induces the formation of a definite tactical system based on sound principles and on a definite standard of technical efficiency, it immensely simplifies problems of construction and ultimately reacts on strategical possibilities and methods'.

The general tenor and enthusiasm of Harding's report leaves us in no doubt that, in 1906, at the time of the agreement, the Admiralty as represented by Jellicoe and Harding, were fully alive to the tactical significance of Pollen's system of fire control.

To Harding, therefore, the system was doubly welcome, first as an aid to gunnery and secondly for its tactical value, and his report concludes on a most enthusiastic note:

> The very simplicity of the solution showing as it does the essential complexity of the problem tends to strengthen the convic-

tion that in principle it is the final solution . . . Its national value cannot be regarded only from the point of view of ingenious instruments for obtaining even a great advance in Artillery technique, but must be looked upon as an essential link in a far reaching chain of development. It is from this point of view that the inventor regards the system, and this now explains much of his apparently exaggerated talk as to its value . . . The system will be of immense national value as a monopoly, and the instruments offered, when their constituents are analysed, make a large group of patents, so that when the intrinsic value of the system and its probable effect on Naval development are considered, together with the value and number of the instruments offered, an apparently large price for the acquisition of the monopoly appears justified.

In the light of after events it is interesting to note that Harding's praise and enthusiasm is all directed to 'the system' and not to any particular instrument.

In later years the idea of a system was lost and not even Wilfrid Greene[8], KC could succeed in reviving it when as Pollen's Counsel, in 1925, he found himself faced with the task of convincing the Royal Commission of Arthur Pollen's right to an award in respect of the system that was used throughout the war, as distinct from the individual instruments. But in 1906 the 'system' was a new and vital conception and valued at a princely figure.

Captain Jellicoe, an orthodox and cautious administrator, knowing the opposition there would be from certain quarters to the introduction of scientific instruments, took the precaution before committing himself to this far-reaching agreement, to invite the support of all the recognised gunnery authorities[9] in the Service. Accordingly, the Captain of the *Excellent*, his Commander and First Lieutenant, the Whale Island Experimental Staff, the Inspector of Target Practice and his Staff, the Director of Naval Intelligence, and the Captain and Staff of the War Course College, had it put to them whether the problem envisaged by Mr Pollen was one to which it was essential to find a solution? Whether the Pollen solution was plausible?

Whether there was any alternative solution? Whether the revolutionary tactical developments anticipated from its success were likely to accrue? To all of these questions the officers consulted replied with enthusiasm. In principle the Pollen system was right and the proposed expenditure on developing its practical application undoubtedly justified.

CHAPTER III

The Fisher Regime

To understand what follows, we must look first at the administrative organisation of the Navy in Arthur Pollen's time. The creative years during which he worked so closely with the Service and achieved so much, namely 1904-09, coincided exactly with Fisher's term of office as First Sea Lord.

Much has been written about this remarkable man, yet the historians remain to this day fascinated by his complex and contradictory qualities. Of the full-length biographies, the first to appear was that by his dedicated disciple, Admiral Sir Reginald Bacon, a man, incidentally, who will figure prominently in our story as Pollen's first and most dangerous opponent. First published in 1930, some ten years after Fisher's death, its uncritical and adulatory tone prompted a strong reaction from a number of former colleagues and shipmates.

Modern historians, with the notable exception of Ruddock Mackay[1], tend to be lenient towards Fisher's failings, but in 1930 there were too many of his contemporaries, and of his victims, still in circulation, for Bacon's one-sided account to pass unchallenged. Service journals opened their columns to the critics and pride of place was given to Pollen's paper, first published in the *Naval Review* of February 1930, and later reprinted for private circulation under the title of *The Tragedy of Lord Fisher of Kilverstone*. Of the many letters of appreciation received by Pollen, that from Captain Alfred Dewar to Admiral W. H. Henderson, the Honorary Editor of the *Naval Review* deserves special mention. It runs:

I have just read *The Tragedy of Lord Fisher of Kilverstone*. May I say that in its vast comprehension, its really piercing insight and its witty style, I think it the most interesting naval article I have read in any review for twenty years. I can discern Pollen in it but am not quite certain it is he. Will you please convey my humble congratulations to him if I am correct. My small holly bush stands under the shade of a vast beech tree.

Alfred Dewar, while less aggressive than his brother Kenneth, was no less respected within the Service as a thinker and writer and it must be rare to find so generous a tribute from one writer to another on his own subject.

Speaking of Fisher's personal characteristics, Pollen tells us:

We can cheerfully concede Admiral Bacon's claim that Fisher was the most remarkable Englishman of his day, if only because his ascendancy, both qualitatively and in point of time, was wholly without precedent and, on the written evidence, wholly inexplicable. In reality his claim to greatness rests not on his work as a 'sea officer', but on the fact that between October 1904 and May 1915 he wholly dominated, as no man had done before, the naval policy of this country. The ten years' ascendancy of Fisher over Court, politicians, Parliament and Press will never be understood by a generation that did not live through it, and is unsupplied with the living evidence of his unparalleled powers of persuasion. That he was a driving and fascinating personality is obvious, and to those who knew him well, not only a most lovable, but a singularly entertaining man. He had gifts that made him a chartered libertine in august circles, where, normally, conversational initiative is an impropriety verging on crime. The most accomplished men of the world, scholars and statesmen, succumbed unresisting to his charm. . . .

It is the fashion today to emphasise Fisher's humble origin and to write as if, for him, life in the Navy had been a constant struggle against aristocratic prejudice. Yet all authorities agree as to the strength of his personality, his ability as a young man to challenge and impress his superiors, and not least to the personal relationship that he established with King Edward himself.

That he had enemies within the Service is undoubtedly true, but these were largely of his own creation and of his own choosing. Among Fisher's contemporaries, if it is permissible to use the expression of a man thirty years his junior, none had a greater appreciation of his capacity or a greater affection for Jackie Fisher than Winston Churchill; but even he, writing of the great reforms introduced by Fisher, tells us, in a much quoted passage[2], that:

> In carrying through these far-reaching changes he had created violent oppositions to himself in the Navy, and his own methods, in which he gloried, were of a kind to excite bitter animosities, which he returned and was eager to repay. He made it known, indeed he proclaimed, that officers who opposed his policies would have their professional careers ruined. . . . 'Ruthless, relentless and remorseless' were words always on his lips and many grisly examples of Admirals and Captains eating out their hearts 'on the beach' showed that he meant what he said.

On the same theme, Pollen tells how 'the ethos of quarter deck obedience to orders became a rule more rigid than Mede or Persian had conceived. Advice and comment was not sought and those who volunteered it came under an imputation of mutiny. The old liberty of discussion, so characteristic a mark of the naval officer off duty, the freedom of speech to which Marryat again and again bears witness, vanished abruptly'.

The effect was to split the service into two warring factions; those in the favoured 'Fishpond', prepared to accept the Fisher rule of favouritism and dictatorship, and those with the courage to express their own views. Leader of the opposition was Lord Charles Beresford, a powerful and courageous character with three medals to his credit for saving life. A dashing rider to hounds and prominent in his young days as a member of the Prince of Wales's social set, his name had figured more than once among the celebrated scandals of the time. Today, there is a tendency to treat him as something of a buffoon, and it must be admitted that in his later years, after he had put on weight, his devotion to his no less corpulent bulldog, by whom he was invariably accompanied, made him an easy prey to the caricaturists. Yet in reality, despite his faults, he was an able and dedicated officer, and one of the earliest and most far-seeing of the many would-be reformers within the Service at the turn of the century. In 1901 he had been one of a small circle to whom Pollen had sent a copy of the proposals he had submitted to Lord Walter Kerr for the plotting of the speed and course of enemy ships. In reply, Beresford had sent a four-page letter, welcoming his initiative and summarising most intelligently 'the collective opinion' of the Navigating, Gunnery and Torpedo Officers of his ship, the *Ramillies*. A rare and interesting example of teamwork, that contrasts sharply with Fisher's later disregard of expert opinion. Nor was this by any means Pollen's only experience of Beresford's willingness to listen and learn. In May 1906 Beresford was among those to whom Pollen sent a copy of the *Jupiter Letters*. In most cases Pollen's friends replied briefly and politely expressing their interest. Beresford, in contrast, wrote a six-page letter which reflected his interest in every aspect of the problem from ship design to fire control and tactics.

To this Pollen responded on the 21st June, elaborating his ideas, correcting misunderstandings and ending with a graceful tribute to Beresford for his continued help and support. 'I shall never forget that six years ago, when everybody else was looking upon me as a blithering idiot, you were practically the only one in the Service to bid me go ahead, so that now when the number of my supporters is really becoming large, I want to assure you again of my genuine gratitude for the sympathy and help which you have given me.'

Also to Beresford's credit was the revelation, in the same letter, that he had given similar early backing to Percy Scott. 'The man who started the gun-layers competition was the man to whom we owe everything for the improvement and advance in Gunnery. I mean Admiral Sir Percy Scott, and it is a curious fact that years ago, before I knew him at all, I wrote to the Admiralty and suggested that he was the only man that appeared to be able to hit accurately with his guns and that he should be sent round to each station to show us all how he did it.'

This, of course, was written prior to the famous row between them when Scott objected to an order to abandon a day's gunnery practice in order to paint ship in preparation for a V.I.P. visit. But it is typical of his concern for the perfection of his weapons and of his keen attention to detail, wherein he once again contrasts so favourably with Fisher who, despite his obsession with material, showed a total lack of interest in the manner of its use. In Pollen's words, 'Fisher had seen the introduction of steam, of armour, of electricity and of machinery of all kinds. He had a flair beyond that of ordinary men for seeing the tendencies and the possible developments of new discoveries in the field he was making his own.' Yet despite the novelty and complexity of the new weapons, he never thought it necessary to set up a Staff System or even committees of experts to examine their design and ensure their effectiveness. 'Nothing,' wrote Pollen, 'is more astounding than the extent to which Fisher perpetually assumed that guns had only to be fired to hit.'

Jellicoe in his post-war account of his stewardship, *The Grand Fleet 1914-18*, freely admits, and laments, an appalling list of defects due to similar neglect; notably the fuses that went off before, instead of after, penetrating the armour and the magazines that, when in use, were unprotected from the flash of exploding shells, and rangefinders through which nothing could be seen in poor light. That the Germans had so many essentials that we lacked was due, so Pollen maintained, not to any lack of inventiveness on our part, but solely to the fact that with the Germans, 'the Staff System kept men at the top teachable'.

It may be objected that Fisher's term of office as First Sea Lord came to an end in January 1910, and that he should not be held responsible for all the defects of 1914. Yet there is ample evidence of the truth of Pollen's assertion that Fisher 'wholly dominated' naval policy from 1904 until his fall from power in 1915. Indeed it is probably true to say that his influence was even greater while out of office.

For one thing, he continued to carry great weight on the Committee of Imperial Defence. In a letter[3] of the 19th January 1911, to A. G. Gardiner, for many years the well-known Editor of the Liberal *Daily News*, we find 'I am more powerful now in the Committee of Defence than when I was First Sea Lord. I had masters then, now I have none and I have a platform,' (meaning the House of Lords.)

When in December 1911, Winston Churchill took office as First Lord, it was to Fisher that he at once turned for guidance, and it was largely on Fisher's advice that new appointments, both Admiralty and Fleet were made.

In *The World Crisis* Churchill recalls how he and Fisher had met for the first time in 1907, in the house of a mutual friend, and how he sat up all night enthralled by the brilliance of Fisher's talk on every aspect of Naval policy. Two years later he fell out with the Admiral by challenging the building programme put forward by McKenna, in the 1909 Naval Estimates. Yet on taking office in December 1911, he knew that he needed Fisher's help and must regain his confidence. Of their reconciliation on this occasion, he wrote[4]:

> I found Fisher a veritable volcano of knowledge and inspiration and as soon as he learnt what my main purpose was, he passed into a state of vehement eruption. . . . It was always a joy to me to talk to him on these great matters, but most of all he was stimulating in all that related to the design of ships. He also talked brilliantly about Admirals, but here one had to make a heavy discount on account of the feuds. . . .
>
> I began our conversations with no thought of Fisher's recall. But by the Sunday night the power of the man was deeply borne in on me, and I had almost made up my mind to do what I did three years later and place him again at the head of the Naval Service. It was not the outcry that I feared: that I felt strong

enough at this time to face. But it was the revival and continu-
ance of the feuds: and it was clear from his temper that this
would be inevitable. Then too, I was apprehensive of his age. I
could not feel complete confidence in the poise of a man of
seventy-one.

Altogether, a fine example of Fisher's 'unparalleled power of
persuasion'. That Fisher exercised similar authority over his
successors is well borne out by his characteristic tribute[5] to
their 'greatness' which we find in a letter that he chose to
reproduce in one of his books of Memoirs:

> I hope Sir Francis Bridgeman will forgive me for hauling him
> into this book – I have no other way of showing him my eternal
> gratitude; and it was with intense delight that I congratulated
> Mr Churchill on obtaining his services to succeed Sir Arthur
> Wilson, the First Sea Lord, who had so magnificently adhered to
> the scheme I left. Sir Arthur refused a Peerage, and he was a
> faithful and self-effacing friend in his room at the Admiralty
> those seven fateful months I was First Sea Lord during the war.
> It was peculiarly fortunate and providential that the two im-
> mediately succeeding First Sea Lords after my departure on 25
> January 1910, should have been the two great sailors they
> were – otherwise there would have been no Grand Fleet – they
> altered nothing.

They altered nothing! Above all was this true as regards
their opposition to the introduction of a Staff System.

As First Lord, Churchill's first public announcement, over
the date New Year's Day 1912, took the form of a memorandum outlining the setting up of a new and extended War Staff.
Yet once again the Service was doomed to disappointment; for
the Establishment, now under the leadership of Fisher's
faithful successor, Admiral Sir A. K. Wilson, proved too
strong for their minister. Churchill in *The World Crisis*
frankly admits[6] his failure.

> It takes a generation to form a General Staff. No wave of the
> wand can create those habits of mind in seniors on which the
> efficiency or even the reality of a staff depends. The deadweight
> of professional opinion was adverse.

Thus it came about that throughout the whole of his time as an inventor, that is to say from 1901 to 1913, Pollen was doomed to remain at the mercy of the arbitrary decisions of Whitehall officials, often in flagrant disregard of expert opinion.

It is against this background that we must now return to the narrative of the events that followed the Admiralty's decision, in 1906, to go ahead with Pollen's system on a basis of monopoly and secrecy.

Under Jellicoe, it will be recalled, Pollen had been treated as a trusted ally, invited to attend the trials of his gear and shown all the reports, records and criticisms. But, alas for Pollen, generations at Whitehall, then as now, were short, and the personal relationships and understanding established between Jellicoe, Harding and Pollen, which had led to the agreement of 1906, were not destined to last many months.

Jellicoe had already served three years as D.N.O., and in the summer of 1907 Pollen learnt, to his dismay, that he was to leave the Admiralty and go back to sea. This meant that responsibility for the all important trials of the Plotting gear, due to be held in the New Year, would pass to his successor, Captain Reginald Bacon, a man with a first-rate brain of whom Pollen was one day to write[7] that 'he had taken all naval knowledge as his province'; and incidentally the author many years later of the biography of Fisher we have just been considering. Yet like so many brilliant intellectuals he was lacking in judgement and administrative ability.

However, in 1907, he was Fisher's special favourite, outstanding in Fisher's eyes even among 'the five best brains' of whom he boasted as advisers.

To make matters worse, Harding, Jellicoe's Gunnery Assistant, who had made a study of A.C. and reported so favourably, was transferred in August, his place being filled by Lieutenant F. C. Dreyer.

Dreyer, before going to the Admiralty in 1906, had served as Flag Lieutenant and Gunnery Officer in the *Exmouth* when she was flying Sir Arthur Wilson's flag during his last command at sea, and later for a few months as Gunnery Officer, under Bacon as Captain, in HMS *Dreadnought*. In 1905 and 1906, *Exmouth* had headed the Fleet listing in gunnery and Dreyer's name stood high with the ruling clique, above all with Admiral Wilson and Captain Bacon, his former Chiefs. Prior to receiving this appointment Dreyer had been on good terms with Pollen and had seemed to welcome the contribution that Pollen was making to Naval gunnery. However, his transfer to the post of Gunnery Assistant to the D.N.O. in August 1907 gave him access to the Pollen papers and thus to the terms of the Pollen contract with the Department. His attitude then changed completely and almost at once he informed Pollen that he intended to compete with him.

Early in November (1907) Pollen received the good news that competitive trials were to be held between his system and Dreyer's: but his joy was short-lived, for within a week it became known that the trials were to be under the sole control of Admiral Wilson. Wilson as we have seen, was a dedicated supporter of Fisher both in policy and methods and not unlike him in his strange mixture of ruthlessness and charm: unfortunately, the likeness did not extend to having an eye for the possibilities of new inventions.

In February 1907, at the age of sixty-five, he had hauled down his flag and was living quietly at his old home at Swaffham in Norfolk, enjoying his well earned retirement and the dignity of his position as an Admiral of the Fleet, when, much to his surprise, he received Fisher's invitation 'to supervise some experiments with Mr Pollen's Aim Corrector.'

Bacon, despite his wide knowledge of the naval arts, was basically a torpedo man, with little faith in long-range gunnery. His ambition at this time was to see the Pollen gear discredited in favour of Dreyer's cheap and simple manual methods. To him, Admiral Wilson, with his tremendous authority, and known dislike of new-fangled and complicated machinery was just the man for the job, and it is easy to imagine that it was he who suggested the name of this mutual friend to Fisher.

In Pollen's account of his first meeting with Wilson we get a good picture of the old Admiral in action:

> In November (1907) I was informed that Admiral Wilson wished to see the instruments. We met at Waterloo Station, and as I had never seen him before, I was told to look out, and if I saw a game-keeper in want of a job, I should be fairly sure of my man. He was there, grizzled and masterful in an ulster of incredible age. We travelled down in the utmost amenity and his conversation was extraordinarily interesting. He had been a torpedo man, and his career as Admiral showed him to be supreme as a navigator while his almost reckless gallantry in the Sudan had earned him a V.C.; in due course we arrived at Portsmouth and spent a couple of hours on board examining the instruments and explaining their purposes. Then Sir Arthur and I went on shore and that night dined with the Commander-in-Chief. Nothing could be more pleasant and amiable than the conversation.

Prior to this meeting Pollen had been warned by no less a man than Admiral Sir Henry Jackson, Controller and Third Sea Lord, that Sir Arthur Wilson would be ruthless in trying to break down his A.C. System — 'If it can be broken he will do it'. Despite this warning the form and savagery of the attack when it came, was positively breathtaking. The scene was once again Portsmouth. There had been a further inspection of instruments and

> After seeing these, we lunched with the Commander-in-Chief, and just after lunch I was saying goodbye to the Admiral, his Flag Lieutenant and other officers, with his butler and footmen standing by, when Sir Arthur Wilson turned upon me and in a peremptory and angry voice and with a very stern expression of countenance, told me he had been horrified at finding no means of getting the data obtained by my plotting table to the guns, and said, 'You will have to explain to me some time or other why on earth the Admiralty should pay you £100,000 more than to Barr and Stroud or any other maker of Fire Control instruments that have got to be used for your system'.

I was completely taken aback by his mentioning before a number of officers who were strangers to me, and the Admiral's domestics, the purchase price which had hitherto been regarded as strictly confidential.

Against this background, Pollen had little hope of being allowed to give a full demonstration of the merits of his scheme. Even so, it was a shock to find himself dismissed after trials in the *Ariadne* lasting barely an hour, in quite irrelevant conditions, and told by Admiral Wilson that his system had been superseded by 'a vastly superior system'. 'Throughout the demonstration' wrote Pollen some time later 'his demeanour was that of a man who would be really angry if the thing were not almost too preposterous for anything except contempt. I appealed to Lord Tweedmouth, the First Lord, on the grounds that the 1908 contract had promised two months' trials and he promised me new trials, but Sir Arthur's opposition prevented the promise being kept.'

This was Pollen's first experience of the kind of injustice which was to become a feature of his later contacts with the Admiralty. To an impartial observer the futility of the procedure was obvious. He had an unanswerable case, but in the presentation of it he allowed his feelings to overcome his judgement and for once gave way to the crushing rejoinder which came to him all too readily, and which in this case gave great offence.

In a memorandum of which good use was made by his opponents we find the following:-

First, three factual but overstated paragraphs –

'Sir Arthur Wilson was not instructed. He did not know what the instruments were expected to do. He was "horrified" at finding them what they were. Five minutes' conversation with anyone familiar with the rudiments would have saved him from this.

'He directed them to an object the instruments were not

designed to achieve. They were designed *to get* data. He tested
them in connection with other instruments as an organisation
for *using* data.

'They were designed for making accurate plots in:

  a)   Roughest weather possible,
  b)   Greatest changes of range possible.

The only test at sea lasted thirty minutes in a flat calm. There
was no change of range at all. It is clear that Sir Arthur did not
know what the instruments were for.'

Next we find commentaries on the qualifications of the three
judges.

'Commander Dreyer was gunnery lieutenant in HMS
Exmouth, and, in the unreal conditions of present Service tests,
kept the *Exmouth* – Sir Arthur Wilson's flagship – at the head
of the fleet for two years. He was also chief gunnery officer in
HMS *Dreadnought*, when Captain Bacon (D.N.O.) was Captain. He is the inventor of much gunnery gear that competes
with the A.C. System. He is also the inventor of the gear said to
supersede the A.C. gear. He was the only officer appointed to
"assist" Admiral Wilson and he was not allowed in the
Ariadne.

'Captain Bacon is the greatest authority on submarines. In
his published essay on strategy – containing some brilliant
passages – he concludes by warning the Service against big
ships. He is therefore, or was, an anti-artillerist. He has never
studied the A.C. System and knows nothing whatever about
the machinery.

'Sir Arthur Wilson had no expert gunnery officer to assist
him in the *Ariadne*. (Fire Control was invented after Sir Arthur
had attained full Admiral's rank.) He also had no mechanical
expert. He showed that in many respects he did not understand
the mechanical principles: or the place the A.C. System fills in
fire control: or the tactical corollaries following from its
success.'

He then recapitulates the weight of opinion that pronounced
in his favour in previous years and compares this with that of
the opposition in 1908.

In 1905-07 the Board had acted with the unanimous support of the six different departments concerned with gunnery, already listed above as having been consulted by Admiral Jellicoe. He names the thirty-two officers, including the heads and staffs of those six departments who had backed him. The list includes a large number of names well known to this day – John Jellicoe, Percy Scott, Charles Ottley, Alfred Chatfield, Henry Oliver, Edmond Slade, Arthur Craig and Frederick Hamilton. As against these thirty-two recognised experts, he claims that he had been turned down in March 1908, only by Admiral Wilson, a full Admiral before Fire Control was invented, Captain Bacon an anti-Artillerist, and Frederic Dreyer the rival inventor.

The thing was preposterous but the pity of it was that he marred the statement of his case by over-emphasis on the personal limitations of the distinguished old Admiral.

At this point it may well be asked where Fisher stood in this matter. How is the rejection of Pollen's system in March 1908 to be reconciled with his assertion, barely eighteen months earlier, as to its 'priceless' importance?

In the early days of the century, knowing that big guns were largely ineffective at ranges over 2000 yards, Fisher had advocated the building of small and fast battleships, or preferably, armoured cruisers, armed with a great number of guns of small or medium calibre, i.e. 6" or 10". By this means, as he explained to Lord Selborne the First Lord, in a letter of 6th October 1901, French battleships would be destroyed at 5000 yards 'by one of the multitudes of quick-firing projectiles that will be flying around . . . even if all the rest are lost shots.'

Four years later, following his appointment in October 1904, as First Sea Lord, he suddenly reversed his policy and persuaded the Board to lay down HMS *Dreadnought*, the first British battleship to be equipped only with 12" guns.

Logically, there could be two reasons for the change of policy. First that he now realised that one quick-firing light projectile would not be sufficient to destroy an enemy battle-ship or alternatively that he now had reason to believe that big guns would be more effective at long range than his 'multiplicity of small projectiles'.

Historically, there are two closely related events that suggest Pollen influence in this matter. First, that in October 1904 a Commission of Inquiry had been set up under Admiral A. C. Parr to enquire into Pollen's proposals. Secondly that before the end of the year Lord Kelvin, who for some time had been in close touch with Fisher, was invited to join Fisher's newly created Committee of Design. Kelvin's biographer, Sylvanus P. Thompson, records[8] that, 'Kelvin took a keen interest in the operations of the Committee and his scientific knowledge, no less than his experience in seamanship, was of distinct value in its deliberations'; and Kelvin was Pollen's co-director on Linotype. Finally, we have already seen that by the summer of 1906 Fisher was convinced of the 'priceless' value of his inventions.

All in all, and given Fisher's known flair for seeing the potentiality of new inventions, it seems reasonable to conclude that at the end of 1904, Pollen's promise of a system of fire control, that could be relied upon to hit at long range, would have been welcomed by Fisher as the missing link in his con-ception of the fastest, biggest and most powerful battleship in the world.

On the other hand, Fisher cared nothing for the rights of individuals. When told two years later by Bacon that Dreyer could produce results as good as Pollen's, by simpler and cheaper methods, he would have rejoiced to think that the great revolution in gunnery which Pollen had initiated could be achieved without going outside the Service, indeed without going outside the 'fish-pond'.

Fisher's faith in Bacon is well known; but seldom can it have been more clearly demonstrated than in the letter quoted below. Pollen, after his rejection in the *Ariadne*, had sent Fisher an elegant and diplomatic plea for an interview. In this he spoke first of the generosity shown to him 'both by direct grants and by giving me two ships to experiment with for weeks together'. 'In the same period,' he wrote, 'we have met only once and that for five minutes. I remember the occasion with the pleasure naturally resulting from the kind things you said. Now I want to see you again . . . I believe I can show you that in backing me, as you have done, you have been right from the start and will be easily proved right in the end.'

To this Fisher sent the following remarkably uncharacteristic reply, dated 26th March 1908:

Dear Pollen,

In reply to your letter just received. As you will remember you much interested me in Sir C. Ottley's room long ago but I don't presume to pit my judgement in opposition to that of far finer brains than I possess. Yet you may be sure so far as my personal influence has play every care will be given to your representations.

Yours sincerely,

J. A. Fisher

That Bacon had not underrated the case in Dreyer's favour is apparent from an earlier letter dated 10th March, in which Fisher, writing to his friend Julian Corbett, the historian, spoke [9] of Dreyer as having 'the brains of a Newton'.

That the brilliant Bacon could really have thought of Dreyer as a genius is unlikely: but his dislike for Pollen's elaborate instruments was genuine and his task was to convince Fisher that Dreyer could produce equally good results.

It follows that the assumption here put forward as to the influence on Fisher of Pollen's inventions is in no way invalidated by his abandonment of Pollen in 1908. All that had happened was that by 1908 the Establishment, in the persons of Dreyer, Bacon and Fisher, had persuaded each other that they could now find their destination without the aid of the pilot.

It should be added that Bacon, from the time he came to the Admiralty in 1907 was greatly aided in his campaign to oust Pollen by the fact that Pollen was known to enjoy the support of Beresford and Custance. For to Fisher consorting with the enemy was an unpardonable offence.

Among the letters published by A. J. Marder, in *Fear God and Dread Nought* (1908-14), is one from Fisher to Arnold White, his close friend and favourite journalist, in which we see Fisher in his most vindictive and spiteful mood. Fisher's quarrel with Beresford had reached the point when Asquith had found it necessary to appoint a Committee of Enquiry, composed of members of the Cabinet, to look into Beresford's charges against Fisher. Fisher complains[10] to White (4th April 1909), that Pollen was taking an active part in the matter:

'I had been told that Pollen's ramifications were extraordinary and his newspaper influence very considerable, and his being a Roman Catholic of immense support to them. I have consistently refused to have anything to do with him or see him.'

A week later[11] he followed this up, in a letter to McKenna, with the cynical comment 'With Jews (Arthur Lee and Ralph D. Blumenfeld, Editor of the Daily Express 1902-1932) and Jesuits (Pollen and Haldane) against one I don't wonder now at the defection of *The Times*.'

By way of contrast to the hostility of Whitehall and as evidence of Arthur Pollen's standing amongst the top young gunnery men of the day let us close this chapter with a 'pretty compliment' from a great man. In a letter to his wife, not long before the ill fated trial of January 1908 Arthur Pollen wrote:

Here's a pretty compliment. Hamilton, Captain at Whale Island, and Chatfield, his commander, came out to Spithead the other day to look at our instruments and inspect some of the tests we have made with them. Both appeared to be surprised and pleased by the results, which indeed have surpassed all expectations. Up to 12 or 15,000 yards it is quite obvious, if there is light enough and the right atmosphere for taking range

at all, that we can get the speed and course plotted on paper of a target within a minute and a half with absolute accuracy, and this quite irrespective of whether the ship is running steadily on her course or yawing in a heavy sea. The results are exactly the same with the ship rolling. After Hamilton and Chatfield's visit, Gipps[12] asked them for a passage back to the beach, and when he came on board again next morning, he told me that as they pushed off Hamilton asked his commander what he thought of it. To which Chatfield replied, 'What am I to think about a fellow who discovers a problem that we did not know existed, and then proceeds to solve it completely? If the rest of his system comes up to what we have seen, he has made good on his promise to revolutionise naval tactics'.
Now what do you know about that?

A pretty compliment indeed, but the real significance of the story is that Whale Island was the Navy's official gunnery school and here we have evidence of the understanding and support that Pollen enjoyed from the men who held appointments that in any normal organisation would have entitled them to a share, if not a decisive share, in decision making. Yet to Arthur Wilson the opinions of junior officers, and their qualifications to express them, were of no consequence.

Furthermore it is remarkable to find a man in such a position, speaking of Pollen having 'discovered a problem which we did not know existed' – an allusion no doubt to Pollen having mastered the problem of the ever-changing rate of change of range.

It is moreover notable that Alfred Chatfield, the young commander responsible for this shrewd observation, was himself a man of outstanding ability, later chosen by Beatty to serve as his Flag Captain throughout the war and destined to rise to the head of his profession and hold office as First Sea Lord from 1933 to 1938.

CHAPTER IV

The Reluctant Inventor

The rejection of Pollen's system by Admiral Wilson in January 1908, however unjustified, marked the entry of Dreyer as a rival inventor and a turning point in Pollen's relations with the Admiralty. Henceforth, for the next ten years, Dreyer was to enjoy the unusual privilege of being retained by the Admiralty as the authorised inventor of Service instruments of fire control, while at the same time being recognised, for the most part officially, as their principal adviser on all aspects of gunnery; in effect placed in the invidious position of being for twenty years judge in his own cause.

It will therefore be helpful at this point, to pause and consider the nature of Dreyer's approach to naval gunnery and how it differed from Pollen's.

It has been shown that in the early years Arthur Pollen's principal achievement had been to persuade Captain Jellicoe, and through him the omnipotent Jackie Fisher, that mechanisation of fire control was not only a practical possibility but inevitable. The agreement of September 1906, with its promise of co-operation and partnership, marked the conclusion of that first vital phase, the fruit of five years patient and imaginative propaganda and intensive research.

Yet within a year his principal supporters, Jellicoe and Harding, had been removed, leaving him at the mercy of the unbelievers, in the persons of A. K. Wilson and Reginald Bacon, both dedicated to ensuring the rejection of mechanisation in general and of the Pollen system in particular; and it was as technical adviser to the unbelievers that Dreyer first came upon the scene in the guise of Gunnery Assistant to the Director of Naval Ordnance.

In his own way, and at a very different level Dreyer, like Wilson, was a typical product of the Fisher era. As a gunnery lieutenant his success had been due to an exceptional capacity for organisation and for the handling of men, combined with a large measure of mechanical ingenuity. He was the embodiment of the qualities and skills that attracted the attention of the senior officers of the day and brought success in the unreal conditions of what in Pollen's phrase was 'sonorously called Battle Practice'. Yet he seemed unable to look further: the 'processes of thought' had unaccountably stopped. To Pollen's thesis that Battle Practice bore much the same relation to true action conditions as clay pigeons to driven grouse, Dreyer turned a deaf ear. His very success in Battle Practice competition made him resent anyone wanting to change the rules of the game.

Dreyer at this stage firmly believed that by his manual methods he could produce results as good as those promised by Pollen, and the rejection of Pollen's instruments after the *Ariadne* trials in the following January had left the field clear for him to show what he could do. With Bacon's support it was arranged that his system should be given an extensive trial during the Fleet's summer exercises. Alas for Dreyer, the trials merely proved, as Pollen had predicted, that his manual methods were totally inadequate.

Much concerned at the failure of the official system and the multiplicity of methods in use during the summer, the War College called upon one of their officers, Captain C. Hughes-Onslow, for an essay on the subject, with specific reference to the question 'whether any of these systems would prove impracticable in action.' Hughes-Onslow, accordingly, addressed a personal enquiry to all the leading gunnery officers of the day to invite their help. At the time he knew nothing of Arthur Pollen's work, and made no reference to him in his enquiry.

He was consequently astonished to receive from Dreyer, by way of reply, a caustic attack on Pollen and his system. In this, Dreyer went out of his way to deny that Pollen had a system and asserted that the so-called Pollen System was nothing more than a revival of the Watkins' System[1] to which had been added a gyro and a lot of complicated machinery. The letter, dated the 18th October 1908, scoffed at the gyro, the complicated machinery, and the whole idea of automatic plotting, and insisted that the simpler we kept our ships the better; a Chetwynd compass, a pointer linked to the rangefinder, a deal kitchen table and a range bar were all that were needed.

At this date in 1908, there was nothing unusual about Dreyer's attitude to mechanisation; it was in fact typical of the reaction of the professional, then and now, who resents and resists the intrusion into his field of new ideas and new methods. On the other hand, from the standpoint of history, the kitchen table letter is invaluable in that it establishes for all time that as late as October 1908 Dreyer had not yet understood the elements of the problem and was in no sense a rival inventor to Pollen. An opponent, certainly, strongly opposed to everything that Pollen was trying to do, but not a rival in the sense that he had at that time the least intention of trying to emulate Pollen in his self-imposed task of devising an automatic system of fire control.

The change to the role of competing inventor of a mechanical system came about much later and solely as the result of the total failure of the manual methods to which he was still pinning his faith in October 1908. He was thus at least eight years behind Pollen in entering the field, a record that must entitle him to rank as the most reluctant inventor in history.

When in 1909, or more probably in 1910, Dreyer at last realised that to compete with Pollen he would first have to mechanise his plotter, he had before him not only Pollen's latest drawings but also the records of Pollen's extensive discussions with Harding, Dreyer's predecessor in the Department in 1905. Among the subjects that had then been debated, one of the most important was the nature of the chart to be produced by the Plotter. The choice eventually lay between what Pollen called the True Plot, that is to say a chart showing the actual track of both vessels, our own and the enemy's, or alternatively two separate graphs, one showing consecutive ranges, the other, the bearings – a method known as Rate-Plotting.

Pollen in 1905 had rightly chosen the former: Dreyer four years later, chose the latter and in September 1910 took out a patent to cover it: and although the idea had not originated with him, the fact that Pollen had rejected it in favour of the true-plot entitled Dreyer to claim it as his own. But that did not prevent Pollen referring to Rate-Plotting as 'our own still-born child'.

The other major Pollen invention that Dreyer embodied in his 1910 system was the use of the gyro to stabilise the range-finder, an instrument about which he had been so contemptuous less than a year previously.

Nothing brings out more clearly the difference in the quality of the minds of the two men than the fact that Pollen, within a year of his introduction to naval gunnery, should at once have perceived the need for gyro control, whereas to Dreyer, eight years later, it was still an unnecessary elaboration and an object of ridicule.

In the next chapter it will be shown that the system that Dreyer developed between 1910 and 1912 consisted like Pollen's of two groups of instruments, the plotting unit and the Clock[2], or Table as Dreyer preferred to call it, and that in the development of the Dreyer Table the Admiralty were even less scrupulous than they had been over the plotter.

Before returning to the narrative of Pollen's negotiations with the Admiralty it will be convenient here to explain the relationship between Pollen and Harold Isherwood his designer. To the layman the distinction between inventor and designer is not always clear. In the world of engineering, the designer is a man whose training in the processes of manufacture should enable him to find the simplest and most practical form in which to give effect to the inventor's brain-child. The inventor is the man who, like Arthur Pollen, has the imagination to think of something at once new and useful. It may take the form of a new device that has never been thought of before: or, alternatively, simply a better way of doing something, or making something, already in common use. Such a man almost invariably needs the help of a professional designer before his idea can be put into production: but only rarely does the professional designer himself produce an original invention.

From the start all Pollen's instruments, other than the gyro, were designed by Harold Isherwood, an imaginative and singularly capable designer who was working for Linotype when Pollen first started in 1901, and remained with that company until 1906, when he resigned to work whole time for Pollen. The association continued on a close and friendly basis until the war brought their activities to a standstill in 1914. Isherwood then joined the RNVR where his technical abilities soon led to his being granted the rank of Commander.

It is a pleasure to record that in 1919, some four years after he had stopped working with Pollen on A.C., Isherwood presented him with a handsome copy of his own book, *The Navy in Battle*, bound in green Morocco leather, with the elegant inscription:

> To the Author, this volume of his own work is presented, by one who, sharing in the successes and many disappointments incidental to inventors, has nevertheless, ever retained a fervent admiration for his genius.

We must now return to the situation that had arisen in 1908 following the rejection of Pollen's automatic system of plotting by Wilson in March. Pollen, as we have seen, had fought back hard, but unsuccessfully, to obtain a retrial.

The Admiralty at this point were confident that Dreyer held the solution to the problem of fire control and that they could safely dispense with Pollen's services. They accordingly asked Pollen what sum he would accept in settlement for his admitted contribution to the subject. To Pollen who needed money for further development of his system the offer of a substantial payment was by no means unwelcome, and a figure of £11,500, together with the return to him of the instrument bought for trial in the *Ariadne*, was quickly agreed. This figure it should be noted included a notional fee of approximately £10,000 over and above his out-of-pocket expenses. Settlement was held up for a time by a last minute demand by the Admiralty that the whole system should remain secret for a further two years, but by mid-June it had been agreed to reduce this to eighteen months.

In accepting this settlement, Pollen had by no means abandoned the hope of eventually selling the whole system to the Admiralty on monopoly terms. On the contrary, he was quite certain that no system of manual plotting would ever prove effective and confident that the Admiralty would have to come back to him. And so it proved, for the Dreyer methods tried out at great length throughout the summer proved totally unworkable.

Meanwhile Pollen and Isherwood had effected important improvements in the design of their gyro mounting and of the plotter, and had also completed designs for a clock. On the 5th January (1909) Pollen, through the medium of the Argo Company which now came upon the scene for the first time as owners of A.C., addressed a letter to the Admiralty advising them of the completion of the drawings for the entire A.C. Battle System, emphasizing that what was now being offered went far beyond anything previously submitted, so that there was no question of their being asked to reopen any matter already decided. Furthermore he reminded their Lordships that the period of secrecy would expire in November and suggested that it would be desirable for them to investigate the whole system prior to that date in case they might wish to acquire the monopoly.

However Bacon was not yet ready to capitulate and Pollen's letter remained unanswered for three months.

Meanwhile, unknown to Bacon, Pollen had enlisted the support of Reginald McKenna, the First Lord, a fellow Liberal, a man of high intelligence and integrity. There is a letter on the file, dated 22nd March, in which Pollen asked McKenna to give him 'sufficient of your time to enable me to put the case so fully before you that you will understand both the problem itself and the history of it, because the history is vital to what is happening and what is going to happen now. This will occupy at least one hour of your time'.

Ten days later Pollen received from the Admiralty a letter dated 2nd April, acknowledging his three letters of the 5th January, 15th February and 10th March, and inviting Argo to tender for a complete unit of their system. By the 21st their tender had been accepted. Judging by the correspondence with the Admiralty and with McKenna, it would appear that Pollen owed this sudden change of policy solely to McKenna's powerful intervention. Yet there is also on the file a rather charming letter from no less a personage than Captain Robert Scott, the ill-fated Polar Explorer, then serving in the D.N.O.'s department, addressed to Captain Hughes-Onslow, whose projected report on gunnery methods in use in the Service was noticed in the previous chapter. The letter dated 17th July 1909 runs –

'Yes, your Essay was downed but not without having created the desired effect. There has been a great change in the whole policy which you would be interested to hear. I will only say that Mr Pollen is in high spirits'. To which he adds as a P.S. 'The D.N.O. went arm in arm with Pollen to Manchester and came back much impressed. He is now sincerely anxious for the experiments to succeed. As regards the Service this is the best possible result of your efforts, but I much regret that your personal share in this campaign cannot be more publicly known'.

Strangely enough, Pollen's own correspondence with the Admiralty during the summer gives no indication of any such change of attitude. For the most part, it reflects Pollen's anxiety as to the form the trials will take and is also much taken up with a minor dispute over the infringement of patents by the Admiralty who had manufactured and issued a device to assist in the process of manual plotting, which was a mere crib of an instrument which Pollen had already sold to a number of gunnery officers. As we shall see, it was not until November that Pollen became aware of Bacon's change of attitude and even then he did not trust it.

The chosen ship for the trials was the *Natal* and the intention was that the gear should be installed during the summer. To be on the safe side, the Admiralty agreed to pay £540 a month to keep open their option on a monopoly should no decision have been arrived at by the end of November, when the existing agreement was due to expire. In the event no trials had been possible by that date although, in practice runs, the gyro and plotter had already achieved outstanding success. The Dreyer Wilson system had in fact been put to shame and for a brief moment it seemed that the entire Pollen system was about to be adopted.

In the course of all these exciting events Pollen had spent a month on board the *Natal* and discovered in Frederick Ogilvy, the Captain, a new friend and a powerful supporter and unquestionably the first naval officer (as distinct from Captain E. W. Harding of the Royal Marine Artillery) fully to appreciate both the strategic importance of his ideas and the mechanical problems involved.

In a letter to Hughes-Onslow, Pollen wrote with unrestrained enthusiasm of his new friend:

1st November, 1909

My dear H.O.,

Never were your good wishes so completely realised. I scarcely dare believe in my good fortune. Ogilvy is not one in a thousand but just one only. His grasp both of principle and detail is, in my experience, unique. We have had great talks. I have not presented him with advocacy. He has studied the pamphlets and descriptions closely; he knows the gear intimately; his eye for a drawing is infallible, it is like a great conductor's for a score – he does not have to hear the music – he can read it. F.O. can see a machine in a drawing and he is even more anti-polyanthropist[3] than I am. It is a new one on me to find a sea captain insisting on making the gear more complete, both as a scientific solution of the problem and as eliminating still more mental and manual operation. But then he is both the best mechanic and the hardest thinker on war that I have encountered. He is ruthless in telling me our shortcomings and defects – all of his suggestions are invaluable. To him the employment of the gun in action – as contrasted with battle practice – is everything.

You cannot realize what it means to me. The great change in our plotting system which we have funked all these years on the grounds that it was an extra complication he, with his urge for sea fighting, insists on as a primary necessity: it is, of course, making the plot irrespective and independent of helm.

The letter ends:

We had great doings Saturday. Atlantic Fleet here en masse, dinner on flagship in my honour in the evening: P.L. vocal in my praises, 'the most important project now proceeding anywhere in the world: the future of naval fighting depends on your success', and so forth, very gratifying.

P.L. was Prince Louis of Battenberg, one of the best brains in the Service, who was later to rise to the head of his profession to serve as First Sea Lord from January 1913 to October 1914.

Yet within ten days of the rejoicings in the *Natal*, Pollen's engineers found themselves peremptorily ordered off the ship, barely twenty-four hours before the official trials were due to begin, a decision that proved to be the prelude to a further year of devastating contradictions and reversals of policy.

The two areas of difficulty were first that the gear in the *Natal*, as with any new and complicated conception, was what is called a 'first-off', experimental set of instruments, good enough when carefully handled to demonstrate its military potential, but too fragile to stand up to Service conditions. As a result, while Ogilvy and his like could see that the idea was right and of great military value, it remained possible for his opponents to point to the poor results as proof of failure.

The second source of difficulty arose out of the disinclination of opponents in the Service to accord full co-operation, or, as they saw it, to share their secrets and their experience with an inventor who was free to take his inventions abroad. The very problem which in 1906 had been so clearly foreseen but to which no solution had been found.

In November 1909 Pollen's reaction to the humiliation of being ordered off the ship had been to demand an interview with Bacon and challenge him to face the issue as to whether and on what terms they would be willing to give him their wholehearted support. He put it to Bacon that no progress could be made if they were to be kept at arm's length and treated as spies, and no less obvious, that unreserved co-operation would never be achieved so long as he was subject to the suspicion of wishing to sell abroad. For his part he was willing, if suitable terms could be arranged, to enter into an agreement under which the Company would be irrevocably bound to secrecy as to present and future inventions, thus renouncing for all time the right to sell elsewhere.

Much to Pollen's surprise Bacon expressed full agreement with Pollen's attitude and asked him to submit his proposals forthwith. These Pollen put forward on the 16th November. At the same time, distrusting the apparent change of attitude by Bacon, he at once wrote off to Ogilvy seeking his support.

Dear Natal,

It would be good if you would write fully to Jellicoe. The fact is I am really worried. To tell the truth I left Weymouth – after watching the good ship steam out – with a very heavy heart. Somehow we seem on the eve of serious trouble. Your parting words that the success of the gear is assured were comforting. I know that the Lords (of Admiralty) at least do trust you. You may counteract Bacon. But he needs counteracting, even after he leaves; for he has bequeathed a legacy of distrust, jealousy, fear – I don't know what to call it – but anyway he has so inflamed the incumbent mass of opposition that I am fairly frightened at times; even when, just as now, things look for the moment better.

Of course, if I can win out and secure co-operation, I shall be absolutely sure. Your belief in it makes me more certain than ever that the show is on sound lines. Eliminate the landsman's errors, and all will be well.

It seems certain that Bacon is going, and that Wilson is to succeed Fisher early in the year. In the back of my mind I have an instinct that if we cannot secure monopoly and co-operation before this last event – the gear will be lost to the Navy as an exclusive possession. Your writing to Jellicoe might do more than anything towards a speedy settlement.

From this letter it appears that while Pollen did not expect Wilson to take over as First Sea Lord until some time in the New Year, he was very doubtful of his chances of finalising negotiations in time.

The situation was complicated by the fact that Bacon had just accepted an appointment as General Manager of the Coventry Ordnance Works and was to leave the Service before the end of the year.

However, to Pollen's relief and surprise, the conference held on the 10th December, under the Chairmanship of Captain A. W. Craig, the Assistant D.N.O., passed off in the same good spirit as his previous meeting with Bacon. Quantities and prices were quickly agreed for a contract worth £176,000 covering seventy-five sets of gyro mountings and indicators and fifty plotters, with monopoly and secrecy assured for a further five years. In a letter[4] to Spender we find 'so completely was I given to understand that this was all settled that I urged Mr McKenna (a fellow Liberal) to have the decision made official before Christmas, so that I might be free to stand for Parliament'.

Writing many years later, in a brief for his counsel at the Royal Commission hearings of 1925, Pollen laid great emphasis on the contrast between the spirit of fairness and honesty which had characterised the Admiralty attitude in 1905 and the treatment accorded to him in later years. 'Only once and then only for a few weeks was this spirit of honest and loyal co-operation restored and that was during the negotiations in November and December 1909, during the last few days of Admiral Bacon's tenure of the Directorship of Naval Ordnance and in the first two weeks of the reign of his successor'. 'Captain Bacon's last act was to admit defeat, and do his best to remedy the blunder for which he was responsible.'

Whether, or to what extent, Bacon's conversion was due to Ogilvy's intervention is not clear, for Ogilvy by this time, was seriously ill with typhoid fever, from which he was to die a week later, on the 18th December. Pollen in his letter to Hughes-Onslow had written of Ogilvy's understanding, friendship and support, 'You cannot understand what it means to me'. Now within a month of the discovery of Ogilvy as friend, counsellor and supporter came the shattering blow of his death. For Pollen the bitterness of the loss was accentuated tenfold by the knowledge that it was his own gift of oysters that led to the fatal illness. Of all the misfortunes that were dealt him by Fate in these critical years, first the ill-luck of Bacon and Dreyer taking over from Jellicoe and Harding just before the *Ariadne* trials in 1908, and now the prospect of Wilson returning to the Admiralty as First Sea Lord at the moment of triumph in the *Natal*, none hit him so hard or seemed so cruel as the loss of Fred Ogilvy. For, in addition to his personal qualities and his unique understanding of A.C., Ogilvy was persona grata at Whitehall and already designated[5] to be the next Captain of the *Excellent*, the Navy's chief school of gunnery. Had he lived to take up this appointment his support might well have proved decisive.

Bacon's successor as D.N.O. was Capt. Archibald Moore, an old family friend of the Pollens, clever enough in many ways but in no sense a real expert in gunnery. To make matters worse, Pollen already had good reason to suspect that while still playing the part of a family friend he was secretly hostile both to him personally and to all that he was trying to do.

On taking over as D.N.O., Moore's first reaction was to accept the obvious and assure Pollen that the order negotiated with Craig in December would shortly be confirmed. This assurance was almost at once belied by a letter dated the 18th January, stating categorically that no order would be placed until further trials had been held.

This was followed on the 11th April, by a further letter, to the effect that following further trials, they were no longer interested in the monopoly of any of the instruments, but would take fifteen gyro mountings at £1,000 each – in effect an order worth £15,000 in place of the order for £176,000 negotiated with Craig. To this there was no possible answer except to appeal once more direct to McKenna.

In this, his second approach to McKenna, Pollen knew that he could count on the wholehearted support of Admiral (later Sir) Richard Peirse the Inspector of Target Practice (I.T.P.). Pollen had met Peirse for the first time in 1909, shortly after his appointment as I.T.P., and found him quick to appreciate the possibilities of A.C. and the futility of the so-called trials in the *Ariadne*. Peirse's support was very valuable because at this time the I.T.P. and his organisation were recognised as the one impartial authority on gunnery methods. Their function was to observe every shot fired in practice, both at home and abroad, and they naturally became the most experienced and best informed critics of the wide variety of methods and ideas with which the fleets were at this time experimenting. A. K. Wilson, as has been said, like Fisher before him, had an unconcealed contempt for the 'Staff System' and it is probably true to say that in their day, the I.T.P.'s Department was the sole exception, a unique example of the kind of standing committee of experts which that term implies. Even so, the status of the Inspector was subject to the anomaly that while totally independent in the administration of his department, his reports had all to be addressed to the D.N.O. with whom the decision rested as to what advice should be tendered to the Board.

Throughout the years 1908 to 1911, so critical to Pollen, the inspectorate remained consistently opposed to the policy of Whitehall. Under Peirse, in particular, it became, in Pollen's phrase, 'almost the focus of mutiny', and remained so under his successor Montague Browning until 1913, when Winston Churchill, as First Lord, allowed himself to be persuaded to abolish the office of I.T.P.; a thoroughly bad decision on which Pollen, writing some years later, commented 'With the suppression of the office of Inspector of Target Practice, there came administrative peace and technical chaos.'

In 1910, however, Peirse was still a powerful influence, and his enthusiastic support provided McKenna with the official backing he needed to cancel the decision of 11th April, insist on further trials, and give Pollen a further two years in which to develop his gear in secrecy. Even so, it would have been out of the question for Pollen to bind himself to secrecy any longer without first obtaining from the Admiralty an order that would keep his factory going while he finalised the system. Wilson and Moore, resentful of their defeat on the principle of maintaining monopoly rights, were ruthless in the terms they offered.

It will be recalled that the plotting gear first tried in the *Natal* in the previous October had produced excellent results as long as the ship was on a straight course, but was unable to do so while turning. Encouraged by Frederick Ogilvy, Pollen had decided to put in hand 'the great change in our plotting system which we had funked all these years, on the grounds that it was an extra complication' and make his plotter independent of helm, or *helm-free*, as it later came to be known. For the same reason the Clock, the first ever produced and known as the Argo Mark I, was withdrawn from trial pending conversion to the helm-free principle.

The terms negotiated in November with Craig had covered seventy-five gyro mountings and fifty of the new helm-free plotters. They did not however include the projected new helm-free Clock which had yet to be designed.

Now, following the farce of the second set of trials in March, and the total rejection of monopoly on the 14th April, Moore, on McKenna's instructions, in a letter dated 29th April, had come forward with an offer to take a mere forty-five gyro mountings, but no plotters and no Clocks. The gyros were for delivery prior to December 1912, with secrecy for the whole system assured to that date. As a stop-gap order this would have been satisfactory enough had the price been right, but Moore's price was £1350 per instrument as against Pollen's tender of £1750.

For Pollen, the choice at this moment lay between taking the system abroad, a course contemptuously recommended to him by the Admiralty on numerous previous[6] occasions, or alternatively, accepting the sacrifice involved and making a new agreement with the Admiralty on Wilson's terms. The situation was complicated by financial commitments. For some time, it had been evident that the Linotype Company, of which he had remained a director, and which had in the past manufactured all his instruments, would have to merge with its American counterpart, the Mergenthaler Linotype Company. This meant that if he was to continue doing secret work for the Navy he would have to find new facilities. In the previous December (1909), encouraged by Moore's assurance that the big orders already negotiated were about to be confirmed, Pollen had entered into a contract to buy control of Thomas Cooke and Sons of York, the leading instrument makers in the country.

Pollen thus found himself under obligation to find £20,000 for the new factory, on which the first instalment of £15,000 was due on the 15th June; and at the same time asked to accept a contract on which the loss over the two years was optimistically estimated at £18,000 but which in the event was to cost him £26,000.

On the face of it the acceptance of such terms was out of the question. Yet he knew that with the exception of Wilson and Moore he had the Service behind him. In a rather bitter memorandum of this date we find the remarkable statement:

> Mr Pollen began his work knowing four officers in the Navy. He is in correspondence now with 132 on the Active List. He has not sought them. They seek him. Why do gunnery lieutenants ask him for gear? Why do they offer to buy [manual plotters] at £1 a month out of their scanty pay? Why do men Mr Pollen has never seen or heard of come to him and ask him to explain his principles to them?

Moreover he believed that Wilson, who had been dragged out from retirement in order to restore the prestige of the Service after the scandal of the Fisher-Beresford row, would not long remain in office. Then again, he had reason to hope that the fresh set of trials (the third in the *Natal*), ordered by McKenna, would be on a more equitable basis and give him a chance to prove what he could do. But above all, the deciding factor was that a number of senior friends in the Service undertook, should need arise, to allow their names to be used in urging the national importance of his work, in support of an appeal for funds from private sources. Encouraged by this, and despite the financial risks involved, he decided to accept.

In the event, the support he received from the Service during the following eighteen months exceeded his wildest dreams.

In the first place, Sir Francis Bridgeman, the Second Sea Lord, taking his courage in both hands and, against all precedent, gave permission for two officers on the active list, Lieutenant Gerard Riley[6] and Lieutenant George Gipps, to go into the employment of the Argo Company for eighteen months, in order to ensure that the final re-designing of the Argo System should, in every detail, be fit for Service conditions.

At a slightly lower level, Craig the assistant D.N.O. had been successful in obtaining in Reginald Hall a first class successor to Ogilvy as Captain of the *Natal*. Hall, who was later to achieve such fame as Director of Naval Intelligence during the war, had a good knowledge of gunnery, and although not yet endowed with the reputation or prestige to enable him to insist on fair play for Pollen, was certainly not lacking in courage or administrative ability. Pollen was again fortunate in the appointment, somewhat later, as Torpedo Lieutenant to the *Natal*, of another first class man in Reginald Plunkett, who later went on to become Beatty's Flag-Commander at Jutland and ended his career as Admiral the Honourable Sir Reginald Plunkett-Ernle-Erle-Drax, DSO, KCB.

Among other supporters was Commander (later Admiral Sir) William James, who as chief gunnery officer in the *Natal* had worked closely with Pollen and his instruments in 1909-1910. In his delightful autobiography *The Sky was Always Blue*, published in 1951, he leaves us in no doubt as to his own reactions to the Admiralty's treatment of Pollen. In the course of a lengthy tribute he remarks:

> Instead of welcoming Pollen as an ally the Admiralty very stupidly treated him as an intruder. One of my instructions was that if I met Pollen or Gipps on shore I was not to speak to them!
>
> The verdict went in favour of the Dreyer system and so fierce internecine war broke out between those officers who were convinced that Pollen had had a raw deal and those who thought Dreyer was on the right lines. Pollen, undismayed by this blow to his hopes then invented a very clever mechanism which was fitted in my next ship, the *Natal*, and followed it with a still better design that was fitted in the *Queen Mary* when I was her Commander. So the man I was told to shun as a leper became a great friend. . . . The irony was that the Admiralty design that eventually emerged was hardly distinguishable from Pollen's design.

When a year later it became necessary to raise £20,000 for the Argo Company, in whose name all his gunnery interests were now vested, Pollen's friends proved as good as their word, and a distinguished group of officers gave him the backing he needed. Their names make interesting reading and appear on the record[7] as follows:

1. Vice-Admiral H.S.H. Prince Louis of Battenburg,
   ex-Commander-in-Chief, Home Fleet.

2. Admiral the Lord Charles Beresford,
   ex-Commander-in-Chief, Home Fleet.

3. Rear-Admiral Slade,
   Commander-in-Chief, East Indies Squadron.

4. Rear-Admiral Peirse, Inspector of Target Practice –
   to be Rear-Admiral, Home Fleet.

5. Captain Brock, Flag Captain, Home Fleet.

Pollen was thus fully justified in his claim that, throughout 1910 and 1911, the Argo Company, 'though to outward appearances an organisation from which the Admiralty held aloof', was yet an organisation which 'counted amongst its closest friends and most intimate consultants many of the most eminent officers of the Naval Service'.

The practical consequence of the seconding of Riley and Gipps, and of the appointment of Hall and Plunkett, was to convince the gunnery officers in the Fleet that Pollen was now accepted, that A.C. would be adopted as soon as it was ready and that meantime they were free to make suggestions to Gipps or ask questions – and as Pollen later recorded, his men were inundated with advice and enquiries – some of it very valuable.

CHAPTER V

Rejection

McKenna's powerful intervention, in particular the promise of new trials, had given Pollen a new lease of life. Nor had he any cause to be disappointed at the constitution of the Trial Committee[1] – chosen and appointed by Sir William May; the C-in-C of the Home Fleet.

Heading the Committee, with the elegant title of Chief Umpire, was the Hon. S. C. J. Colville, a much respected figure who possessed the advantage that he was not a gunnery specialist and therefore not already involved in the A.C. controversy. The other members were Captain A. P. Stoddart, Captain C. M. de Bartolomé and Commander (later Admiral Sir) William Fisher, Colville's Flag Commander in the *Dreadnought*. With Plunkett[2] at the same time in the *Natal* as Torpedo Lieutenant, reporting direct to Fisher, Pollen could not have asked for a fairer Tribunal.

A welcome and unexpected development was the decision to submit the two current Service systems for trial at the same time. Both were dependent on manual plotting, a fact that supports the belief that even at this late date neither Dreyer nor any other inventor was in the field with a mechanical system.

On the other hand Pollen had cause to be apprehensive in that his gear had deteriorated sadly since its installation in the *Natal* in the previous autumn. In particular the wooden table, frequently exposed to water and heat, was badly warped.

Pollen, who at the time knew little of the arrangements, feared the worst and protested strongly when his engineers were again ordered off shortly before the trials began, arguing that his gear could not be expected to function adequately in strange hands.

In the event, his fears proved groundless. The Committee's report dated the 1st July opened with an unqualified condemnation of the two manual systems, and showed that, despite the malfunctioning of the Argo gear, they were fully alive to its military potential. Their recommendations were as follows:

First, the immediate adoption of the gyro-controlled range-finder mounting

Secondly, the adoption, when available, of the 'improved model clock as proposed by the makers', and

Thirdly, that there should be further trials of the plotter but not until after it had been further developed. That when available the improved models should be fitted in four ships in order to expedite development.

In effect the recommendations met all Pollen's demands, particularly the final proviso that the ships officers should cooperate with the makers with a view to the production of 'the most efficient instrument as quickly as possible.'

But alas, this report – the first by an ad hoc Committee of experts since 1905, and destined to be the last – was kept a tight secret. Pollen, usually well informed of even the least favourable events at the Admiralty, never knew of its existence, not even when presenting his case to the Royal Commission in 1925.

All he knew of its contents was what could be deduced from the official letter of the 19th August, by which he was informed that 'as a result of the trials in HMS *Natal* with the plotting gear installed by you in that ship, my Lords Commissioners have decided not to adopt your automatic Plotting Table.' Wilson's contempt and disregard for expert opinion have often been noted and condemned but it would be difficult to find a more reprehensible case than his rejection of the finding of the Colville Committee in regard to the A.C. plotter.

In contrast, their attitude towards the clock was helpful and co-operative in that they sent Pollen a detailed report on the working and the weaknesses of the instrument[3] tried in the *Natal*. In his acknowledgement Pollen thanked them for their criticisms 'which appear to us perfectly just and extremely valuable.'

But the successful concealment of the clause in favour of the further development of the plotter was a disaster from which he never recovered.

In the event, the conversion of the Mark I Clock to helm free gave rise to unexpected difficulties of design which resulted in a delay of twelve months before Pollen found himself in a position to advise Admiral Moore, the D.N.O., that he was about to start construction.

The sequel, as recorded by Pollen some years later, makes curious reading:

> In May 1911 I informed the Admiralty that I was beginning the construction of an instrument, the Argo Clock II, afterwards known as the Argo Clock Mark IV. I told Admiral Moore, the Director of Naval Ordnance, how its functions would differ from those of my first Clock, submitted in 1905 and demonstrated in 1910. Admiral Moore at once asked me for the confidential loan of my drawings for his personal perusal and I lent them to him without hesitation. I did not know at this time that Commander Dreyer was the Admiralty's Chief Adviser on this branch of Fire Control, nor that he was actively co-operating with Sir Keith Elphinstone, in the production of instruments to compete with my expected solution of the whole Fire Control problem. It appears that Admiral Moore promptly handed over my drawings to Elphinstone and Dreyer and that, in the words of the Royal Commission, 'the transformation of the Mark III Dreyer Table which did not integrate into the Mark IV which did', was brought about by these persons plagiarising both the purpose of my Clock and the means by which that purpose was effected.

Unaware of the activities of Moore, Elphinstone and Dreyer, Pollen and Isherwood went ahead with the construction of the

Argo Mark IV, and by March in the following year (1912) were able to report that the first completed instrument was ready for inspection at the Company's Adelphi office. There it was seen in operation by all the leading gunnery authorities of the day, and by the Lords of Admiralty in person, including Winston Churchill himself.

Among friends behind the scenes at this time, was Reginald Hall who as Captain of the *Natal* in 1910 had seen at first hand what the Pollen Plotting System of the day could do, and the lengths to which Whitehall had gone to discredit it. In 1912, as Assistant Controller, he was at Whitehall when the Argo Mark IV Clock was first offered to the Admiralty, and many years later[4] testified to the impression it had made at the time and to the prompt decision of the Controller, Sir Charles Briggs, to appoint a top level Committee to advise on it.

As in 1906, the Committee included all the recognised gunnery authorities in the Service, namely the Captain of HMS *Excellent* and his experimental Staff, the Inspector of Target Practice and his Staff and the Gunnery Officers of the Naval Ordnance Department. This Committee was unanimous[5] as to the vital importance of monopolising the new invention, and plans were at once made for an exhaustive demonstration at sea.

All this was achieved between March 1912, when the Clock was first shown, and the middle of June. At this moment there occurred yet another of those dramatic changes of personnel that was to reverse the course of history. For no apparent reason Sir Charles Briggs was removed from the Controllership and his place taken by Archibald Moore the D.N.O. To Pollen, Moore's promotion to this key post on the Board was a grievous blow for by now he had ample proof of Moore's secret hostility. To make matters worse, Moore at once decreed that all major questions of Fire Control would be dealt with direct by himself as Controller and not as hitherto by the D.N.O.

A week or two later he let it be known that monopoly of the A.C. Clock, which as D.N.O. he had recently recommended, would be abandoned at the end of the year and the company given freedom to sell it abroad. Formal intimation of this decision was not given until the 20th August but by that time Pollen's plans for a counter attack were already far advanced.

The two men to whom he had turned for support were first his old friend J. A. Spender, the influential editor of the *Westminster Gazette*, and secondly Admiral Peirse, the former Inspector of Target Practice, who had saved the day in 1910.

Earlier in the year, in May, while Pollen's relations with the Admiralty were still normal, Spender had brought Pollen and Winston Churchill together at lunch and Churchill, in his grandiose way, had promised not to let A.C. go without exhaustive tests, even if they cost £100,000. The Admiralty letter of the 20th August abandoning monopoly without trial of any of the latest instruments, showed that Churchill had failed to follow up his early show of interest. The problem now was to find some way to get him back to his earlier position.

With that end in view, Pollen, with Spender's aid, concocted a letter[6] which Pollen was to write to Spender and of which Spender would forward a copy to Churchill.

The presentation of the case was broadly as follows. On the three previous occasions when the Board had thrown over secrecy without trial, the decision had been based not on the merits of the case but on the issue as to whether the Board could give a decision contrary to the advice of a distinguished officer – Wilson in 1908, Bacon in 1909 and Wilson again in 1910. Each time it was dealt with as a personal issue; a matter of discipline not of doctrine. Now history was repeating itself with Moore as his distinguished opponent. 'I cannot believe,' wrote[7] Pollen, 'that Churchill – so clear-headed on the functions of a General Staff in what he admits to be the less important fields of strategy and tactics, should be blind to the wants of a similar organ in what he describes as the vastly more important field of the individual efficiency of ships.' And again, 'for obvious reasons I do not wish to go to him and be forced into the ambiguous position of seeming to make charges against a colleague he rightly trusts. The moment I am compelled to abandon the defiant role of the patriot, I must assume the obsequious part of the shop-walker and avoid angry discussion with the patrons to whom it is my commercial interest to cringe. Luckily my commercial interests are safe. I am left with a fine property that owes much to Service help. It can only be against my commercial interests if the system is monopolised.'

A curious feature of the situation was that the Admiralty had just taken delivery of one of Pollen's Clocks and were intending to go ahead with the promised trials despite the abandonment of monopoly. The Clock was installed in the *Orion*, one of the latest big-gun battleships, under the command of Captain A. W. Craig (later Craig-Waller). Craig had been Assistant to Bacon, the D.N.O., at the time of the *Natal* controversy at the end of 1909, and was a great believer and keen supporter of Pollen's instruments. On hearing the story he at once realised that much might depend upon his obtaining good results before monopoly ran out at the end of the year and he threw himself with great zeal into perfecting the clock and adopting it to Service use. In the six weeks from the end of October to mid-December he and Pollen exchanged no less than a dozen highly technical letters on such matters as the shape and location of the dials and methods of control. What really worried Craig, no less than Pollen, was not the details of the Pollen Clock, but the total inadequacy of Dreyer's Rate-Plotting method of obtaining the data. For the value of any computer depends on the accuracy of the information fed to it. The capabilities of the Argo Clock could not be fully demonstrated so long as it was harnessed to a Dreyer Plotter. With Pollen's help, Craig himself prepared and submitted a strong restatement of the case for True-Course plotting, but once again it fell on deaf ears.

Parallel with all this technical work, Pollen and Peirse were busy planning their top-level campaign to obtain a stay of execution. Behind the scenes Reginald Hall played a big part in these discussions and Craig was kept fully informed.

All were agreed that letters were unlikely to meet with any response and that they must aim at personal interviews at the highest level, if possible with Churchill, the First Lord, Bridgeman, the First Sea Lord, Prince Louis, already named to take over from Bridgeman at the year-end, and Jellicoe, now back at the Admiralty as Second Sea Lord after two years in command of the South Atlantic Fleet. The difficulties would clearly be tremendous; not least the fact that Dreyer had for the past two years served as Flag-Commander to Jellicoe, to whom every stage of his gear had been submitted. Indeed, it was freely said that Dreyer's system was virtually Jellicoe's. Nor was Dreyer very scrupulous or accurate in what he reported to Jellicoe in regard to Pollen's Argo Clock. Among other things Peirse discovered that Jellicoe had been led to believe that Pollen had given up his system of True-Course Plotting and adopted Dreyer's system of Rate Plotting. Had this been true it would have represented a tremendous victory for Dreyer and fully justified the Admiralty's 1910 decision in favour of Dreyer's system of plotting. In fact it was absolutely untrue and on the 27th September Peirse reported to Pollen that he had just been writing to Jellicoe to put him right and had told him that in reality he and Pollen thought that Rate Plotting was 'an abomination'.

Then again there was the further factor of Moore's hostility to Pollen, of which they were all by now fully aware.

Happily, Peirse was personally on good terms with all the top men and able to assure Pollen that he would have no difficulty in arranging the necessary interviews.

Armed with a strongly worded memorandum he called upon Winston Churchill. Churchill received him very kindly but was clever enough to have an urgent appointment[8] at the House of Commons which cut the meeting short. Peirse had therefore to be satisfied with the promise of further enquiry and of a careful study of his Memorandum. In this Peirse had boldly asserted that in the Service 'we are now relying on guesswork as a means of obtaining the rate when we ought to be straining every nerve to perfect a system based upon scientific principle. . . . In my opinion, the only instruments which hold out any hope of success in the attainment of this are those devised by Mr Pollen.'

Copies of this memorandum were sent to Bridgeman, Prince Louis, Jellicoe and Montague Browning, Peirse's successor as Inspector of Target Practice. In the covering letter[9] to Prince Louis written from HMS *Thunderer*, in which the Director was being tested, Peirse wrote:

> To throw over Mr Pollen now, and allow him to give the fruits of his ten year experience (all gained at our expense) to some Foreign Power would in my opinion be nothing short of a National Disaster.
>
> The Director, from what I have seen of it here, undoubtedly promises to give us the best system of firing and, one might add, the only system where the ship is rolling. What we still require is the means of placing these concentrated broadsides on the Enemy and keeping them there.
>
> Pollen's apparatus is without any doubt whatever the one best calculated to give us this.

Peirse later went to see Prince Louis to reinforce his letter but had to report to Pollen that the Prince had frankly confessed that Moore had succeeded in persuading them all that the Dreyer System was just as good.

Meanwhile Pollen himself had been no less active, covering much the same ground but with a rather different approach. To the impartial observer the most glaring omissions were, first, the failure to establish the facts by competitive tests, and next the refusal, despite the conflicting views of the Briggs Committee and those advanced by Moore his successor, to appoint a well qualified Committee of experts to investigate the issue. Yet neither Pollen nor his advisers thought it wise to press for these obvious measures. They had been cheated too often in the past. There was the risk, if not the certainty, that any new Committee would be packed: alternatively that the tests as in 1908 would be so contrived as to show what the

Dreyer System could do and not what it was unable to do.

In June Pollen had written direct to Fisher, who was no longer in office, to ask for an interview. In reply he received a very courteous telegram regretting that 'circumstances made it impossible for him to intervene'. His next move, to seek an interview with Churchill, also failed and there was nothing for it but to present his case in writing. With a story that would require several thousand words to re-tell, it was not easy to decide what to include or in what manner to present his material. Various drafts were prepared and discussed at length with Peirse, Hall and Spender. The final product, in simple letter form, was despatched to Churchill on the 21st October. Too long to be quoted in full, the following extracts deserve special mention. First a reminder that 'successive Boards have retained me now for eight years to work on the problem . . . in the ships where our gear has been tried we have profited by the criticism of many of the ablest specialists in the Navy. The opportunities given to us in experience, co-operation and money have been unique. It is no wonder that we have succeeded in doing what we were of set purpose subsidised to do, and have actually produced the perfect Fire Control System.'

Next, 'he ventures to suggest' that 'the real obstacle to adoption is not its price nor its supposed unsuccess, but that the official conception of the kind of fire control necessary in action differs radically from what we (and those naval officers who think with us) think necessary.' He continues:

> Take the two divisions of the subject, range, speed and course *finding* and range *keeping*.
> We maintain that range, speed and course *finding* must be available however high the relative speed, (so as to enable a *Lion* at top speed to fight another *Lion* at top speed if she wished). And next, that to be ready for war the *Lion* must be able to get the data for doing this, whether she is on a steady course or under helm.
> The proposed Service methods of getting speed and course cannot do either of these things, because they are not designed to attempt to do them. Yet their military value is incalculable.

Prophetic words when we recall that four years later the battle of Jutland did in fact open with Beatty in his flagship the *Lion*, steaming due East at top speed, to cut off Hipper coming down from the North, also at top speed, in *'another Lion'*; and when we remember too, that it was in the opening twenty minutes, while making a large turn to the South, that Beatty had so much the worst of it, the *Lion* being repeatedly hit and the *Indefatigable* sunk, following an explosion in her magazine.

After describing the manner in which trials had been conducted in 1908 and again in the *Orion*, he comments that it is not surprising that so many Naval officers who, after years of study, have come to the conclusion that his system provides the only solution, should now have written to say that for him to take it abroad would be a national calamity. 'So strongly do I feel this myself that I now make the following proposal to you'.

The proposal was nothing less than an offer to undertake, in advance of any enquiry, 'to accept any financial arrangement that you personally may decide on in the event of monopoly being shown to be necessary to national safety.' In the light of this offer to the First Lord it is difficult to believe in the good faith of the stories subsequently put about in the Fleet, of his having tried to blackmail the Admiralty into paying him vast sums for his monopoly – sums once referred to by Moore as 'hush' money.

Finally, there is an important postscript to the letter in which he argues that the reopening of the case could be justified on the grounds that since the adverse decision was taken in August three new factors had been imported. These he listed as follows:

First, the Sea Experiments in the *Orion*.
Next, Professor Boys' report and
Thirdly, the unreserved submission of terms to the First Lord.

The 'Sea Experiments' referred to had indeed produced results which of themselves should have been sufficient, without any further argument, to ensure adoption. First, there was the demonstration given late in September in the *Orion*, of the rate-*keeping* (as distinct from rate-*finding*) capacity of the Clock: of this Pollen's description, written shortly after the event ran as follows:

> We were given the range of a fixed mark, whose distance from the ships had been exactly ascertained. Our Clock was set to its bearing and range and to our own course and speed. Our ship, the *Orion* then described a quadrilateral figure, whose sides measured between eight and nine miles, and the three turns executed in describing it were made under full helm, and aggregated more than three full right angles. And, in the course of these nine miles, speed was worked up from cruising speed to the highest speed possible in the time. As the experiment was carried out at the entrance to Bantry Bay, it was easy to complete it by steering the ship to the exact point at which it commenced; and this was a point which, in the circumstances, could be, and was, exactly fixed by the navigators; thus verifying, beyond cavil, the margins within which we could do what we had set out to do. The task was to keep the range of the fixed mark and its line of aim throughout the run, without having transmitted to us any range or bearing corrections of any kind whatever. At the end of the run, it was found that we had the range within twenty-five yards, and the bearing within half a degree. And, as we had been without further data about the target, we had, in fact, proved that we could have kept an invisible target under accurate indirect fire just as easily as a visible target under direct fire throughout the run.

Of the second demonstration which took place a month later, this time with guns in Battle Practice, Pollen wrote[10] 'with no other gear have firing tests ever been carried out in such difficult conditions or with more novel and startling results. Never until the A.C. Clock was tried in the *Orion*, had firing at high speed during a six point turn been attempted. By hitting a fast and distant target continuously at a high rate of change with the firing ship under full helm the *Orion* has achieved what all gunnery experts would, a few weeks ago, have said was impossible.'

In a later chapter it will be shown that the failure of the Navy four years later at Gallipoli, to silence the Turkish forts was due solely to the inability of their guns to keep the forts under fire when their ships were forced to circle round for their own protection. Yet in 1912, Moore's only reaction to these remarkable results was to finalise the order which had been under discussion for so many months for an additional five A.C. Clocks at a price of £2300 each. Well might Pollen say, in 1912, that the Admiralty's idea of the kind of fire control that would be necessary in action was very different from his: and at Gallipoli, as we shall see, it was merely a stationary not a moving target that proved to be beyond the capacity of the Service gear.

It should be added that while Pollen's team were not permitted to attend the trials, they were allowed to visit the *Orion* prior to the trials to make certain the gear was in order. Pollen himself paid one visit following which he wrote[11] to Peirse, 'It really is gloriously inspiring to go down and talk to fellows like that with the smell of Whitehall still in one's nostrils.' Pollen never failed to react to the confidence and gratitude of the men who had used his gear and knew what it could do.

The second new factor mentioned in Pollen's postscript was the report by Professor Sir Charles Vernon Boys FRS. Born in 1855, Boys, by 1912, had already established himself as the outstanding physical scientist of the day. A recognised authority on integrating machines he numbered among his more fascinating achievements the invention of the moving lens which made possible the study of the speed of lightning.

His report on A.C. embraced the whole system including the new Plotting Unit which was still under construction and not destined to be offered for trial until the following March, when the Admiralty, true to form, refused even to inspect it. Also included was the Pollen-Cooke rangefinder[12] of which only an early experimental model had ever been inspected by the Admiralty. Of the use of these two instruments in combination Boys reported:

I consider that you have done well in making a simultaneous attack upon the optical, electrical and mechanical problems, the right solutions of which are necessary to the solution of the first half of your Fire Control problem. . . . The complexity of the problem you have solved cannot be disputed but in analysing it correctly you have surmounted the principal difficulty of all. . . . Taking the mechanism as a whole it is perfectly adapted to do the work required of it.

Passing to the second unit of the system, he writes:

I regret that in the matter of the design of your 'Clock' I am not able to make any suggestion for its improvement, and perhaps this is another way of saying that in my opinion it is as near perfection as any mechanism which I have ever examined critically. The records of its accuracy which have been brought to my notice seem to show that its indications will always be correct in the terms of its setting.

I have followed the development of the integrating machine in its various forms for over thirty years, including the ball, disc and cylinder integrator used by Lord Kelvin in his harmonic analyser. I have no hesitation in saying that the integrating mechanism used in this Clock is the most perfect of all that has been done in this direction.

I should like to add that it is surprising that you should have reached so perfect a conclusion in the short time of six years since you first consulted me. The problem is one of such difficulty that it must have required immense perseverance to have kept in mind the main desideratum and to have persuaded Mr Isherwood to find the mechanical solutions of a series of problems of great technical difficulty.

Professor Boys's reference to Lord Kelvin's harmonic analyser and to an earlier conference with Pollen is a reminder of the extent to which Pollen and Isherwood were helped in the early days by these two distinguished scientists. Moreover Boys's comments on the difficulties with which they had been faced and his congratulations on their having produced so perfect an instrument in the short space of six years are all in line with Kelvin's earlier forecast of 'ten years hard work'.

Meanwhile to those interested in the history of computers

the Argo Clock will no doubt now assume a new importance as, being by many years, the first electrically driven analogue computer ever employed or designed.

Pollen's next move was a letter to Jellicoe who was believed to carry most weight with the Board on technical matters such as fire control. Here again, with Jellicoe so closely involved personally with Dreyer's system, and after so much glaring injustice in the technical field, it was no easy matter to decide where to begin or what to leave out. After much consultation within his own small circle, it was decided that a simple one-page letter, concentrating on the significance of the actual performance of the Clock in the trials would best serve their purpose. With no mention of Dreyer or of past misunderstandings, Pollen pinpointed the technical advantages of the functions which A.C. alone could perform and confined himself to the one pungent comment, 'It seems to me most extraordinary that there should be no willingness of any kind to enquire into claims as far reaching as these, when they are backed by actual demonstrations of what we have done and by the opinion of the finest mechanical authority in Europe'. (A copy of the Boys report was forwarded as soon as it became available, ten days later.) Enclosed with this letter of the 9th November was a copy for Jellicoe's eyes alone of Pollen's letter to Churchill. In reply Jellicoe wrote[13] from the *Hercules*, that the enclosures interested him a great deal but that as both his Clock and Dreyer's System were on trial in ships in his own squadron, he must refrain from comment until the trials were concluded.

Meanwhile the failure to obtain any reply from Churchill was a big disappointment which led to the suggestion that perhaps Arthur Pollen's brother Stephen, now a member of the Argo Board, might be more fortunate. Colonel Stephen Hungerford Pollen[14] was a soldier by profession who, in 1899, had served on General Buller's headquarters Staff in South Africa. In 1902 he had retired to go into business as representative of Sir Julius Wernher of Wernher Beit & Co, later the Central Mining and Investment Corporation of South Africa.

His experience of big business and his sound judgement, coupled with the fact that he had met Churchill in South Africa and could write as a brother officer, were valuable assets at this critical moment and his request for an interview was at once granted. They met on 6th December, with Moore in attendance. After first correcting a few misconceptions and misstatements by Moore, Stephen asked the First Lord whether he was satisfied as to the wisdom of allowing his brother's system to go abroad. The point was not simply whether it was right for the British Navy to have a system slightly inferior to Argo, but that Foreign Powers who at present had nothing in any way comparable to either would now have one admittedly superior. 'The point seemed to have some weight with the First Lord' wrote Stephen in his rather formal minute, 'and he asked whether it would be possible for Argo to quote for a large number of clocks on the basis that the Admiralty should be our only customer.'

The minute ended with the significant statement that 'Mr Churchill also agreed that if, in view of a final decision by the Admiralty, the Argo Company was to supply their gear to Foreign Powers, they would by (the Admiralty's) decision be acquitted of all obligations imposed by patriotism.'

Five days later the two brothers called on Moore the Controller, to submit a tender, on the following basis:

Either 150 clocks at £1600 each – £240,000
or   200 clocks at £1525 each – £305,000

It was no great surprise when a week later the offer was formally declined on the grounds that the price was excessive. To this comment the best answer is that within a year the company was receiving orders for far more Clocks than they could build, at £2000 each with no restriction as to market. It is hard to believe that the request for a quotation was more than a gesture of co-operation towards a brother officer: alternatively perhaps Admiral Moore was glad to have a quotation which he could say was excessive.

Time was running short and Pollen now played his last card,

in the form of a final appeal to Prince Louis, who was due to take over as First Sea Lord at the turn of the year. For many years Wilson had been the insuperable stumbling block and Prince Louis his most influential supporter. In 1909, it will be recalled, after the successful demonstration in the *Natal*, Prince Louis had spoken of A.C. as 'the most important project now proceeding anywhere in the world.' A few months later, on 11th May 1910, he wrote to Pollen 'I am delighted to hear what you tell me and only have time to say that I may possibly be in a position by-and-by of practically ensuring your being accorded the recognition which is your due.' To this Pollen had replied, tactfully but firmly, questioning the advisability, from the standpoint of the maintenance of secrecy, of his name appearing in the Honours list. Yet such was the enthusiasm of the Prince, that he wrote again on the 25th July expressing the hope that the King would take the opportunity to see Pollen's gear during his forthcoming visit to the Fleet. A year later the Prince headed the short list of officers who signed the testimonial to the value of his work that enabled him to raise the money needed by the Argo Company.

The month of April 1912 saw them still on friendly terms. The new Mark IV Clock had just been inspected by the Lords of Admiralty in person and by the heads of the various gunnery departments and schools, and no adverse decision had yet been taken. On 24th April Pollen addressed to Prince Louis a long memorandum, arguing the technical case for his system and submitting a well reasoned plea for closer co-operation.

> If your Board think monopoly necessary you can have it on the terms that you and some past member of the Board, representing me, agree are fair . . .
> A word on co-operation between ourselves and the Service. It cannot be disputed that we hold the field in Fire Control in spite of much opposition. Should we not be more advanced still if we had official help instead? Without monopoly this co-operation cannot exist: there will always be the natural fear that foreign powers may profit by our navy's hard won knowledge. And the

experience of the Service both in this and other fields will justify that fear. On the other hand we are only on the threshold of our work. There is relatively as great an advance to be made in night fire control as in its big brother the daylight art – and I do not doubt that we are on the right lines to make it. In both arts there will be continuous progress. Is it not worth retaining the exclusive services of those who have proved both their goodwill and their capacity? and to regularise our position by domesticating us; anyhow I have carried on all these years in the hope that it is inevitable.

There is no record in the file of any reply to this eminently sensible, and far-reaching proposal. All we know is that he failed to obtain a favourable response. Nor is there any reason to believe that any notice was taken of the fact that Pollen was already working on methods of night fire control. The battle of Jutland was to reveal that in the technique of night-fighting we were at a tremendous disadvantage against the Germans, having neither adequate searchlights nor any other means of finding the target. Here again Pollen seems to have been at least four years ahead of the Admiralty in his thinking. Had the Admiralty adopted the system in 1912, night fire-control would certainly have been one of the developments that would have been far advanced before Jutland.

In September Pollen wrote again to the Prince, this time to express his great regret that the Board should have taken a decision about monopoly without even waiting for the result of the trials in the *Orion*.

In October Pollen sent him a copy of his letter of the 21st October to Churchill, without response, and by mid-December can have had little hope of winning his support. However, unwilling to surrender, he wrote requesting an interview. This resulted on the 18th in what must have been a very tense conversation over the telephone, of which Pollen left the following record:

The Prince called me up and said he could not understand what there was I could tell him in conversation which could in any way alter the Admiralty's attitude towards monopoly. The question had been thoroughly thrashed out, and their decision was made in the light of all the facts. I replied that I believed from what I had been told that the trials had not been entirely thorough. He said he did not think this could be the case as they had been carried out under Admiral Jellicoe's directions, and that Admiral Jellicoe's opinion, that the Dreyer gear was for practical purposes as good and as accurate as mine, had decided the Board not to accept our offer. I asked the Prince if the Admiralty intended to make any counter offer as I understood it was admitted that our Clock was more accurate and could be used in more difficult conditions than the Dreyer Clock. The Prince said that was not disputed, but that nobody wanted a Fire Control system that could be used when there was a change of range of 2000 yards a minute, which was not a practical possibility, and that the Dreyer Clock was sufficiently accurate for all conditions which would arise in war.

Next day, in self-justification, Pollen wrote:

> I have long been so positive that a proper trial of my Clock would show its tactical advantages to be overwhelming that I asked Mr Churchill eight weeks ago to institute enquiry. If trial or enquiry show that I am right, monopoly can only be to my commercial disadvantage, for foreign Navies will certainly adopt an overwhelmingly superior system and the English Navy will have to follow suit to regain equality. In challenging enquiry, I am deliberately risking the adverse verdict which would gravely prejudice my commercial prospects. Whether, therefore, I am right or wrong about the relative methods of the two systems I have everything to lose and nothing to gain by the line I am taking now. Should I be unsuccessful in my appeal and the question arise as to my conduct as a loyal citizen, either at this juncture or on any of the four previous occasions when I have successfully asked the Board to reverse decisions come to on insufficient evidence, I will ask Your Highness to bear these obvious facts in mind.

There is an interesting commentary on Prince Louis's attitude at this date in a letter written twenty years later (23rd October 1934) by Pollen to Custance. Admiral Mark Kerr's[15] biography *Louis of Battenberg* had just appeared and had attracted favourable comment. To Pollen the most interesting aspect of the book was the confirmation it afforded of the fact that none of the ruling clique, 'not even P.L. who had the best brains of the lot, were really awake to the true meaning of war.' P.L.'s three most important letters of 1902, 1909 and 1911, respectively to Fisher, King Hall and Churchill were 'all organisation and no real war doctrine. No emphasis, that is to say, on the relentless determination to bring about battle, which would have prompted equal determination to have officers, crews, and leaders with minds always envisaging fighting and its essentials. The Staff and the War College are to be occupied with everything except the crucial activity of war – namely, battle.'

On the personal issue of P.L.'s attitude to him in 1913, the letter recalls the support P.L. had given him from the earliest days and how when on half pay early in 1911 'he came to see me at Buckingham Street, his interest in the thing higher than ever. And almost as soon as he came to the Admiralty in December of that year he sent for me again to know how I was getting on. Yet, when it came to the point in 1912 and he was on the verge of becoming First Sea Lord he was not prepared to risk falling out with Jellicoe and Moore. There was too much at stake and he was not sure of his hold over Churchill.'

Among other friends with whom Pollen was in touch at this difficult time was Percy Scott the inventor of 'Director Firing' and other devices. Admiral Sir Percy Scott Bt., KCB,KCVO, as he eventually became, was one of the great reformers and rebels of the time, and remained till the end of his days a thorn in the flesh of the Admiralty.

In his entertaining autobiography *Fifty Years in the Royal Navy*, he tells of his attempts to break down the old fashioned routine of scrubbing and polishing, and train his men in the arts of war. 'Gunners not housemaids' is what he wanted and many a reprimand it earned him.

Scott's reforming efforts were exactly contemporary with Pollen's, and his scathing attacks on the Admiralty's attitude to new ideas are very relevant to our story.

In 1903, having attracted attention by the success of his experiments on the China Station he was brought home and made Captain of the *Excellent*, the Navy's Gunnery School at Whale Island. Of his experiences in that appointment, he writes 'As Captain of the *Excellent* it was quickly brought home to me what a flood of opposition I should have against me if I attempted to improve the shooting of the Fleet'.

Scott's second and more important contribution to gunnery was the invention and introduction of what was called 'Director Firing'. The Director was a device which made it possible 'to lay all the guns in parallel and fire them simultaneously', thereby producing a spread of fire in the target area on the principle of the shot gun.

Director Firing was an old idea first put forward in 1885 by Richard Peirse who twenty-five years later, as we have seen, was to play so prominent a part in the Pollen story. Unfortunately for the young Peirse, changes introduced in 1897 in the design of casemates made it impracticable to make use of his invention, which accordingly lay fallow and forgotten until revived by Percy Scott. Of the delays and boycotting of this invention from 1905 when he revived it, till its adoption in 1913, Scott, with typical lack of restraint, wrote – 'The boycott was not because the Admiralty was ignorant of its efficiency. It was boycotted simply for professional jealousy'. The ultimate adoption of the Director in 1914 he attributes to Admiral Jellicoe who had held the office of Director of Naval Ordnance in 1905-06, when Scott was Inspector of Target Practice. In *The Grand Fleet* Jellicoe tells us, with justifiable pride, that on his return to the Admiralty, as Second Sea Lord at the end of 1912, he had insisted that Scott's Director must have a fair trial. Despite delays and opposition Jellicoe fortunately succeeded in getting it adopted before the Battle of Jutland was fought.

It so happened that the decisive trial of Scott's Director was held in November 1912 and took the form of a competitive shoot between the *Thunderer* on which the Director was mounted and the *Orion*, which carried the Argo Clock and was reputed to be the best gunnery ship in the Fleet.

After the shoot Pollen wrote[16] a spirited letter to Scott from which the following is taken:

> I gather from the papers that your courageous work of the last eight years is really crowned with success at last . . .
>
> The real truth about the cursedly inept gunnery policy that has prevailed since 1907 is that neither Bacon nor Moore were either of them in the minutest degree Artillerists; by this I mean that there was not a single branch of practical naval artillery technique in which – I won't say they were experts – in which they were even competent to understand the leading points. . . . The consequence is they have been bang off the track and absolutely wrong on every point in connection with both (gunlaying and fire control).
>
> It certainly gives me a most venomous delight to see you down those b——y know-alls, who for years have had the whole aegis of official infallibility to conceal the imbecile folly of their childish heresies.
>
> A bas Bacon, Conspuez Dreyer, Moore à la lanterne, for the rest, full speed ahead.

It is interesting and also indicative of the magnitude of their subject to find that despite the wide range of the work in which each was engaged, there was no overlap, and that even in 1912, in the final stages of development, these two great reformers each saw the work of the other as complementary and not competitive.

A more important example of their fellow feeling, and more relevant to the subject of this chapter is provided by a difference of opinion that arose earlier in the year in regard to a series of articles, written by a friend of Scott's, condemning the Admiralty's incompetence in matters of gunnery and in particular their attitude to Pollen. Scott had kindly sent the articles to Pollen to seek his consent to their publication. This drew from Pollen a five-page reply, correcting a number of misstatements in the articles but above all arguing against publication. 'One of the chief elements in the value of my system for the Navy will be the fact that it is secret – not only in the design of the instruments but in the far more important sense that the very purpose of the instruments is unknown. Any public discussion at once demolishes the second form of secrecy'.

He next makes the point (perhaps optimistically, but this was written on the 3rd June) that 'the Board can be persuaded to do the right thing but they can't be dragooned'. Any public attack on Moore would mean that his policy would never be reversed.

This was a line of thought which would not normally have limited Scott's activities but on this occasion he was good enough to respect Pollen's veto and, as we have seen, they remained on good terms.

Pollen's failure to win Prince Louis's co-operation marked the end of the battle, so far as he was concerned, and by the end of the year he was writing to his closest friends to tell them the sad news.

> If I was entirely without obligations to others, as was the case in 1908, I might try to carry on as I did then, by keeping my system secret on my own account, and so wait for better times. Unfortunately, however, the thing has grown to such dimensions that it has been necessary both to get the financial support of shareholders and to employ a large number of people. I cannot throw these last upon the world or neglect the interests of the former. I have no alternative but to go forward as the Admiralty direct me. I hope that the transition from working solely for the Navy to being a mere tradesman will not affect our friendship.

All without exception wrote assuring him of their sympathy and their friendship; and in the years that followed all were as good as their word. Craig went further and expressed strong indignation at the suggestion that his friendship would be affected. Custance consoled him with the assurance that he had nothing whatever with which to reproach himself and begged him to remember that all inventions soon became public property. To Arthur Leveson, at once his closest and most remote friend, he wrote rather more fully and frankly ending with the old American story of the New York dealer in imported dry goods, who after the high tariff was put on, advertised his business in the following terms, 'With one brother in the Customs house and another Sheriff, we defy competition.' To which Leveson replied in his characteristic, elliptic, clipped and unpunctuated style, 'In spite of the Ad Let warning you off the course my personal Affection for you is undiminished.'

CHAPTER VI

Recognition Abroad

With the turn of the year, Pollen's monopoly contract with the Admiralty came to an end, leaving him with nothing to show for his loyalty to the Service but a handful of letters of condolence from the small circle of friends in whom he had confided; and, seemingly, with nothing to be done but go ahead with the arrangements for registering his patents abroad.

However, news of the breach spread rapidly through the Fleet and all at once he found himself besieged by letters from the much wider circle of supporters who knew the value of his inventions and refused to believe that they could be rejected and allowed to go abroad. Knowing nothing of his gallant struggle for survival of the previous three months, the writers protested vigorously at the Admiralty's decision, and begged him to use every means in his power to persuade the Board to reverse their decision, and save the system for the Navy.

To the Pollen brothers the strength, volume, and, above all, the quality of these unsolicited testimonials brought new hope. For Churchill to brush aside the opinion of a single expert, however eminent, such as Peirse, was one thing but could he ignore such a wave of protest as was now coming from the whole professional body of gunnery men, headed by no less than ten Admirals on the active list, and thirty Captains?

Of the two brothers, Stephen clearly had the better chance of a hearing; on the 20th January he wrote to 'My dear Churchill' to tell him of the new development and show him the evidence. Extracts from twenty of the letters, including those 'from seven or eight Admirals in commands or employed' were enclosed, the intention being that all names, whether occurring in the text or as signatures, should be cut out. Unfortunately, one got through in which Jellicoe's and Moore's names appeared in a disparaging context. This inevitably gave offence, with the result that an initiative which might have borne fruit served merely to fan the flames of anti-Pollen prejudice. The only pleasing feature of the incident was the friendly nature of Jellicoe's response to Pollen's apology in which, while pointing out that such correspondence was hardly conducive to good discipline, he wrote 'My dear Pollen, I quite understand that you had no intention of doing anything that might be offensive to me. I know you too well to imagine you would do anything intentional in that way.'

From Masterton-Smith they received a formal reply stating rather curiously that the First Lord was 'not in a position' to depart from the decision already conveyed to Mr Pollen on a number of occasions and reminding him of the obligation under the Official Secrets Act 'to refrain from any step that would be in the nature of an improper disclosure of British naval secrets.'

This strange piece of verbiage proved to be the prelude to a change of attitude on the part of the Admiralty that was shortly to bring a new dimension into the dispute.

Meanwhile, undaunted by the failure of his direct appeal to Churchill, and unwilling to believe that the strength of the Service reaction to his dismissal could be ignored indefinitely by Whitehall, Pollen had fought back with vigour and imagination. As intermediaries, Peirse having gone abroad, he now enlisted in addition to Spender, first his elder brother Francis, a sailor who had retired some years earlier with the rank of Commander, next his old friend John Walter, the principal owner of *The Times* and, thirdly, E. G. Pretyman, who had been the Financial[1] Secretary to the Admiralty at the time of Pollen's confrontation with Wilson in 1910.

The intention was that Walter should make a direct appeal

to Churchill; that his brother Francis should submit the whole story to Geoffrey Robinson the editor of *The Times* and that Pretyman would advise on the possibility of invoking the aid of the leader of the Opposition. In each case the emphasis was to be on the folly of allowing the Pollen inventions to go abroad, as distinct from the quite different and largely technical issue as to whether the Pollen system should be preferred to Dreyer's.

John Walter sought and obtained an interview with Churchill and wrote twice. In the second letter he wrote firmly 'It is clear from the Admiralty letter, which states that the Argo Company's patents contain an important secret, that I was right in holding that these patents should not be published. It is equally clear that they will be published unless some arrangement is come to.' Yet the only answer[2] he received was to the effect that the letter from the Argo Company's solicitors would be replied to at the earliest possible date, and that in the meantime 'you may entirely dismiss from your mind the idea that the point at issue involves the risk of national disaster such as you appear to imagine.'

Pretyman's response[3] to Pollen's enquiry was to the effect that he knew Jellicoe well, as they had served at the Admiralty together; he had the highest respect for his ability and good judgement and would like permission to write to him personally. A week later Pollen received from Pretyman a short but significant letter reporting that he had been informed that 'A.C. depends upon other secret patents which are Government property and which cannot be communicated elsewhere' and adding that 'they seem to be quite alive to the necessity for secrecy.'

From these two letters it would appear that before the end of February both Churchill and Jellicoe had been informed that Pollen would be unable to sell abroad because of these secret patents on which his clock was dependent. Yet it was not until the 30th April that the Admiralty were equally frank with Pollen. This was followed by four weeks of inconclusive argument between the lawyers, at the end of which it was decided, on the advice of Sir Robert Finlay, that the Admiralty must be challenged to prove their case. The story is well told in a letter[4] written a year later to Peirse, now C-in-C East India Station.

> (Late in January) I was in the Admiralty and had occasion to ask Tudor /the D.N.O./ certain questions. In the course of conversation he said that some question had been raised as to whether our clock included some Service secret which ought not to be allowed to go abroad. On that I went straight to Moore /the Controller/ and asked him if he had heard anything to this effect, and he replied that my question was the first he had heard of the matter. I then wrote to the Admiralty quoting Moore and Tudor, and asking for an immediate answer on the point raised. A month afterwards we got a letter saying that the linkage for converting speed and course into rates, or rates into speed and course was based upon confidential information, and that its publication would endanger the existence of an important Service secret, as if a well known mathematical truth could be a Service secret. As the matter seemed to threaten me personally with imprisonment (under the Official Secrets Act) if I took out a patent or showed the Clock to foreigners, I put the matter into our lawyers' hands, and after making a very full statement to the Admiralty, and getting no retreat from the positions they were taking up, we finally took the advice of Sir Robert Finlay, the ex-Attorney General, as to the course we ought to pursue.

The letter giving formal notice to the Admiralty was dated 8th July 1913. The Admiralty protested but declined the challenge. Their bluff had been called. Instead they adopted the cowardly course of striking the Argo Company off the Admiralty list of contractors and issuing a secret Fleet Order warning officers to have nothing to do with Pollen.

Meanwhile, prior to the issue of the ultimatum to the Admiralty Stephen Pollen made one last attempt to settle direct with Churchill. In the course of two admirable letters, the first dated 2nd June to Churchill personally, the second of the 13th June to Masterton-Smith[5], Private Secretary to the First Lord, he reminded Churchill that as early as in March of the previous year, he and his colleagues had personally inspected the Clock in London; that by July the patents had been in the hands of the Admiralty and that in December Churchill had personally invited the Argo Company to quote for a supply of Clocks on monopoly terms. 'For the Admiralty some months later,' he wrote to Masterton-Smith, 'to claim that we have not the power to dispose of the very property which they themselves had negotiated to purchase, is to mark those negotiations as unreal, and must leave us under a sense of the deepest injury, and that we have been dealt with with what must appear a lack of sincerity. I know how foreign anything of this nature is to the character of Mr Churchill but his refusal to hear our case permits no other conclusion.'

Of Francis Pollen's attempt to win the support of the editor of *The Times*, it can be said that he met with partial success in that *The Times* did give considerable publicity to Argo matters when the case was raised[6] in the House of Commons at the end of June.

Pollen had for long been in two minds as to the wisdom of allowing the matter to be publicly discussed in Parliament, as will be seen from the following letter of 30th January to Alfred Spender:

> I am coming rather strongly to the opinion that this matter ought to be brought before the Prime Minister, as the most important member of the Imperial Defence Committee. Since seeing you last, I have been urged by an important body of men – amongst them the Editor of the '*Spectator*', one member of the House of Commons and one of the House of Lords – to assist in having the matter raised in Parliament. I have told them quite frankly what seems to me must obviously be my policy in this matter. I will do anything I can to assist in keeping the thing *secret* – that is to say, just as I have appealed from the Ordnance Branch to the Board of Admiralty, and from the Board to the First Lord, so I am prepared to appeal from the First Lord to the Prime Minister if I have any encouragement to believe that he would pay any attention to me. But I am not prepared to assist in having the matter publicly discussed, because a public discussion would defeat my main object –

namely, secrecy, – and, if I cannot secure secrecy, I shall
certainly do nothing simply from motives of revenge, as any unnecessary opposition to the Admiralty might damage the commercial prospects of myself and my associates.

A further objection to invoking the aid of the Opposition
was the fact that he was himself a Liberal and still hopeful of
having the time and opportunity to get into politics and it went
against the grain to have his case used as a political weapon
against his own party. However, it is to be presumed that by
the middle of June he had come to the conclusion that intervention through questions in the House must be risked as the
last remaining possibility of compelling Churchill to give way.

On the 29th June, in reply to a question asked by Mr Harcourt, Churchill gave the following misleading and damaging
reply. The principal question was whether the good firing
results obtained by the *Orion*, to which attention had been
drawn in the Press, were attributable to the Pollen system and
the secondary question whether it was intended to adopt the
Pollen system. Churchill replied:

> I am informed that some portions of Mr Pollen's apparatus were
> used, but they were not used in accordance with the Pollen
> System. The good shooting was not attributable either to the
> Pollen apparatus or to any employment of the Pollen System. It
> is not intended to adopt the Pollen System, but to rely on a
> more satisfactory one which has been developed by Service ex-
> perts. In reply to the last part of the question, the Admiralty has
> given Mr Pollen considerable assistance in the hope of obtain-
> ing a valuable system of fire control for the Navy. The results
> obtained with his system and the principles underlying it are
> such that it is not proposed to take any steps to prevent his mak-
> ing public use of all its essential features. This he can do
> without divulging official secrets connected with the Service
> system and he will, of course, be precluded from disclosing Ser-
> vice secrets of which his connexion with the Admiralty has
> given him knowledge, or from any infringement of the Official
> Secrets Act, which I have every confidence will be respected. I
> should like to add by way of caution that all these questions con-
> nected with fire control are of a highly technical character, and

their discussion in the newspapers could not lead to any intelligible conclusion or be attended by any public advantage. So far as the relations between the Admiralty and Mr Pollen are concerned, I shall be quite prepared on a suitable occasion, if desired, to explain them fully to the House. So far as the technical aspects are concerned, I must decline on behalf of the Admiralty to take any part in their public discussion. I can only say that in coming to the decisions which I have stated to the House, and for which I accept full responsibility, I have been guided by the representations of my naval colleagues and the advice of the experts on whom the Admiralty must rely.

On the 30th June, the day this statement was published both *The Times* and the *Daily Mail* published the following letter over Pollen's signature:

I understand that Mr Churchill, in replying to Mr Harcourt today, said that, after assisting me for some years to produce the A.C. system, the Admiralty, in view of the results obtained with it, had adopted a more satisfactory fire control system developed by service experts. A meaning, which, I am sure, Mr Churchill did not intend, might be conveyed by these expressions – namely, that two fire control systems had been in competition with each other, and the more satisfactory one accepted. As this is an inference which might prove damaging to an enterprise in which a large amount of capital had been invested, I ask to be allowed, without waiting to see the text of Mr Churchill's reply to make the following statement in your columns:- The A.C. Fire Control system, invented by Mr Isherwood and me, consists principally of –

(1) A group of instruments for ascertaining the target's range and movements, generally known amongst experts as the plotting or 'ratefinding' unit; and

(2) Of a device known as the Argo 'Clock', which uses the information gained by the first group, to control the sights of the gun automatically.

Both processes are essential to Fire Control.

The first group has never been supplied for trial; the clock alone was tried for the first time about two months after monopoly had been abandoned.

At this point, Sir Inigo Thomas, the former Secretary to the Admiralty, whose help Pollen had previously solicited, intervened with a remarkable letter that was published by *The Times* on the 2nd July. For a retired Civil Servant to write so frankly and so fully about matters which in their origin had come to his knowledge in the course of his duties, was in itself courageous even when disguised, as on this occasion, behind the pseudonym, Emeritus. But the letter is even more remarkable for the piercing and delightful irony with which he presented his indictment. For example:

> Mr Churchill in speaking of the results obtained by the A.C. System could merely have been alluding to the opinion of the Admiralty experts in question, for as it happened no trials had taken place. The very explicitness of the First Lord's statement makes one wonder whether he himself realised this fact.

And again:

> I note Mr Churchill says he had been guided by the advice of experts on whom the Admiralty 'must' rely, a curious and apparently defensive phrase. Had his predecessors felt this compulsion, secrecy would have been abandoned in March 1908, in February 1909 and again in the spring of 1910, when there was no Service system in the field at all. The secrecy of the A.C. system was saved by the fact of the disagreement of the experts being brought to the notice of the First Lord on each occasion. . . . That there is a strong feeling in the Navy in favour of the A.C. System is undeniable . . . the believers in the Pollen system are quite as eminent in their professional attainments as the official experts who are once more in opposition to it.

And, finally,

> The wisdom of giving up a fire control system acknowledged to be the foundation of our own, developed entirely within the Navy and largely at public expense, must be very questionable, especially in the absence of any evidence that foreign powers possess any system as scientifically thought out or as thoroughly developed.

The Naval and Military Record, the most influential Service journal of the day, underlining the significance of the letter from 'Emeritus', expressed themselves in unusually strong language. 'There is no reason' they wrote 'why the Admiralty should suck the brains of an inventor and then reject his invention, pirate it and call it a Service invention. This is the implication made by 'Emeritus' but not by Mr Pollen himself.' *The Times*, having published Sir Inigo's letter refused to press the matter any further. It must be presumed that they accepted Mr Churchill's view that 'further discussion would not be attended by any public advantage'.

In these days, when it is the established practice to set up a Government enquiry to silence embarrassing criticism on even the most trivial matters, it seems surprising that Pollen's supporters were unable to carry the matter any further. But in 1913 the Navy enjoyed a prestige that rendered the Board of Admiralty immune to the demands of justice or reason.

For Pollen this was the end of his twelve year struggle to keep his inventions for the sole use of the British Navy, the battle of which he had written[7] to Spender in 1910 'I am fighting for all I am worth to make them keep the secret and rob me of the fortune they are trying to thrust upon me. For a poor man was there ever, outside comic opera, a more preposterous role?'

Six months later[8] he was writing to Hall to say, 'The Argo Company is being run off its feet. We have sold the whole of our output for the next twelve months and I shall be disappointed if in a week or two's time we shall not have hypothecated our output for another year as well. Does it not seem to you a queer thing that hardly a year ago Jellicoe should have said to me, with I think quite a genuine sympathy that he feared we should never sell any of our stuff abroad.'

In a similar letter of the same date[9] to Peirse he added the comment that it was of course a great personal triumph to find that all the foreign experts had accepted his views but that it was 'a triumph that brought singularly little pleasure or real satisfaction. That we must make an immense fortune out of the thing seems now obvious, but the apple of discord, even when made of gold, is a sapless and tasteless diet.'

In a rather more technical letter to Craig, he enlarges on the views of the foreigners. 'It is funny that Dreyer should have based his system upon the plotting of the two rates, which seems to be the basis of practically all foreign fire control. Almost every Commission has asked us whether we can adopt our plotting system to rate plotting, if we have tried rate plotting and what our opinion of it is. So far I have not found one case where they wish to persist with it after they have heard the argument pro true course plotting and contra rate plotting. . . . It is curious that the French have gone so far as to produce a linkage which they tell me is very like ours, for converting the two rates into speed and course. . . . I imagine the French system is almost pure Dreyer.' And he was writing after negotiations with the Americans, Brazilians, Chileans, Austrians, Italians and Russians, with talks pending with the Swedes and the Greeks.

It will be shown later that when put to the test of war the Dreyer instruments proved just as ineffective as Pollen had forecast: that as a general rule the officers in charge preferred not to use them in action and simply did without: and finally that when after the war, Beatty as First Sea Lord, brought the Pollen and Dreyer designers together, on the newly-created 'Admiralty Fire Control Committee', the new instruments which they introduced in 1926, embodied both the true course and the helm-free principles for which Pollen had fought in vain in 1912.

If then it was obvious to all the foreigners in 1913 that Pollen was right in these matters, and no less obvious to our own Admiralty ten years later, how are we to account for the refusal of the Admiralty in 1912 to give Pollen a hearing?

Happily for the historians the answer as to how it happened, if not as to why, is to be found among the Battenberg Papers[10], in a letter addressed by Admiral Moore, the Controller, to

Prince Louis who was due shortly to take over from Sir Francis Bridgeman as First Sea Lord. It will be remembered that Prince Louis was among those to whom Peirse addressed himself in September 1912, in his brave attempt to save the Pollen system for the Navy. Prince Louis had sent Peirse's letter of the 7th September, together with the accompanying memorandum, to Moore for his comment and Moore's reply of the 19th to which we must now direct our attention, may be accepted as a statement of the argument by which the Board was persuaded to abandon Pollen at the end of the year.

Having told[11] the Board in August that Pollen's True Course method of Plotting 'had been tried over and over again and always failed' and that 'the Service' (sic) preferred Dreyer's 'Time and Range' and 'Time and Bearing' curve systems, it must have been somewhat embarrassing to Moore to be faced with the definite assertion by so high an authority as Peirse that Pollen's True Course method was 'without any doubt whatever the one best calculated' to produce the desired results: and in addition that 'To throw over Pollen now, and allow him to give the fruits of his ten years experience (all gained at our expense) to some Foreign Power would be nothing short of a National disaster.'

In his reply Moore very cleverly contrives to convey the impression that he is open-minded about the merits of Pollen's gear. 'I believe that both Dreyer's and Pollen's systems will produce about equal results. Dreyer's is the more developed at present but Pollen's worksmanship is probably better and less liable to get out of order. If Pollen can produce a better plotting table/than the one that failed in *Natal*/there would be no objection to trying it in conjunction with the Clock and rangefinder and Mr Pollen is quite mistaken in thinking I oppose this.'

On the other hand he reveals a positive phobia on the subject of the monopoly prices demanded by Pollen and makes the ugliest insinuations about Pollen's motives and integrity. 'By placing Mr Pollen in the position of a favoured inventor we have put him in possession of the most confidential items of our Fire Control system and we are being constantly pressed by Mr Pollen to pay him large sums of money to keep that information for our exclusive use. Each time we pay him thus (monopoly rights) he gains more confidential information . . . it is a chain round our necks being forged more and more relentlessly . . . it might be called Hush money.'

As to the vital technical problem of the relative value of True Course and of Rate plotting, he dismisses Peirse's very strong views with the casual comment 'I don't think Peirse is conversant with the latest details of Dreyer's gear, although, as he is an advocate of True Course and Speed plotting, such knowledge would not altogether change his opinion.' He does however commit himself to the statement that Pollen knows that he (Moore) does not think that Pollen 'has yet or is ever likely to produce equal results with True Course and Speed plotting.'

In general it is fair to say that the letter is weak on the vital technical issue and dishonest in its expression of willingness to try any of Pollen's gear that may be offered. For, as we have seen, the trials of the Clock held in the *Orion* proved its ability to perform functions which the Dreyer Clock could not even attempt – yet it was the Dreyer Clock that was adopted: and when in the following March, the new Pollen Plotter was offered, the Admiralty refused even to inspect it. Nor must we forget that Moore as D.N.O. in July 1910 must have played an active part in the pigeon holing of the Colville report advocating the active development of the Pollen Plotter.

In contrast the letter is very powerful in its condemnation of Pollen's exorbitant demands, of his prying into Naval secrets and of his threats to sell abroad, and there can be little doubt that the prejudice aroused by these allegations played a big part in the ultimate decision. On the question of prices alone there are no less than six offensive references to 'monopoly prices'. 'What I am opposed to is paying him monopoly prices when we have practically the same principles at work in Dreyer's system.' 'I have been trying for nearly a year to get contracts placed for five Argo Clocks but Pollen has always held out for a prohibitive price.' 'Pollen has always made a great parade of his patriotic feelings but . . . threatens to go abroad and trade upon confidential knowledge he has acquired by reason of his specially favoured treatment.' 'If Pollen's table proves better than rate plotting then it is a question of how much better compared to price.' Speaking of the 1910 contract for forty-five gyro-controlled rangefinder mountings which, as explained above, involved the Argo Company in a loss of £26,000 on a job costing £88,000, he claims to have paid a 'very handsome monopoly price'.

If we disregard the prejudice that permeates Moore's presentation of his case, the grounds on which he recommended rejection may be summed up as, first, that the plotting system had always failed, secondly that 'the whole of the Argo Company's knowledge of Fire Control necessities had been derived from the exceptionally privileged position in which Pollen had been placed by the Admiralty', thirdly that Dreyer, with his much cheaper instruments could produce much the same results as Pollen.

On the question of prices, the most significant item in Moore's letter is the comment that if Pollen's plotter proved better than Dreyer's then it would be a question of how much better in proportion to price.

The price of Pollen's plotting unit was about £1000. If we assume that Dreyer's plotter cost as little as £600 the saving per ship would have been £400. The Russians paid £40,000 per ship for the complete system. Moore's statement amounts to the admission that for a saving of 1% of that total, the British Admiralty were prepared to settle for a second best and let the best be sold abroad.

If we turn now to the important statement that A.C. had always failed, Pollen's answer would have been somewhat as follows:-

'In the development of an entirely new scientific conception it is necessary to proceed step by step. In industry it is the common practice for tests of an entirely new invention to be carried out with mock-up instruments of flimsy design, and light, easily worked materials, designed to show that one particular function or requirement has been mastered. Such tests should not be confused with tests of reliability, which must rightly be made before any new device is put into service.'

In 1905, in accordance with this principle, tests had been made to establish the possibility of plotting speed and course; the 'results' obtained were grossly inaccurate but Jellicoe had been intelligent enough to perceive that the possibility of plotting speed and course had been established and that the inaccuracy of the 'results' were due in large measure to ignorance of the extent of yaw. He accordingly recommended further experiments. In July 1910 the situation was very similar in that the re-trials ordered by Wilson had to be carried out with instruments that had badly deteriorated and under the control of officers with no experience of the apparatus. Yet despite these handicaps, the Colville Committee had been sufficiently impressed by the military potentital of the gear to recommend that four units should be ordered in order to assist and accelerate its development. Shocked at this unexpected conclusion, Moore, as Controller, backed by Wilson the new First Sea Lord, had ordered the Colville report to be disregarded and pigeon holed. When in March 1913, with no help from the Admiralty and no opportunity for tests at sea, Pollen produced his new and improved plotter, Moore refused even to have it inspected.

We are thus forced to the conclusion that Moore's statement that the Pollen plotters had always failed was fundamentally dishonest.

As regards the special relationship accorded to Pollen by the Admiralty, of which Moore complained so bitterly, there is an interesting paragraph in one of the memoranda[12] which Pollen prepared for the use of his supporters in February 1913

In this he points out that in 1910, after the rejection by

Wilson and Moore of the Pollen system of plotting, the Service was left without any instrumental form of Fire Control whatever. Furthermore that it was during this period that two officers on the active list, George Gipps and Gerard Riley, were officially seconded to the Argo Company in order to ensure that the development of the gear should be in a form acceptable to the Service. In the circumstances, he wrote, it seemed so obvious to every gunnery man in the Service that the Pollen system, once perfected, would be officially adopted, that 'for the next eighteen months the Argo Company was inundated by criticisms and suggestions for bringing the system to perfection.' Thus it came about, so he maintained, that the Argo Company, 'while not indebted to the Service for any of the mechanical inventions which had made the production of their gear possible, had, by the experience gained at sea which the Admiralty had given them, and by the criticisms and suggestions of many of the best experts in the Service, been able to push their original analysis of the requirements of Naval gunnery to completeness.'

In the more private context of a letter to Peirse dated 16th September 1912 we find the point put more simply and forcibly. 'The idea that there is anything in the fittings of the *Orion* which it would be a danger for me to see is surely too ludicrous for words. After all, my whole raison d'être is that I want the entire Fire Control of the present Navy superseded by my system, and Service methods have no interest for me whatever.'

Yet perhaps the most remarkable thing about the situation that arose in 1912, is that it had been clearly foreseen from the outset. The reader will recall that the agreement reached early in 1906 between Pollen and Jellicoe, for the joint development of the Pollen inventions, had hung fire for many months while the lawyers fought over the terms. From the Admiralty side it had been openly argued that by working with the Navy Pollen would learn so much about Service methods that they would eventually have to buy him out at his own price, whether they wanted his gear or not. To this Pollen had replied that all he would ask for his own protection was that the Admiralty should formally recognise that the inventions they were working on were his; and that while it might seem superfluous and a matter of elementary honesty to undertake not to appropriate his property without compensation, the fact that the inventions were his might not be so obvious in years to come.

Prior to 1912 there had been nothing comparable to Pollen's mechanical system, and despite many differences and attempts to depart from the scientific approach, Pollen had succeeded in keeping the monopoly agreement alive. 1912 saw the arrival of a competing system, allegedly a Service invention, and all at once they found themselves in the situation foreseen in 1906, with Moore accusing Pollen of seeking to sell Admiralty secrets abroad and Pollen accusing Dreyer of having plagiarised his inventions.

Two questions now faced the Admiralty. First as to which was the better system, secondly what to do about Pollen's if Dreyer's were preferred. In the early days, both Jellicoe and Prince Louis had had the imagination and the understanding of the problem to see the possibilities of his system and both, with varying degrees of enthusiasm, had backed his demand for full investigation.

By 1912 the situation was very different. It was no longer a simple matter of science v. guesswork. Faced with instruments which had overcome the problem of continuous change of rate by the use of second order differentials, neither Jellicoe nor Prince Louis had the technical knowledge to challenge the supposed expertise of the D.N.O. when he assured the Board that the Pollen and Dreyer systems worked on much the same principles and that there was nothing to choose between them. In reality there was all the difference in the world, as was later proved when put to the test of war, but of those who had access to the Board only Peirse and Craig really understood the essential superiority, in the vital qualities of speed and accuracy, of True-Course Plotting over Rate Plotting; and by 1912, Peirse, no longer Inspector of Target Practice, had no official standing and was relying only on his personal prestige. Craig, as Captain of the *Orion*, had no standing at all other than that of an expert witness to the performance of the Clock, a witness who might or might not be asked for his opinion.

To Pollen, it remained to the end inexplicable that Peirse with his knowledge and experience of gunnery failed to carry more weight with the Board. For, as we have seen, he had the ear of the top people, and the courage to state his views clearly and forcibly; and, as we now know, the backing of Fisher, on whom Churchill, the First Lord had relied so heavily in his first year of office. Among the Fisher papers quoted[13] by Arthur Marder in his *Fear God and Dread Nought*, is a lively letter to Churchill dated the 5th March 1912, in which he warns that 'The gunnery of the Fleet is not in a satisfactory position at present.' '*You want a clean sweep*. Controller, D.N.O. and Inspector of Target Practice' must all go. 'You must make Admiral Peirse Controller whether you like him or not.' Fisher, as is well known was ruled by flair rather than reason, and in the present case it was probably faith in the man rather than any particular belief that inspired his advice. But to followers of Pollen it is tantalising to know that once again the one appointment that would have assured the adoption of his system had been so near to fulfilment. Furthermore, the fact that Fisher's urgent advice was rejected in March helps us to understand, and to accept at face value, his reply to Pollen's appeal for help in the following June when he telegraphed 'Regret I am unable to see you as circumstances make it impossible that I can intervene.'

To revert to the situation with which Prince Louis and Jellicoe were faced in September 1912, it is relevant to recall that in the world of private industry there is nothing unusual about a Board of Directors having to take decisions on matters on which they are entirely dependent on expert advice. There are recognised procedures by which the experts can satisfy their directors by argument and practical demonstration. The surprising thing about the Pollen story is that the Board accepted the personal opinion of the Controller without regard to the strong technical evidence as to the performance of the *Orion*, without regard to Professor Boys's verdict as to the Argo gear being 'the most perfect of all that has been done in that direction' and, finally, in total disregard of strong evidence as to the support enjoyed by Pollen among leading gunnery men in the Service, all of which factors had been resolutely brought to their individual notice in recent months.

For a technical explanation of the Board's strange decision, as distinct from the prejudice created by Moore, we must go back to Pollen's letter to Churchill of the 21st October 1912, in which he told Churchill that,

> The real obstacle to adopting my system is less its price and its supposed unsuccess, than that the official conception of the kind of Fire Control necessary in action differs radically from what we (and those officers who think with us) think necessary.

The further we look into the evidence the clearer it becomes that there can be no other explanation. For one thing, Pollen from his earliest days had promised to revolutionize not merely gunnery but tactics. In 1909-1910, parallel with, but quite independently of his work on his helm-free clock, an enterprising group of young officers led by Captains H. W. Richmond and K. G. B. Dewar, strongly supported by Admirals May and Sturdee, had been campaigning for more fluid, or divisional, tactics. By 1912 their proposals had been firmly rejected by the ruling clique at Whitehall, including both Jellicoe and Prince Louis, who pinned their faith to the traditional single line of Battle under centralised command. The controversy had been hard-fought and there is little doubt that to Jellicoe the mere mention of fighting under helm was sufficient to cause apprehension. It would certainly have occurred to him that to fit his battleships with fire control specifically designed for fighting under helm would be to encourage divisional thinking and re-open the whole issue.

In support of this theory there is a very interesting letter, written as far back as 18th November 1908, by Pollen, to George Gipps who had been gunnery Lieutenant in the *Ariadne* at the time of the ill-fated trials, but was now serving in the *Hindustan*:

> I have for some years given up trying to argue about the tactical results of the A.C. system, as it seems to me that we have to convice them of the gunnery revolution before carrying them on to the tactical developments. The tactical developments are not otherwise than reasonably obvious to those who will take the gunnery developments for granted, but I am tired of asking people to take things for granted; and I find that the majority of Naval officers – it is at once their weakness and their strength – are not fond of exercising their reasoning faculties in a region to which the only entry is by hypothesis. It is hard enough to get them to reason correctly from the facts; but on truths following from hypotheses they are as helplessly at a loss as in uncharted waters. Their speed drops to four knots, and they cannot attend to a word you say, for the reason that all hands are out heaving leads.

Looking back, it is possible to see in this typically light-hearted and humorous comment, the key to the whole sad story of the rejection of A.C. From the start of his investigation in the year 1900, Pollen had been inspired by the knowledge that throughout history, new weapons had led to new tactics. He never doubted that, if successful, the A.C. System would lead to a revolution in naval tactics. In the early years, as we saw in the *Jupiter Letters*, he assumed that an imaginative description of the tactical developments that would flow from A.C. would stimulate interest in his gunnery inventions. By 1909 or earlier, as we see from his letter to Gipps, he had come to realise that he must proceed more slowly and logically, step by step. In this he was right, but where the whole plan went wrong was in the mis-timed move by Richmond and his friends who, independently of Pollen, tried to introduce the tactical revolution without due consideration of the gunnery problem.

The point is well put in a letter from Pollen to Richmond, written many years later, on the 19th August 1927, in the course of a discussion on this very point, that followed the publication of Churchill's account of Jutland in *The World Crisis*. 'My first point,' he wrote, 'is that flexibility of tactics cannot exist without a correlative flexibility in the use of artillery, a truth more than ever obvious if you add that tactics are the creation of weapons and not vice versa.' 'You failed to get the higher command interested in tactics being made more flexible, largely because they knew that flexibility in action meant artillery out of action. This single piece of knowledge stood like a stone wall between them and the kind of tactics you saw to be essential if fleet action was to be fought to a finish.'

In other words, unlike Pollen who had long since realised, as he wrote to Gipps, that the gunnery revolution had to come first, Richmond and his friends had their priorities wrong in seeking to introduce fluid tactics without waiting for, and fighting for, the necessary flexibility in gunnery. The stone wall which they erected by their misunderstanding of the problem remained standing and immovable when Pollen, in his turn, proffered the gunnery solution in 1912.

However, as we have already seen, Pollen fought back against the 1912 decision and by the spring of 1913 the issue was still undecided. Moore, anxious as to the outcome, called for a report from his Department. As Controller, this was his responsibility, but one can hardly imagine that it would have been Churchill's wish that an enquiry into the relative merits of the two systems should be conducted by the inventor of one of them, F. C. Dreyer, together with his successor as assistant to the D.N.O. at Whitehall. Yet it was typical of Admiralty mentality at the time.

The report, by Captain F. C. Dreyer and Commander C. V. Usborne is entitled *Pollen's aim Correction System. A Technical History and Technical Comparison with Commander F. C. Dreyer's Fire Control System*. From interior evidence, it was produced in April 1913 or soon after. The report opens (Part I, Chap II) with a table headed 'Assumptions as to the conditions under which actions will be fought.' Of these the two most significant are first,

> That the accuracy and rapidity of gunfire is greatly interfered with by alterations of course and that while a ship is under helm her gunnery must suffer in both respects owing to the increased difficulty of aiming.

Next,

> That as an Admiral will always be fully cognisant of the capabilities and limitations of the guns and fire control fittings and arrangement of his fleet, he will guide his tactics accordingly, endeavouring so to control the tactical situation that the task of the guns will always be one to which they are fully equal.

In effect these two paragraphs reflect, in technical language, the attitude of mind which, it is here contended, governed Jellicoe's decision against Pollen. That is to say an outright refusal to examine or consider the possibility that the hitherto insuperable difficulty of maintaining rapidity and accuracy of gunfire while altering course, might already have been overcome, coupled with a readiness to accept the tactical limitations implicit in the Dreyer system. By announcing at the outset of the report that the difficulty was insuperable, the authors relieved themselves, at any rate to their own satisfaction, of the obligation to examine the evidence to the contrary, to which no reference whatever is made throughout the report.

To fill the void left by the failure to discuss the essential point of difference between the two systems, they provided sixty pages of highly technical detail.

As regards the Argo instruments, the report presents a curious mixture of contradictory statements. The general tone reflects Moore's condemnation on the grounds of unreliability. Yet the comment on the individual instruments is perfectly fair[14]. 'The rangefinder, following the alterations now in hand, will be . . . a great improvement on the Barr and Stroud.' As to the Plotter (which the Admiralty had declined to inspect) they say 'we must assume that Boys is right and that it is mechanically perfect'; and of the Clock 'on the whole it solves in an effective and reliable manner the problem it undertakes.' But, of course, not a word to indicate that the Clock will undertake functions that the Dreyer Clock could not even attempt.

Among a number of mis-statements the least excusable appears in the reference to the report of the Colville Committee which had been so unaccountably suppressed by Wilson and Moore in 1910. To Dreyer and Usborne, whose mandate it was to justify Pollen's rejection, the existence of that report was a serious embarrassment. To ignore it entirely was out of the question. They therefore compromised by omitting any reference to the positive recommendations in favour of the gyro, the clock and the plotter, and concentrating attention on the one indicisive phrase:

> If it is necessary in order to hit an enemy that her track shall first be drawn on a chart, the automatic method of doing it, as arranged for in the *Natal*, is far superior to any other method.

Building on this statement, they make the quite unjustifiable comment[15]:

> They /Colville 1910/ could not recommend that such a track was necessary. There is no doubt that /they/ considered the question thoroughly, and purely from a war point of view, and had they seen any real advantage to be gained by such a track, they would have recommended it to the Admiralty.

In reality, any uncertainty as to Colville's belief in the desirability of plotting, if an effective means could be found is dispelled by the strong statement on the second page of his report to the effect that:

> Further trials are necessary to test the automatic plotting arrangement when that portion of the installation has been further developed: and in order that it may be developed as quickly as possible, the Committee recommend that it should be

fitted in four ships and the officers of these ships and the makers should co-operate to produce the most efficient instrument.

After this example of deliberate misrepresentation there is an element of light relief in the patronizing conclusion, attributed to Usborne, that:

> /The Dreyer instrument/ is in every way a practical instrument designed to meet the real requirements of Naval action, in so far as we can foresee them, and no one but a Naval officer working with ample experience of fire control behind him, could have produced it.
>
> Similarly the A.C. System is the embodiment, perhaps the perfect embodiment of a system conceived by a civilian. The system is an attractive one, and may have real advantages, but it is not based on a full apprehension of the real conditions of action and cannot be compared in value with the Dreyer.

To sum up, it seems fair to say that the Dreyer-Usborne report is valuable, first in that the assumption that it was axiomatic that 'while a ship is under helm its gunnery must suffer', exactly expresses, in technical language, the attitude of Jellicoe and the Board to Pollen's inventions, and, secondly, in that it affords an excellent example of the ignorant and prejudiced propaganda to which Jellicoe was subjected, first by Dreyer, while serving in the South Atlantic, and later, after his return to the Admiralty as Second Sea Lord, by Moore.

All in all, it provides the final proof of the truth of Pollen's statement that 'the real obstacle to the adoption of our gear is that the official conception of the kind of fire control necessary in action differs radically from what we and those naval officers who think with us, think necessary.'

In Chapter XI, it will be shown that Jellicoe remained faithful to Dreyer and his inadequate instruments throughout the war, and that it was not until October 1918, ten months after his retirement from the office of First Sea Lord, that the gunnery officers of the Grand Fleet, through a Committee appointed by Beatty as C-in-C, were given the opportunity to say what they thought of the Dreyer Table and demand a new design that would permit them to fight under helm; or as they expressed it, one that took account of the fact that 'frequent alterations of course at high speed are now the accepted conditions in action.'

There we must leave the question as to why Dreyer was preferred to Pollen in 1912. There remains the quite different, but no less important, question as to how or why the Board came to allow, or rather to compel Pollen to take his system abroad. We have seen that Moore was fanatical on the theme of the cost of Pollen's instruments and the price demanded for monopoly; but by 1913, when the decision was taken, this was no longer an issue. For in his letter to Churchill of 21st October 1912 Pollen had offered to let him have the monopoly at any price he thought fair — surely an unprecedented sacrifice to have made in the interest of his country, when we realise how confident, and rightly confident, he was of the fortune awaiting him if he took it abroad.

Moore's contribution to this vital question, as it appears in the letter to Prince Louis of the 19th September 1912, discussed in the previous chapter, is almost unbelievable.

> I agree that it is unfortunate that Mr Pollen should have acquired so much confidential information but I think the time has long since arrived when we should shake ourselves free and let Mr Pollen prove the truth of his contention that he has a waiting market elsewhere.

If, as Moore himself had told the Board, the Pollen system was as good as Dreyer's, what possible justification could there be for presenting it to foreigners, who were believed to have nothing comparable of their own?

We have seen that attempts were made later to block sales abroad by claiming that Service patents were involved: but that was surely not in Moore's mind when writing to Prince Louis in September: and the idea that he could be stopped by these threats had been exploded long before the final decision was taken at the end of June 1913. Finally there is the fact, later recorded in a letter to Hall already noticed, that Jellicoe had shown genuine sympathy over the improbability of Pollen's ever finding a market abroad, thus showing that he had accepted Moore's negative assessment of Pollen's prospects of doing so.

Up to this point it would have been easy to imagine that Moore's hostility to Pollen stemmed mainly from a prejudice in favour of a fellow officer; but this final challenge to let Pollen prove that he had a market abroad must be genuine and, if genuine, a reflection of his own and the Board's total failure to understand the magnitude and significance of Pollen's achievement.

CHAPTER VII

The Royal Commission
Gives Judgement

To Pollen the outbreak of war in August 1914 came as a bitter
blow. Despite his involvement with the theory and weapons of
war he had never believed that the Germans could be so
wicked. To him, the maintenance of a powerful Navy was a
form of insurance against the possibility of war rather than a
preparation for it. The present writer has a vivid recollection of
Hilaire Belloc coming to dine in the early days of the war, at
the cottage at Walton Heath, prior to giving a lecture in the
neighbourhood, and of Belloc's comment on the outbreak of
war: 'The worst of it is that all the fools are right'. A comment
with which Arthur Pollen was in wholehearted agreement.

Before going on to consider Pollen's reaction to war, we
must leap forward ten years and allow the Royal Commission
on Awards to Inventors to write the last chapter on A.C., the
last round in the long drawn out rivalry between Arthur
Pollen and Admiral Sir Frederic Dreyer, GBE, KCB.

The Royal Commission was set up in March 1919 to adjudi-
cate on claims for inventions used by the Crown, with express
authority to make ex gratia awards in cases not covered by
patents. The need for such a Commission arose quite
understandably from the circumstances of war but its mandate
was not confined to wartime inventions or wartime user.

At first sight the appointment of this Tribunal must have
looked to Pollen like the answer to prayer.

In 1912, as indeed in all the previous crises Pollen's recur-
rent plea had been for the setting up of an independent

unbiased committee to examine his claims; here, thanks to the accident of war, was precisely the Tribunal for which he had asked. However, further examination was to show that the presentation of a case would not be so simple. The problem before the war was to determine the relative merits of the Pollen and the Dreyer systems, and decide which would best serve the interests of the Navy. The Royal Commission's mandate was very different. It was to decide the origin of inventions that had been used by the Service and apportion the awards accordingly. What had to be proved, therefore, was not that the Pollen inventions ought to have been used but that inventions which had been used were Pollen inventions.

It will be recalled that in 1912, after seeing the demonstrations in the *Orion*, the Admiralty ordered six of Pollen's Argo Mark IV Clocks, while adhering to their previous decision to adopt the Dreyer Table as standard equipment. The fact that these six Argo Clocks had been bought and paid for in 1912, at an agreed price, ruled out the possibility of making any further claims, through the Royal Commission, in respect of that instrument.

To establish a claim for an extra payment he had to show either that the whole system of fire control, i.e. both plotting unit and Clock, used by the Service during the war, was based on his inventions or alternatively that some essential instrument in their system was based on his submissions. He was confident that both these propositions could be proved, if only, and it was a big 'if', he could establish for certain what system the Admiralty had used. In all other claims before the Commission, and this was evident from their reports, the Government Department concerned had made the fullest disclosure of the various appliances and devices they had used. But not so in Admiralty v. Pollen. The Admiralty took the line that Pollen, in 1913, had been guilty of disclosing Admiralty secrets abroad. Accordingly he was not to be trusted. His Counsel could see what was now being used but not Pollen nor Isherwood nor their Patent Counsel. In thus taking advantage of their powers under the Official Secrets Act the Admiralty were yet again, and at Pollen's expense, pre-judging the issue. In simple terms, the case before the Tribunal was to decide whether these secrets had in fact belonged to Pollen or to the State. In the event the Court decided that they had belonged to Pollen. Yet from the outset disclosure of vital evidence was withheld from Pollen on the grounds that the secrets were State secrets.

The sequence of events in the handling of the claim was by no means lacking in interest. Pollen's first application for a hearing was made in 1920. The final hearing took place in 1925 and in the meantime, much had happened. The case actually came before the Tribunal on two occasions – the first being in October 1923 and the second in the summer of 1925. For the first hearing only three days were allotted. To make matters worse, the Chairman, Mr Justice Sargant, without previous warning, decided that the claim would be divided into two parts – the first as to the system in general, and the second, as to the specific instrument known as the Dreyer Table. The three days allotted to the case were clearly inadequate, but the Chairman overcame the difficulty by announcing on the third day that the claim in respect of 'system', as such, was too general to come within the terms of their mandate, and that the second part of the claim, in respect of the Clock, must be re-submitted as a separate claim. This decision was resisted by Pollen and his advisers, who pleaded for a new hearing of the entire case. After much argument, their appeal succeeded and a rehearing of the entire case was conceded. This in itself was something of a triumph, and the irony of it was that the principal factor in getting a complete rehearing, was the fact that Admiral Dreyer, having returned from the Far East and having heard of the failure of Pollen's first claim, had now himself submitted his own claim in respect of the Dreyer Table. Thus it came about that at the new hearing in the summer of 1925 both Pollen and Dreyer appeared simultaneously as claimants; Pollen claiming for the whole system, including the clock,

Dreyer claiming only in respect of the clock, known in the Service as the Dreyer Fire Control Table. The intervention at this late stage of Admiral Dreyer, now one of the Lords of Admiralty, provided a dramatic setting for the final trial of strength; an ideal setting but for the fact that Pollen was once more being cheated, this time by the Admiralty's refusal to disclose essential particulars of the system they were using. For the Admiralty, the Attorney General, Sir Douglas Hogg, later Lord Hailsham, appeared, supported by Sir Duncan Kerly, KC, a formidable character with much experience in defending the Crown against the claims of inventors. Pollen and the Argo Company were represented by Wilfrid Greene, KC, and Mr Carrol Romer. Wilfrid Green, a future Master of the Rolls, was undoubtedly one of the ablest men of his day, but in so technical a matter and so vast a field, the prohibition on consultation with his client, who alone knew the whole long history of the case, was a tremendous handicap.

In his opening remarks, Wilfrid Greene left the Court in no doubt as to his own view of the injustice of this unprecedented procedure:

> Now I am in a singular position and it is a position in which I venture to think Counsel has never found himself before. I cannot complain of it because, of course, it is the result of the ruling of the Chairman based on the view of the Admiralty. I have been put on terms that I am not to discuss my own case with my own client, except so far and to the limited extent of discussing so much of it as appears on his own side of the curtain. The result is I come into this contest with one hand tied behind my back. However, there it is. It is going to operate against me very much. It is going to operate against me during the course of the case just as severely as in attempting to get it up.

As to the merits of the case, the fundamental difficulty was that in the early days a number of alternative methods of doing the same thing were freely and openly discussed between Arthur Pollen and Captain Harding, the Assistant D.N.O.

The 1906-08 Agreement had established what was virtually

a partnership between Pollen and the Admiralty, and the intention had been that they should work out the solution of their problems together. The contract was drafted in such a way as to include within the definition of the Pollen system every form of plotting.

The contract also included the very remarkable provision that the Agreement would remain binding whatever modifications might be introduced in the instruments, whether they emanated from Pollen or from the Admiralty. All this was done deliberately, because neither side wanted the other to be able to claim that the contract was invalidated because of some mechanical modification.

However in 1910 there was a major breach in the relationship between Pollen and the Admiralty, and it was a term of the settlement made in April of that year that the 1906-08 Agreement should be regarded as a 'dead letter'. Once that Agreement had been abandoned, the difference between the two alternative methods of plotting, which had been so freely discussed by Pollen and Harding, was found to assume a new importance.

Pollen, supported by Harding, had from the start preferred and advocated the making of what was known as a True Plot, i.e. a chart representing the actual course of the two ships, our own and the enemy's; Dreyer on the other hand had advocated the plotting of what were known as 'Rates' i.e. two separate charts, one of successive bearings, the other of successive ranges. It was agreed that both methods owed their origin to Pollen, as far back as 1905. However, not even Wilfrid Greene's ingenuity could overcome the simple fact that Pollen had advocated the one, Dreyer had advocated the other and that it was the second that had been used; and it was on this point alone that the Tribunal in their award concluded that the system in use by the Admiralty was not Pollen's system. By way of consolation, Wilfrid Greene's advocacy did win from the Judge the remarkable tribute, 'May it not be this, that a conception of a great mind is gradually penetrating bit by bit into another mind; but it does not follow that you can treat that conception as something entitling you to an award'. Very flattering to Pollen as the inventor but discouraging to him as claimant.

On the second part of the claim the Tribunal's finding (*see* Appendix) was as sweeping and conclusive as anybody could wish:

> As to the second part of the claim we are satisfied that Mr Pollen and the Argo Co. Ltd. were the first to produce a mechanical integrator of the kind hereinbefore referred to, namely the Argo Clock and that the clock mechanism of the Dreyer Tables Marks IV and V works substantially on the same principles although there are differences of mechanical detail.
>
> Further we are satisfied upon the facts that the principle and details of the Argo Clock were communicated to the Admiralty and to those who were at work on the Dreyer Tables and directly contributed to the evolution of the clock mechanism of the Dreyer Tables Marks IV and V. The knowledge so acquired made plain the feasibility of converting the clock mechanism of the earlier types of Dreyer Table into a form which served the same function and was based upon the same principle as the Argo Clock and while we acquit all concerned of any intention or desire to copy or take unacknowledged benefit of the claimants' work (and any suggestion of the kind was disclaimed at the hearing) we think it impossible to question the influence of that work upon the ultimate result.
>
> There are other elements in the Dreyer Tables which in our judgement owe their origin to communications by Mr Pollen to the Admiralty.

The simple factual style of these findings is disarming. To be told that the Commission is 'satisfied upon the facts', that the principles and details of the Argo Clock were communicated to those who were at work on the Dreyer Tables might mean no more than that Pollen and his Counsel had succeeded after fourteen days of argument and evidence in establishing that Dreyer and his colleagues had drawn their inspiration from Pollen's 'great mind', and gradually adopted his ideas. For

Wilfrid Greene had indeed devoted long hours to the patient assembling of 'straws in the wind', whereby he showed the extent to which the so-called Service system had drawn upon the conception of Pollen's great mind.

But there came a moment on the thirteenth day of the hearing when Pollen was electrified to hear[1] that the drawings, designs and specifications of his Mark IV Clock had actually been handed by Captain Henley, an assistant to Admiral Moore the D.N.O., direct to his competitors thereby enabling them to transform the very inadequate Mark III Dreyer Table into a genuine integrator, which 'served the same purpose and was based on the same principle as the Argo Clock'.

To Pollen this admission revealed with dramatic suddenness the whole dark story, of which for fourteen years he had remained in ignorance. The facts quite simply were as follows:-On the 15th May 1911 Pollen had called upon Captain Henley to tell him that he was about to start production of his new clock, later known as the Argo Mark IV, and explain its unique and revolutionary capabilities. Working drawings and sketches were enclosed with the letter. Further drawings which completed the specification were furnished two weeks later on the 27th May. The letter so dramatically produced at the hearing had been written by Dreyer to Sir Keith Elphinstone of Elliotts, the leading Government Contractors in the manufacture of instruments. The date of the letter was the 4th July and from the context it was clear that by that date both Sir Keith Elphinstone and Captain Dreyer were already fully informed as to the contents of the Argo communication to the D.N.O. of the 27th May, and familiar too with the mechanical detail of the Argo Clock. It then emerged that unknown to Pollen, Dreyer and Elphinstone had for some time been engaged in designing a new clock that was intended to compete with the instrument that Pollen was known to be designing. At that time Dreyer was serving as Flag-Commander to Jellicoe in the *Prince of Wales* and but for the fortunate circumstance of Dreyer being then at sea, and the consequent need for Dreyer and Elphinstone to communicate by letter, the truth about their acquisition of the Argo ideas would never have emerged. Even more fortunate was the fact that Dreyer's Counsel had thought fit to include this letter in the papers submitted to the Commission, in support of his own claim. The letter certainly proved that he was a leading contributor to the design of the Dreyer Tables, but both he and Counsel apparently overlooked the fact that it also disclosed the source of his ideas. Commenting on the situation disclosed by this letter Mr A. M. Langdon, KC, a member of the Commission remarked:

> What weighs on my mind is that Captain Henley was possessed of the material matters concerning the construction of the Argo Clock and was in daily consultation, as far as I can make out, with Sir Keith Elphinstone who was designing the matter which Admiral Dreyer left in his hands. Neither Captain Henley nor Sir Keith Elphinstone have been called to give evidence. I do not blame you for not calling them but what I want to know is: What inference am I to draw from the fact that, as from the material date of the communications by Mr Pollen to the Admiralty on 27th May Captain Henley is in daily consultation with Sir Keith Elphinstone who is designing the table which is in question here?

This led on to the disclosure that Sir Keith Elphinstone was a frequent visitor to Cooke's Works at York where the Argo Clock was being made, and in particular that when Captain Henley paid a formal visit to York in October, to see the clock and study all the drawings, Sir Keith Elphinstone went with him.

It must have been a relief to all concerned in the case that, in this story of the communication of Argo ideas to the rival designers, the villain of the piece, if there was one, emerged as the Admiralty rather than any individual whether Sir Keith Elphinstone or Admiral Dreyer. Sir Duncan Kerly, the Admiralty Counsel did his best to brazen it out, but the Chairman had heard enough. Addressing Sir Duncan, he closed the discussion with the following observation:

What puzzles me about your argument is, that it reduces mechanisms which are admitted apparently on all hands to be very ingenious and very clever mechanisms, to the level of the obvious. I should have thought myself that the Argo Clock was a new idea. It for the first time produces mechanically that which hitherto had not been thought of by anybody or done by anybody. . . . The whole point is that it crossed the Rubicon which none of the other things had done because none of the other things had mechanically generated the rates with success. That is the whole point. They got over that which hitherto had been a frontier line.

Thus did the Judge after twenty years of prevarication by the Admiralty bring the argument to conclusion and compel them to face the facts.

It will be recalled that the Tribunal, under the Chairmanship of Mr Justice Tomlin, which heard Pollen's claim, also had before it at the same time, Admiral Dreyer's own claim for the Fire Control Table (or Clock) that bore his name. A peculiar feature of the case was that Admiral Dreyer who had acted for the Admiralty in the pre-war phase from 1907 to 1913, and again after the war when he was brought down from Scotland to attend the first hearing of Pollen's claim in 1923, now appeared not as an Admiralty witness but as the rival claimant. One of the first questions that Wilfrid Greene addressed to the Admiral was, 'The case which the Admiralty has put up both at this and the previous hearing is really in substance a case put up under your advice is it not?' To this Admiral Dreyer replied, 'No. I was asked as to my knowledge of the history of the case but actually as regards the framing of whatever opposition to Mr Pollen the Admiralty has put forward, I had nothing to do with it. It is not in the function of the Director of Gunnery'. After a number of further questions Wilfrid Greene returned to the point expressing it slightly differently, 'Is the case which the Admiralty put up substantially in accordance with what you reported?'. Without loss of dignity and with the frankness and simplicity which distinguished all his evidence the Admiral replied, 'Yes, I think it must be as I should not be likely to make a wrong report'. As to his first introduction to Pollen's inventions, he was reminded by Wilfrid Greene of his visit to the Linotype Works at Broadheath in June 1907, when he accompanied the Controller Sir Henry Jackson and the D.N.O., Captain Jellicoe, on a formal visit of inspection of the Pollen gear; in reply he maintained that he had no recollection of seeing the Pollen gear – 'I have certain recollections such as seeing the Linotype gear (printing machines) and so on and I am only prepared to give evidence with regard to what I can recollect'. However, he did go so far as to say that he would not traverse Mr Pollen's evidence as to what he had seen and, in as much as the whole purpose of the visit by this high-level delegation was to see the Argo gear, it would have been difficult to discount the possibility that they had done so. With the tact and courtesy so characteristic of the lawyer and incidentally so effective, Wilfrid Greene modified the question saying, 'I will put it to you hypothetically. Assuming Mr Pollen's recollection is right about it, that would have been the first time that such an idea had ever been put before you?' Again the Admiral goes down with flags flying, 'Let me say the complete solution of it, yes. I think that is a very fair way of putting it'. The question to which Dreyer was then assenting was, 'Had you ever before seen or heard of an integrating mechanism which, when set to own course and speed and enemy course and speed and an initial bearing and an initial range, automatically generated the range and bearing?' Wilfrid Greene's final question to the Admiral was, 'There is one other question I want to ask you, rather a personal one. I notice that you had your award of £5000 in 1916, but your claim was not put forward till 1924. What was the reason for that?' To this the Admiral replied, 'I was waiting for Mr Pollen to have his case heard before I put in my claim. I thought his case had been heard. I had no idea he would have a rehearing and I sent in my claim as Captain of the *Repulse* in 1923'.

To conclude the story of the hearing of Pollen's case before

the Royal Commission, here are Wilfrid Greene's final comments on the manner in which the case was fought by the
Admiralty.

> The first thing I should like to deal with is the suggestion that
> Mr Pollen's system is not new. You must not take it that this
> defence is put forward lightly. It is put forward with the greatest
> vehemence. Where are the people who should have been called
> before the Court to give evidence as to what novelty there was
> in the years when he came on the scene? The only person
> whose evidence about that the Court has heard is not an
> Admiralty witness at all. It is Admiral Dreyer. Where are the
> people who were there at the time? Where is Admiral Jellicoe?
> Now that he has come back to England (from New Zealand) I
> suggest that he ought to have been called to say that in the
> years 1906 and 1907 what the Admiralty was doing was
> something which was old, obvious and useless. Where is Ad-
> miral Crook, now Director of Ordnance at the Admiralty, one
> of the members of the committee on which Colonel Harding
> sat? We on our side have called Colonel Harding, Admiral
> Peirse, Admiral Craig Waller, Admiral Sir Reginald Hall and
> Captain Hughes-Onslow. When Mr Pollen goes into the box
> there are pages and pages of cross-examination on the subject of
> novelty or no novelty, and that the thing was stale and old. But
> the contemporary people on their side are not called, and the
> contemporary people on my side are not cross-examined about
> it. Did they dare to suggest to Colonel Harding that the whole
> of this thing was not new but obvious, and that there was no
> merit in suggesting it? Admiral Jellicoe, if he had been asked
> these questions would have laughed at the whole thing. That is
> the sort of way in which the case has been dealt with by the
> Admiralty.

The award of which the full text is given as an appendix
left a number of points in the air, particularly in regard to
future user of the Pollen inventions and in addition, there was
the whole question of the publicity to be given to the Commission's findings. The hearing had all been held in camera and
even the amount of the award had not been made public
although it would be listed in due course in the Annual

Report, which it was customary for the Royal Commission to publish. After some unsatisfactory correspondence, a conference was held at the Admiralty as a result of which, the following very courteous exchange of letters took place between Pollen and the Admiralty:

11th February 1926.

Sir,

I am commanded by My Lords Commissioners of the Admiralty to refer to the recommendations and report of proceedings of the Royal Commission on Awards to Inventors on the subject of your claim last summer, and to the frank discussion on the whole matter which took place on your recent visit to the Admiralty, when it appeared that it would be acceptable to both parties that this long dispute between the Admiralty and yourself should be treated as at an end and that any questions left outstanding should be settled without acrimony and litigation.

2. Their Lordships note with satisfaction that in the course of the proceedings, you spontaneously volunteered the statement – endorsed by the Commissioners' findings – that you had been convinced of the good faith of those who had maintained opposing claims to your own, and Their Lordships understand that this applied not in an individual case only but to all concerned.

3. Their Lordships on Their part are glad to acknowledge that neither during your confidential relations with the Service, nor since, are They aware of anything in your conduct that justifies any reflection on your personal honour or loyalty, and They associate Themselves with the Royal Commission's recognition of your service as of great value to the Admiralty and to the country.

4. My Lords also desire to refer to the recent conversation between you and Sir Oswyn Murray as to the steps which might be taken to give effect to the wish of both parties that any possible difference of view as to the correct interpretation of the scope of the Commission's findings and award should be amicably adjusted as soon as possible. I am to confirm the suggestion then made that, in the event of any difficulty in arriving at such a settlement by friendly discussion, the matter

should be referred by agreement to the Royal Commission, or preferably to the Chairman of the Commission sitting alone if he should be willing to deal with the matter.

> I am,
>> Sir,
>>> Your obedient Servant,
>>>> O. Murray.

12th February 1926.

Sir,

The receipt of yours of the 11th February has given me the utmost pleasure. I cordially welcome the reconciliation so handsomely conveyed. I beg you to convey to Their Lordships my sincere thanks for the generosity of Their expressions and to assure them that what was said on my behalf at the recent hearing was intended to apply to the whole action of the Admiralty from 1912 until the present time, and to all its representatives.

I welcome and agree to the method which you suggest of settling any outstanding matters.

> I am, Sir,
>> Your obedient Servant,
>>> A. H. Pollen.

It would be pleasing to be able to record that this exchange of letters had brought the long standing dispute to a close. Unfortunately there remained one all important point of interpretation on which they were far from agreement.

In 1912, as has been shown, Dreyer had embodied in his Dreyer Table all the essential elements of the Argo Clock except for the helm-free functions which he thought superfluous.

In 1920 Lord Beatty became First Sea Lord and at once set up[2] a Committee of all the talents 'to study the whole subject of fire control and evolve a new design'. The Committee included Sir Keith Elphinstone of Elliotts who had designed the Dreyer Table and Arthur Pollen's two former colleagues Harold Isherwood (now Lt. Commander RNVR) and a Swede by the name of Landstad, the latter being specifically named as designer to the Committee.

This committee, known as the Admiralty Fire Control Committee, was actually the first standing committee ever set up to deal with the subject of fire-control, a fact which goes far to explain the surprising statement made by Admiral Custance in his *Land and Water* article of April 1917, to the effect that prior to the War Arthur Pollen 'by his mastery of the subject had forced himself into the position of Chief of the only constructive staff the Navy possessed for the study of fire control'.

Among those co-opted to the Committee in 1920, was Hugh Clausen, an electrical engineer, who on the outbreak of war had joined the RNVR and later served as Gunnery Lieutenant in the *Benbow* at Jutland. After the war he transferred to the civilian staff of the Admiralty and later rose to the rank of Senior Principal Scientific Officer, and chief designer to the Fire Control Committee.

In March 1947, in the course of a lecture to the Naval Ordnance Department, which was then stationed in Bath he expressed strong views on 'the pernicious practice of attaching personal names by service people to inventions.' 'The very fact,' he said 'that Commander, later Admiral, Dreyer called his alternative to the late Mr Pollen's Argo fire control, the Dreyer Table, put back the development of gunnery material by many years. This is a classic example, but others may be quoted showing the same result in lesser degree.'

In 1926 the conclusions of the Committee would no doubt have remained a closely guarded secret had it not been for Pollen's dispute with the Admiralty as to the interpretation of the Award, which brought to light information that the Admiralty had sought to keep from him.

The agreed procedure for disposing of the dispute was for each party to submit a statement of their case to Lord Tomlin, who had sat as Chairman of the Royal Commission's enquiry.

Pollen's submission, dated the 28th July 1926 included the following statement:

In his draft on our communications, required for transforming the Mark III which could not integrate, into the Mark IV and

Mark V Tables which could, Admiral Dreyer in 1911 and 1912 stopped short of borrowing the slipless drive used in conjunction with the necessary linkages, by which combination alone the foregoing helm-free functions could be realised. The deficiency, therefore, had at once to be made good. The new design accordingly was put in hand under the direction of a strong committee, and with the assistance and advice of Lieutenant-Commander Isherwood and Mr D. H. Landstad – the designer and draughtsman of the original Argo Clock.

The Admiralty's counter submission to the Commission, dated the 7th October 1926, contained the following by way of reply:

> In view of the numerous references to the mechanisms incorporated in the Argo Clock, especially to the Slipless Drive, and to the statement made on behalf of the Admiralty that these mechanisms had been adopted in a new design of Fire Control Table then under construction, My Lords are satisfied that all the facts necessary for the consideration of Mr Pollen's claims were presented to and appreciated by the Commission and that in consequence the use by the Admiralty of this device is covered by the award.

The formal admission by the Admiralty that the slipless drive had already been adopted contrasts strangely with Sir Duncan Kerly's twice-repeated statement in the course of his cross-examination of Arthur Pollen, that the Admiralty had never used the slipless drive.

However it transpired that the admission that it was to be fitted in 'two ships now building' was made at a hearing from which Pollen had been excluded. The ships in question were the *Nelson* and the *Rodney*.

As an attempt to settle the dispute these submissions were of no avail. The Chairman refused to go into the question as to whether the new instrument could be regarded as a 'future modification of the Dreyer Table', and, therefore, covered by the award, or whether, as Pollen maintained, the adoption of the slipless drive, the vital element that distinguished his clock from Dreyer's, had created an entirely new situation. In the event, Pollen, unwilling to face the risk and expense of seeking his remedy in the Civil Courts, had to give way.

However, the dispute over the interpretation of the award had at least served to establish the remarkable fact that in 1926 the Admiralty, freed from the shackles of the ancien régime, had at last admitted the validity of the helm-free principle and of the mechanisms which they had rejected in 1912; furthermore that these mechanisms were to be embodied in ships now under construction.

Fourteen years is a long time in the history of a young science and it is hard to imagine clearer proof of Arthur Pollen's claim to the title 'Pioneer of Naval Gunnery'.

By way of explanation of the long delay in obtaining recognition of his work, it is interesting to note that the Royal Commission's award to Pollen and his company was made, not in respect of the comprehensive Pollen system first submitted in 1906, nor even in respect of the perfected Argo Clock that was offered to the Admiralty in 1912, but solely in respect of ideas and mechanisms communicated to the Admiralty in 1911 and subsequently embodied by Dreyer in the 'Dreyer Table' adopted by the Admiralty in 1912.

With the two rival claimants before them, the Commission made an award, in respect only of the Dreyer Table, of £30,000 to Pollen and his Argo Company, this being in addition to the sum of £11,500 paid to Pollen in 1908. To Dreyer, to whom £5000 had been paid by the Admiralty in 1916, they made no further award.

By comparison with the sum of £150,000 that would have been payable under the 1906 contract for the monopoly of the Whole System, £30,000 was a small sum; but the Royal Commission was concerned only with what had happened and not with what should have happened.

CHAPTER VIII

War

Few men can have been called upon to face so many total reversals of fortune as Arthur Pollen. We have followed him through all the ups and downs of his conflict with the Admiralty and have seen that when driven abroad by Whitehall in 1913 he had been at once acclaimed by the foreigners and had his order books filled. Yet the greatest paradox of all was yet to come, when, on the outbreak of war, with its promise of fortunes for the manufacturers of the instruments of war, his business was brought to a halt.

Pollen's first reaction to war had been to place the resources of his companies at the disposal of the Admiralty with the offer to work throughout the war without profit – a gesture which led Reginald Hall to observe, in the memorandum he addressed to David Beatty in 1922, 'I have yet to learn that any other person or firm in armaments volunteered to work throughout the war without any profit at all.'

True to form, the Admiralty rejected Pollen's offer out of hand. War or no war, a personal feud was to them more important than the services of the leading instrument makers in the country.

There remained the possibility that the value of the Pollen system might yet be so conclusively demonstrated by allied navies as to compel the Admiralty to reconsider their attitude. But here again he was thwarted by the refusal of the Departments concerned to say whether he would be allowed to give delivery, even to our Allies. In the end only the Russians, who

146

had already started taking delivery before the outbreak of war, actually received a complete unit. The neutrals of North and South America saw no prospect of early delivery and our Allies, other than Russia, were too occupied by other wartime pressures to feel disposed to experiment with a new system of gunnery.

While these problems were being worked out, Pollen found an outlet for his restless spirit in writing. In a letter to his old friend Alfred Spender, written at the end[1] of August, we find:

> Would you care for a weekly, or more frequent contribution from a naval specialist, to wit me? The fact is that the war keeps me hanging about London without very much to do, and I should like to be more occupied and picking up a few pennies by the way. There has not been a great deal of naval news yet but every scrap that does come out has an important bearing. If you think I could be useful I should be grateful.

In the crisis of 1913, Spender had done his best to help resolve Pollen's dispute with the Admiralty and now jumped at the opportunity to enlist so knowledgeable a critic as Naval Correspondent. By return of post came the reply 'The idea is an excellent one – by all means go ahead with it and fire in your first article'. Yet for some time he had no thought of writing professionally and remained hopeful of finding a more warlike and active appointment where his knowledge and experience could be more effectively used.

In November, the good news reached Pollen that Reginald Hall, after taking part in the Battle of the Heligoland Bight as Captain of the *Queen Mary*, had been obliged by ill health to withdraw from active service, and had now been appointed to the responsible office of Director of Naval Intelligence (D.N.I.). After all the disappointments of their former association, in the *Natal* in 1910, then again in 1912, it was a happy chance that brought the two men together once again at this time. Of the understanding established between them during the war, Hall was later to record[2]:

It was my special business to keep a watch on the Press and its influence on public opinion. By the time I came to Whitehall, as Director of Intelligence at the end of 1914, Arthur Pollen was already established as the Naval writer of the day and I made it my business to keep in close touch. When I wanted the Press to take a certain line I learnt to rely very greatly on his advice as to how it could best be done. Nor did he ever seek exclusive information to his own advantage.

When, in April 1915, Pollen was invited by Neville Foster to join Hilaire Belloc on *Land and Water*, he realised at once that to accept a post as one of the two feature writers on a specialist weekly would be a very different matter from writing a weekly article for a daily paper, and that he would be virtually committing himself to the role of naval critic for the duration of the war.

However, he had by this time established a good understanding with his old friend Masterton-Smith, the First Lord's Private Secretary, and felt confident that as a journalist he would not be handicapped by previous differences with Whitehall over rejection of the System. On the 8th May 1915 he appeared for the first time as the author of 'The War at Sea' and from then until the end of the war shared the headlines with Belloc.

Another means of influencing opinion, long since displaced by television and radio, was the lecture. In 1914, well-known military critics were much in demand as lecturers and to Pollen, who by nature preferred talking to writing, the opportunity to make a name for himself as a lecturer on a subject he knew so well, was by no means unwelcome.

Among a number of testimonials to his gifts as a lecturer there is one, by E. C. Tobey, the chief representative of the U.S. Navy Department in London, which merits quotation in full. It was written in May 1917 to a colleague in Washington to announce Pollen's forthcoming visit to the States, and urge him to make use of Pollen's services as a lecturer:

I have been to one of his lectures and went in a mixed party of

soldiers, journalists, British and American statesmen and
people of fashion. The audience, for the most part, was
wounded soldiers and nurses.

The subject was novel, complicated, technical to a degree and it
was made as enthralling, as intelligible and as easy to remember
as a fairy tale. It is a simple fact that when after an hour and
forty minutes, the thing came to an end, there was not one of us
who could believe that we had been listening for half an hour. I
was sitting almost alongside of the Editor of the *London Times*,
the kind of man, one would think, who could not easily be
worked to rapturous approval. 'It was the best lecture,' he said,
'I have ever heard on any subject in my life.'

As a journalist the two big events in Pollen's life were first
the Battle of Jutland and secondly the crisis of May 1917.
Paradoxically he appears in the first case as Jellicoe's best
friend and supporter and in the second as prosecutor demanding the removal of Jellicoe and his team from Whitehall.

Today it is only in his role of critic that he is remembered.
Indeed, Professor A. Temple Patterson, Jellicoe's latest biographer, and Editor of the Jellicoe Papers, goes so far as to write
him off[3] as a disappointed and disgruntled inventor. Yet the
reality was very different, for Pollen was a serious journalist
well aware of his responsibilities as the leading naval writer of
the day. The following letter to Lady Beatty dated the 21st
October 1915 is typical of his attitude:

Your letter and mine must, I think, have crossed. I am in entire
agreement with you on the broad question that we should do far
better with younger men right through the Government. On
the other hand, it fills me with the greatest possible distress to
see the country and particularly London being brought into a
kind of hysterical condition by perpetual attacks on the Government, because they disturb the public mind without the country
having any means of making its criticism effective. I am afraid it
is a great deal better to bear the evils that we have than fly to
others that we know only too well.

The real trouble of the present position is that Harmsworth
through *The Times* and *Daily Mail* has made the task of sane
critics extraordinarily difficult by keeping up an atmosphere in

which almost any criticism runs the danger of being thought alarmist. So that really one has to devote a great deal of one's time to calming the public when really one would much prefer to be bringing the pressure of an instructed opinion upon the Government. Do read in the present number of *Land and Water*, Belloc's couple of columns on 'Seeing things as they are' on page 11.

Although I have not been in close consultation with Belloc, I can see that he feels as keenly as I do, the cramping effect of having to counteract Harmsworth. He has, I am sure, many points of military policy that he would like to criticise, just as I have many points of naval policy. But while the Government is under fire of a perfectly ignorant criticism, it is not only useless but quite dangerous to supply these gentlemen with new weapons.

That his attitude as supporter rather than critic was fully appreciated at Whitehall, is shown by the fact that when in May 1916, Masterton-Smith and Arthur Balfour, the First Lord, became anxious about Jellicoe's health, and wanted to ascertain Jellicoe's wishes as to his own future as Commander-in-Chief, it was to Pollen that they turned for help. It had been arranged that a party of Naval journalists were to pay a visit to the Fleets at Rosyth and Scapa, and Arthur Pollen was to go as representative of the *Westminster Gazette*.

A day or two before we started, Masterton-Smith, the First Lord's private secretary, asked me to go and see him. It seemed that the First Lord wanted certain information about the Commander-in-Chief's attitude towards maintaining his command, or alternatively going to the Admiralty as First Sea Lord. He had been under extreme strain for more than eighteen months, and he was by some years the oldest officer afloat. Had the strain so told on him that the physical and mental change to less strenuous duties would be welcome? If he wished for a change what would his attitude be towards the restoration of Lord Fisher to a position of influence and authority at Whitehall? Again, whom would he designate as his successor? On matters of this kind the First Lord was quite unable to obtain any disinterested access to the Commander-in-Chief.

Nobody was in a better position than Masterton-Smith to assess the Pollen-Jellicoe relationship and Pollen, a working journalist at that time, would certainly not have been entrusted with so sensitive and personal a mission had there been the least suspicion of ill-will between them. Moreover it is clear from Reginald Hall's record of their talk that when they did meet at Scapa Jellicoe had opened his heart to Pollen. Hall's account[4] reads as follows:

> At Scapa, Pollen had a long talk with Jellicoe that he reported to me on his return. As a result he made strong representations that Jellicoe should be superseded as soon as possible and the Vice-Admiral of the Battle Cruiser Fleet, Admiral Beatty, put in his place.
> This step was discussed between Masterton-Smith and Pollen but naturally the discussion dropped after the Battle of Jutland which took place on the 31st May.

Prior to Jutland there had been time for an exchange of letters with Jellicoe and Pollen had drawn from him the revealing comment[5] that no man living knew Fisher's weaknesses so well or was less anxious to see him have any influence on war strategy. He added that it amused him to find that he was not considered proof against Fisher's blandishments and that he would like to see all the old Admirals of the Fleet dropped at once.

As a sidelight on the Press tour, it is characteristic to find Pollen in a hasty note to his wife from Rosyth complaining 'I am always put next to the host as principal person! I have had to protest!' As a propaganda effort the tour miscarried in that it was overtaken by the Battle of Jutland which took place the following week. But to Pollen the ascendancy he established over his colleagues was to prove invaluable when the time came to rally them from the near-panic into which they had been thrown by Arthur Balfour's first grimly factual report of the Battle.

The Battle of Jutland had ended with the Germans making good their escape under cover of darkness, and returning to a heroes' welcome. Having faced the full might of the British Navy and inflicted more damage than they suffered, they had reason to be satisfied with the result. The British, under Jellicoe, had not covered themselves with glory but they had put to flight the enemy's main fleets thereby confirming their long established mastery of the surface of the sea. Materially nothing had been altered, but psychologically the situation was wide open. The Germans with time on their side, having returned to port some hours ahead of the British, seized the opportunity to proclaim a great victory, deliberately concealing the loss of the *Lützow* and *Rostock*, and greatly exaggerating the losses of the British. In truth, neither side could be very sure of the enemy's losses, but the British Admiralty went too far the other way, admitting all their own losses while at the same time underestimating the enemy's. British losses were put at ten possibly sixteen ships in all, including three battle-cruisers, while of the Germans', our claim was limited to one battle-cruiser certain, one battleship and two light cruisers probable, plus a number of destroyers. The actual losses were fourteen British ships against eleven German.

Arthur Balfour, the First Lord, who accepted full responsibility for the announcement, subsequently defended himself on the grounds that it had been right to give the public the facts as then known to him. Coming from an intelligent man, and Arthur Balfour was renowned alike for his intellect as for his eloquence and skill in debate, this was a very inadequate answer. For in making his announcement he had given not one word of explanation or reassurance and left the critics and the public to interpret the unsavoury facts as best they could.

Pollen's account of his unavailing efforts to forestall the first blunder and of the steps that he took subsequently to remedy the situation, makes interesting reading, and incidentally throws a revealing light on his status among the naval writers of the day.

Friends in the Admiralty had told me on Wednesday 31st May (the day of the Battle) and again on Thursday of certain news that had come in, and on Friday I called up the First Lord's Secretary, Masterton-Smith who was a great friend of mine, to ask when they were going to publish the news. He said, 'What news?' I replied, 'Well, we are both thinking of the same news.' 'Not till tonight.' I said, 'Can you give me a first view of what is to be published before it goes out?' to which he replied, 'I will if I can.' Later he called up to say that if I would come round to the Admiralty I could see the bulletin. I read it with consternation, and he then told me that my brother[6] was reported seriously wounded, and if I liked to go round to a certain department I could get any later news that had come in; that he had to go off, but would come back in a quarter of an hour. On his return I asked him if it was possible to modify the bulletin in any way. He said he thought not, as it had been agreed on by the Lords concerned, but asked me what modification I would suggest. I said that the difficulty of the situation was this, that the Admiralty expressed no opinion or judgement of any kind on the event, and to publish it as it stood threw upon the naval writers the obligation of taking a side. The escape of the enemy implied a censure, especially as the list of casualties did not include the loss or apparent damage of a single ship in the Battle Fleet. It was impossible on the text to avoid an inference that Beatty had got into action and Jellicoe had not. This was a matter that would certainly have to be explained.

I then went off to ask about my brother; discovered that he had been taken to hospital at Rosyth suffering from severe burns; returned, saw the Secretary again, and was told that there was no hope of any modification or addition to the bulletin. I then came back to my office, secured a sleeping berth to Edinburgh to reach my brother by the night train, and telephoned to the wisest admiral on shore, (Sir Reginald Custance) to meet me at my Club at once to advise me as to what I ought to do. . . . We agreed that if the Germans were allowed to get away with a sea success, the loss of morale on the Allied side and the discredit to Great Britain in the eyes of the world might bring about results too awful to contemplate. We discussed this matter for some time, and then called up Admiral Sir Cyprian Bridge and put the case to him as to what my duty was. He could see the intellectual dishonesty involved, but thought that in the circumstances it was my duty to make the most of the obvious point that the retreat of the Germans to their own harbours was an adequate proof that they had been defeated, and thwarted in any object they might have had in coming out. Having swallowed a hasty meal, I went back to my office and dictated an article for the *Westminster Gazette*, and called up all the newspapers in turn, urging the naval writers and editors to take the same line. Most of them were reluctant to do so, and in fact in the first editions of some of the papers Beatty was somewhat bitterly attacked for his rash tactics, but these were recalled in the later editions, which took the line that I had advocated.

This account, although not written until after the war, is supplemented and corroborated by a contemporary letter of the 12th June to Reginald Plunkett, an old friend from the days when they were working together in the *Natal*, and now serving as Beatty's Flag Commander.

It appears that Pollen had seen Plunkett during his brief visit to Edinburgh, and that they had had a hurried and not wholly satisfactory talk. On his return to London, Pollen felt it necessary to put the record straight, and set out in brief what he had done both in London and Edinburgh to establish Jutland as a victory.

On Friday night /the 2nd June/ I had done everything I could to get the Sea Lords and Mr Balfour to change the form of their statement and announce a victory definitely. When I failed in this I wrote an article for the *Westminster* explaining that the Germans had been beaten and sea command vindicated, and on arrival in Edinburgh the first thing on Saturday morning at once sent to the *Evening Despatch* for an interviewer and gave out the statement which before evening was in every afternoon newspaper in England, Scotland and Ireland. This interview was reprinted in almost all the Sunday papers also. If then there was any section of the Press that failed to see things in their true light it was the section that preferred their own views to mine.

In reply Plunkett, in a brief note writes 'I note your remarks and was fully aware of your point of view, which had already commended itself to the V-A'. The statement that won the Vice-Admiral's approval had been reported in the *Edinburgh*

Evening Despatch of Saturday 3rd June, as follows:

> The salient point is this. . . . For the first time we have had a chance of forcing them to fight. That chance has been instantly and gallantly seized. Naturally the opportunity fell only to our fastest squadrons, and of our latest capital ships, the battle-cruisers are the weakest in defence . . . It was a splendid and gallant fight against heavy odds. The determination of the British Navy to fight always and at any cost has been vindicated, and whatever lies the German Government may tell the German people about it, the German Navy knows as well as we do that if they give us another chance it will be seized in the same way.

Brave words to have used to a public stunned by the Admiralty's inept communiqué. Little wonder that his message was at once seized upon by the Press and broadcast country-wide.

Among the Jellicoe Papers recently published by the Navy Records Society, there is a letter from Arthur Balfour, the First Lord, to Jellicoe, dated Tuesday the 6th June, in which he writes:

> If the Grand Fleet had some reason to feel disappointed over the public attitude on Friday night and Saturday morning they certainly have no reason to be dissatisfied now. Opinion has undergone a revolution both rapid and complete.

Some credit for the improved atmosphere must be given to the Admiralty who had followed up their first disastrous announcement, of Saturday 3rd June, with two further communiqués, one issued on Sunday morning and the other the same evening; but the real weakness of the first report had been the failure to concentrate attention on the simple fact that the Germans had fled from the scene of battle, and there can be little doubt that Pollen's attitude and the reproduction, throughout the provincial press, of the bold statement he had given out in Edinburgh, did more than any communiqué to rally opinion.

At Whitehall, certainly, the authorities were under no illu-

sions as to the value of his contribution and in return gave him
some real facts on which to work, with the result that his
article in *Land and Water* of the 8th June, which covered no
less than six pages, was at once recognised both at home and
abroad as the first really authentic account.

From the standpoint of history, the most interesting page is
that devoted to 'The News and its Reception'. Without minc-
ing his words he castigated both the Admiralty and that
section of the Press which had insisted on treating the Battle as
a defeat. *The Times* had spoken of 'our heaviest blow at sea';
the *Daily Mail*, *Daily Chronicle* and the *Observer* were named
as having spoken of failure and even the *Telegraph*, 'exceptionally sane as a rule on naval subjects, warned us not to be *too*
gloomy or to indulge in *undue* pessimism'.

Nearly all the big names are there, with the notable exception of the *Morning Post*, the *Westminster* and the *Sunday
Times*. Not content to name the offenders and record their
comments he goes on to tell his readers of the bitter reactions
of the returning sailors whom he had met in hospital up North.
'It was certainly pitiful when one of them said to me "We were
a bit bucked with ourselves when we came in here, but look at
these papers! They tell us we have been beaten".' He comments, 'It was once considered characteristic of the English
that we did not know when we were beaten. Now it seems we
do not know when we have won.'

It is perhaps too much to claim that it was Pollen who turned
defeat into victory. Yet the evidence is impressive. The rival
fleets had been within gun-range for four hours: the German
forces, carrying a broadside of less than half that of the British,
had inflicted the heavier losses, both in men and material and
retired in good order. The Admiralty communiqué, by reporting the casualties without comment, had tacitly admitted
defeat and it had been so interpreted by the Press both at home
and abroad. Had Pollen not issued his inspiring statement in
Edinburgh, had he not thrown the whole weight of his influence behind the specious argument that the day was ours

because the Germans had fled from the scene, or, worse still, had he joined forces with *The Times*, the *Telegraph* and the *Observer* and admitted defeat, would there have been a sudden revival of confidence? Would opinion, in Balfour's words, have 'undergone a revolution both rapid and complete'?

Be that as it may, there is ample evidence to show that throughout the summer Pollen was far from happy about the state of opinion abroad and taking every opportunity and using every argument to restore the prestige of the Navy.

CHAPTER IX

Mr Churchill Intervenes

Working in close collaboration with Masterton-Smith, Pollen had made some progress in his war of words against the Germans, when all of a sudden, in the last week of September, there appeared an article by Winston Churchill which, coming from the former First Lord, undermined his whole case.

Churchill, it will be recalled, after a brilliant and successful start as the wartime First Lord, had fallen out with Fisher in May 1915, over his handling of the attack on the Dardanelles. Fisher, exasperated beyond endurance, had suddenly resigned, at the same time informing his Tory friends that Churchill throughout the operation had ignored his professional objections. Fisher, at the time, in the words of Bonar Law the Tory leader, was 'the darling of the Tory Party' – while Churchill had become its 'Bugbear'. The upshot of the whole affair was a major political crisis which resulted in the formation of a Coalition Government with strong Tory participation: and part of the price that had to be paid was the dropping from the Government of Winston Churchill.

Uninfluenced by their pre-war differences, Arthur Pollen in conformity with his general policy of backing the Administration, had from the start of the war supported Churchill and refrained from criticism of his pre-war policies: and when in May 1915 he fell from power, it was to his courage and not to his mistakes that Pollen drew attention. In *Land and Water* of the 12th June in addition to his regular article, there was a special feature headed 'The Courage of Mr Churchill'.

Upon Mr Churchill has fallen the humiliation of relinquishing the post of First Lord just when the British Fleet was discharging the main purpose of its being – namely, the complete command of the sea, with a thoroughness unparalleled in history. The assertion of supremacy was made on the first day of the war, and all our subsequent military operations have been made possible by it. Mr Churchill has been the leader through all this time, and is surely entitled to some of the credit of so overwhelming a success. The minor set-backs in the first five months of war hardly affected that success at all. It is the unsuccess of the expedition in the Dardanelles and the disagreement with Lord Fisher that have brought him down. In speaking at Dundee, therefore, he came before his constituents in the character of a beaten man, and he spoke at a crisis when the country has been more depressed in spirit than perhaps at any time since last August. A man who at such a moment as that can deliver the best of his fighting speeches, indeed the best fighting speech that we have had in ten months, is something more than able, clever, or brilliant. Throughout this crisis Mr Churchill has shown the loftiest sort of moral bravery.

Had Pollen been the kind of man who harboured resentment or liked to pay off old scores, what better opportunity could he have had than at this moment of crisis in May 1915, with Churchill discredited and defeated? Instead, we have this fine tribute to qualities not much appreciated at the time, but which a generation later were to win the acclaim of the whole Western world. As a wartime First Lord, whatever his previous failings, Winston Churchill had shown courage and leadership: the thanks of the country were, therefore, due to him and must be expressed handsomely and without reserve.

Now, more than a year later, with the propaganda battle against the Germans in full swing, there appeared in the October issue of *The London Magazine* an article expounding British Naval policy in terms that made nonsense of Pollen's campaign. Churchill's argument ran as follows:

Although the battle squadrons of the Grand Fleet have been denied all opportunity of decisive battle, yet from the beginning they have enjoyed all the fruits of a complete victory. If

Germany had never built a Dreadnought, or if all German Dreadnoughts had been sunk, the control and authority of the British Navy could not have been more effective. . . . There was no need for the British to seek battle at all. . . . A keen desire to engage the enemy impelled, and a cool calculation of ample margins of superiority justified, a movement not necessarily required by any practical need.

This passage has been generally regarded as the origin of the theory that later came to be known as Churchill's 'heresy', the belief that a decisive victory at Jutland over the enemy forces was not necessary to us, since we were already enjoying all the fruits of victory without the hazard of battle. In reality, the underlying fallacy that the destruction of the enemy's forces is not necessary to victory, can be traced back thirty years to Admiral Mahan, the great American writer on Naval strategy, whose most famous work *The Influence of Sea Power on Naval Strategy* was published in 1889. By a strange coincidence it was another distinguished American, Captain W. S. Sims of the U.S. Navy who was responsible for its revival in 1916, and from whom, in all probability, Churchill had borrowed the idea.

Arthur Pollen had been the only British writer to take note of Captain Sims at the time. In the two issues of *Land and Water* dated the 14th and 21st September he had exposed the fallacy and gone to some lengths to prove that our Grand Fleet was tied down, and would remain tied down, to a watching and defensive role as long as the Germans retained a powerful fleet capable of sallying forth at their 'selected moment' to attack our small craft, our trade and our coasts.

In these articles Pollen showed good judgement in his references to Captain Sims, who, within little more than a year, was to be appointed Commander-in-Chief of the United States Naval Forces in Europe. He introduced him as 'probably the most distinguished officer of his standing in the United States Service' and went on to say that he would probably never have used the argument had he been addressing a professional audience. Captain Sims had in fact been the victim of an unfortunate coincidence in that the Battle of Jutland had hit the headlines while he was engaged in giving evidence before Congress in support of a proposal to build a number of battle-cruisers. Three British ships of this class had been lost in the battle, and his opponents at once claimed that this proved the inadequacy of their armour. Early reports suggested, quite wrongly as it turned out, that the battle-cruisers had at the time been engaged against battleships. Sims quite naturally retorted that Beatty had neither the right nor the need to take such risks. No need, because the British were already enjoying, without a battle, the fruits of victory.

To Pollen, Sims's statement, based as it was on a misunderstanding of what had actually happened at Jutland, had done no particular harm but for Churchill to repeat it was a very different matter, and in Pollen's view a disaster of the first magnitude. He saw at once that the critics abroad would regard this admission by the former First Lord, the man responsible for Jellicoe's appointment, as tantamount to the admission that the Commander-in-Chief had no mandate to risk his fleet in battle.

The following week[1] (28th September), in *Land and Water*, he switched his attack from Sims to Churchill and went so far as to set out the initiatives which would become possible if the German Fleet were effectively immobilised.

> If there were no German battleships nor battle-cruisers a passage into the Baltic could be forced; complete destruction of the German fleet would make possible an Anglo-Russian invasion of Germany from the Baltic . . . If no German Fleet existed, we could establish a short range blockade. Instead of the defensive policy of mining their submarines out of our waters we could mine them into their own harbours. . . . Instead of devoting the whole resources of our ship-building industry to building warships we could produce something like 180,000 to 200,000 tons of merchant shipping a month.

At this point it is interesting to note in passing that Pollen's point as to our Fleet remaining tied down to a watching and defensive role by the constant threat of a German sally, was subsequently confirmed almost word for word by Jellicoe in the official account of his stewardship, *The Grand Fleet* 1914-16, which he published immediately after the war.

On page 39 we find the purely factual assertion that

> The German High Command realised that if Germany adopted a defensive role with the Fleet, it created by far the most difficult situation for us. Repugnant as this might be to high-spirited German naval officers, it was unquestionably the worst policy for us, for whilst the German High Seas Fleet remained 'in being' as a fighting force we could not afford to undertake operations tending to weaken our Grand Fleet, particularly in the earlier period of the war when our margin of superiority at Germany's 'selected moment' was not great.

It is also very interesting and relevant to find among the Jellicoe Papers a letter dated the 4th February 1917, written by Jellicoe as First Sea Lord, to Beatty of all people, 'You are wrong about the blockade of Germany, it will not win the war. The war will not be won until the enemy's armed forces are defeated, certainly on land and probably on sea'.

Yet to this day there are writers who seek to persuade us that at the time of Jutland, Jellicoe had no reason to believe that a crushing defeat of the High Seas Fleet would materially help the allied cause and therefore no reason to take risks to achieve it.

The Times, true to form, now picked up the scent and on 4th October published a letter from Lord Sydenham attacking Churchill's heresy in much the same terms as Pollen had used the previous week. Pollen and Sydenham were old allies, in frequent correspondence, and completely of one mind in condemning the defensive attitudes of the Admiralty Administration. They had been brought together in February 1915 by a common attitude to Admiral Sir Archibald Moore's failure to bring the Dogger Bank engagement to a successful conclusion after Beatty and his flagship had been forced to drop out; it was the first occasion on which a British capital ship had retreated before the threat of torpedoes and both Pollen and Sydenham lamented the abandonment of the ancient practice of holding Courts Martial after any engagement not crowned with success. The purpose of a Court Martial, as Pollen pointed out, was primarily not punitive, but to determine points of principle such as arose at Dogger Bank. Only through such a tribunal could an officer clear his reputation and in the old days there were numerous examples of Commanders demanding enquiry by Court Martial.

Incidentally, Pollen was very proud of the little pat on the back he received from Custance on this subject. 'You are very good in the *Sunday Times* today. The mongrel crew who have controlled the Navy of late have never understood and never will understand the inner soul of the Profession. There is much in heredity.'

Under Lord Northcliffe, it was the practice of *The Times*, when they wished to take up a campaign already initiated elsewhere, to make their intervention through the medium of some distinguished figure not already involved. Lord Sydenham who, as Sir George Clarke, had served as the first Secretary of the Committee of Imperial Defence was an eminently suitable choice to open a discussion on strategy. It is doubtful whether *The Times* would have paid much attention to Churchill had there not at the time been considerable public dissatisfaction, on other grounds, with Balfour's conduct of the naval war. Channel raids on our shipping and on our coasts, ineffective in themselves, had attracted attention out of all proportion to their military significance and submarine losses were already causing serious concern. The belief was growing that Balfour and Sir Henry Jackson, the First Sea Lord, had lost their grip.

Pollen had started the attack on Churchill and it suited Northcliffe to pick up the argument as a stick with which to beat the Balfour-Jackson régime. Pollen's methods were very different. When something needed doing it was his custom to start by discussing the matter with Masterton-Smith and, if necessary, follow up with a memorandum for the eye of the First Lord. On this occasion the paper he sent in ended with the following paragraph:

The whole of my policy for dealing with the situation tumbles down like a pack of cards in the presence of W.C.'s give away of the whole show in the October 'London'. All the world now sees that, for two years and a quarter, the strongest single military force in the world has by the deliberate policy of its Commander-in-Chief, been kept neutral. This makes it a matter of immediate urgency to change the policy, and this cannot be done while preserving its exponents in responsible command or office. In my humble and always to be despised opinion, the First Lord is faced by the most difficult problem, the solution of which will carry with it one way or the other, the greatest responsibility that has fallen on any single individual in the war. By far the most significant sign of the times is the complete silence of all the professed naval writers on the greatest naval issue of the day. Not a single one of them has dared endorse, comment on or criticize my articles on Sims and Churchill. I think they know that they are completely out of their depth, but the moral of the situation is clear. The truth will dawn upon all the plain men, editors and proprietors here and abroad with great suddenness, and then if the situation has not been dealt with drastically at Whitehall there will be a land slide. At the first sign of this it will be absolutely necessary to tell the whole brutal truth to the public, or we may be landed in a situation worse than the present. The only way to save everything is for the revolution to be accomplished from within, before the public has appreciated its necessity.

P.S. You know it is said that J.J. has it on record at the Admiralty since the beginning, that he did not intend to face German mines with British ships in any event. There may have been some excuse for this when our margin in capital ships was small, but the increases of the last two years have altered the situation completely. Nor is this all. The success of the German *guerre de course* has entirely altered the urgency of destroying the German Fleet, for without such destruction between two hundred and two hundred and fifty of our fast light craft are necessarily tied down to Grand Fleet duties. Destroy the German Fleet and the bulk of these are free for protecting commerce and hunting submarines. The situation then has undergone two changes, both pointing to a single policy.

When he spoke of a revolution from within, Pollen had in mind two immediate objectives. First, to obtain from the First Lord of the day a specific repudiation of his predecessor's false doctrine: secondly, the changes in command that had so long been envisaged and to which the Churchill gaffe had now given a new sense of urgency. On the first point, as we have seen, Pollen had for some weeks been waging a vigorous campaign in *Land and Water* and success was nearer than he had dared to hope.

On the 16th November, the Admiralty at last came forward with the formal repudiation for which he had for so long been pressing. Lord Lytton in the House of Lords, replying to Lord Sydenham and Lord Beresford[2], gave this categorical reply:

> If the noble Lord asks whether it is a fact that the policy of the Admiralty with regard to naval strategy at the present time is governed by the view that it is not necessary to seek out and destroy the enemy, and by a feeling that we have at the present time gained all we want by confining the enemy to their ports, I most emphatically repudiate on behalf of the Admiralty any such suggestion. Neither is it the opinion of the Commanders of the Fleet, nor of the War Staff of the Admiralty that it is not our main and first business to seek out and destroy the enemy fleet.

On this, Pollen commented that:

> It is particularly gratifying that Lord Lytton in his repudiation spoke not only for the Board of Admiralty but included the Commanders-in-Chief at sea and the War Staff.

To Pollen's amazement this rebuff, instead of settling the issue, evoked an even more embarrassing statement from Mr Churchill, which drew from Pollen a devastating rejoinder[3]:

> My readers, I fear, may be a little wearied by recurring expositions in these columns of the vagaries of Mr Churchill. . . . His latest outbreak occurs in his reply to the critics who pointed

out the stupefying absurdities of his statement that without a decisive victory we could enjoy all the fruits that victory could bestow. He now tells us that this was not an announcement of principle, but an argument which we have all failed to understand. He never meant us to understand that victory was unimportant. It was his delicate way of telling us that it was wholly unattainable. It was the argument, in short, that the grapes were sour.

Mr Churchill's former heresy, bad as it was, was better than this. It only said that a fleet need not fight because victory was without value. The new doctrine that the fleet cannot fight but must always run away, really strikes at the root of everything. It is the sheer insanity of nonsense.

And it is announced to the world at a most unfortunate time. It will be received by the enemy with that satisfaction reserved for those who can truthfully employ those words of comfort – 'I told you so'! For it is exactly upon this reluctance to take risks that the Germans have built all their naval hopes. They even have the effrontery to say that this hope was realised at the Battle of Jutland. The whole thing is beautifully set out in the writings of Captain Hollweg of the German Press Bureau. It was adumbrated in an article in the *Scientific American* of last July. *The Times* of Saturday last printed a series of extracts from a recent and more elaborate exposition of the theory by the same writer. The theory is briefly this. The Germans were never such fools as to suppose that with a fleet of sixteen battleships and five battle-cruisers, they could attack and defeat a fleet of twenty-eight battleships and nine battle-cruisers. But they were quite prepared to take on the battle-cruisers with all their forces, if we could give them an opportunity; and quite confident that if the engagement, so produced, ended by an encounter with the Grand Fleet, they could stand the Grand Fleet off by torpedo attacks and so escape from the overwhelming gunfire of the more numerous and more powerfully armed squadron. We know, of course, that they did make two organised torpedo attacks at Jutland, and that these, amongst other manoeuvres, enabled them to open the range. But they achieved this end, not because no British Admiral dared risk an under water attack upon his ships, but because the falling mist, the peculiar conditions of light, and the lateness of the hour made the obvious reply to these manoeuvres impossible.

It will be seen that Captain Hollweg's exposition of the German objectives at Jutland, and of their achievement, follows very closely the views that Pollen had expressed to Masterton-Smith. Yet Pollen in this article gives nothing away and remains resolute in Jellicoe's defence: nothing but bad visibility deprived us of full victory. He thus successfully steered a course between the Scylla and Charybdis of admitting on the one hand that we had got the worst of it at Jutland or on the other, that we were satisfied with the result.

For two years Pollen had said nothing of Winston Churchill's failure as an administrator in the days before the war; his failure to insist upon the creation of a Staff System; his failure to ensure that machinery was set up for the study of the new weapons and devices with which the great ships of the day were to be equipped; his failure, in effect, to make adequate preparation for war; for to have done so would have lowered the prestige of the Navy. But now, in November 1916, the position was reversed. Churchill was no longer in office and the prestige of the Service, particularly abroad, demanded that the false doctrines on which he continued to insist should be demolished.

To the generation that knew Winston Churchill in the days of his greatness, as the saviour of our country and of Europe during the Second World War, it must seem strange to find him cast, first, as the Minister responsible for the pre-war follies of Whitehall: and then, in 1916, expounding false and untenable doctrines of strategy. But it must be remembered that on taking office at the end of 1911 he had made a determined effort to introduce a Staff System only to be defeated by what he called 'the deadweight of professional opinion'. Thereafter he had succumbed to Fisher's 'unparalleled powers of persuasion' and become an active supporter of Fisher's materialist policies, thinking only in terms of weight of broadside without regard to the capacity to hit.

Meanwhile, Lord Lytton's repudiation of the 'heresy', although vital, was only the first step towards the restoration of the prestige of the British Navy. There remained the problem of leadership. Politically, the complete retirement of Jellicoe would have looked like surrender to the German claim to victory at Jutland, and the only practical solution was for Jellicoe to go to Whitehall as First Sea Lord and for Beatty to take over as Commander-in-Chief.

These changes, long approved in principle, were being daily rendered more urgent by the revival of the submarine war on a basis more ruthless and more effective than ever before. Once again Arthur Balfour was indecisive and dilatory.

When at last Jellicoe's appointment as First Sea Lord was announced, Arthur Pollen greeted it with characteristically discriminating approval (7th December 1916):

> A good many writers in the Press, I observe, have invited us to put confidence in the new First Sea Lord *because of his long experience of Admiralty Administration* under Sir John Fisher and later as Second Sea Lord under Winston Churchill. . . . My own faith in Sir John Jellicoe's success rests entirely upon the belief that two and a half years of the realities of war must have made him unlearn the teachings of ten years Admiralty experience.

The article concludes by welcoming the appointment to the Board of Sir Cecil Burney and Captain Lionel Halsey, as Second and Fourth Sea Lords respectively. Burney had been Jellicoe's second in command of the Grand Fleet and Halsey Captain of the Fleet, and Pollen 'looked forward to the further introduction of men with fighting experience'. Yet, as Pollen well knew, these men all belonged to the Fisher school and the likelihood of any major change in policy at Whitehall was virtually nil.

What Pollen and his friends really thought at this time is best reflected in his correspondence with Custance, who wrote:

> The Government seems to be giving Jellicoe a free hand in the formation of the new Board. This is a wise proceeding as no plea of want of opportunity will be possible when the inevitable crash comes. Then all will fall together.

CHAPTER X

Failure of the Service System in Action

Preoccupied as he was after Jutland, with his campaign to restore the prestige of the Royal Navy, Pollen would have been less than human had he not been haunted by the vision of what might have happened had his great contribution to gunnery not been frustrated by Dreyer's machinations. Inevitably he saw in the disappointing events of that day, the proof of his theories, the realisation of his prophecies and the justification for the long years of hard work that had gone into the development of his instruments.

Friends in the Service made no secret of the general dissatisfaction with the Dreyer System and urged him to return to the attack. Encouraged by their attitude he drew up a memorandum, tactfully rehearsing the history of the previous rejection of his system and arguing that the experience of war had proved that the problems of fire control in action would never be overcome 'except by a system that is theoretically complete and mechanically perfect'. On the 16th August he forwarded this paper direct to Jellicoe, with copies to a number of known supporters, whose names make interesting reading today. They are listed as Admirals Beatty, Brock, Leveson and Evan-Thomas, Captain (later Admiral Sir Herbert) Richmond and Commander (later Admiral Sir William) James: all, without exception, now numbered amongst the best brains in the Service.

Herbert Richmond replied[1] characteristically, 'I wish I could think there was some chance of your being listened to but you

169

know as well as I do who will have a voice in the reply'. And, sure enough, Jellicoe's answer, inspired by Dreyer, his flag captain, was to the effect that his instruments had served him well.

Beatty, on the other hand, replied[2] that he was much interested: the Argo Clock was undoubtedly superior to the Dreyer Table and he assumed that the Commander-in-Chief would give the proposal the close consideration that it deserved. He went on to say that he was not in touch with the latest development of Pollen's system, and not acquainted with anybody who was. He added very significantly, 'The difficulties against taking ranges with the rangefinder are so great under present conditions that we must learn to do without them'. Pollen at once wrote back to say:

> This is 1908 all over again. In 1908 Wilson made the Service adopt Dreyer's system of manual plotting and then, when it failed, announced that all plotting was dead. Now you have the Dreyer Table and the Dreyer system of Finding Ranges and because that fails you say that you must learn to do without. This merely proves what I have always maintained, that an instrument is either perfectly accurate or perfectly useless.

Pollen's attempt to get Jellicoe to reconsider the adoption of Argo failed, but, in our present context, the significance of this correspondence lies in the fact that Beatty's comment reflects and confirms the general disinclination within the Service to employ the Dreyer instruments in action.

The story of Jutland has been told too often and too well to need telling yet again. On the other hand it is fair to say that illustrious writers have for the most part shown a total disregard of the elements of gunnery technique that lay at the root of the Pollen-Dreyer rivalry. While paying lip-service to the differing conditions of visibility they have in the main been content to base their verdicts on the bare statistics of shots fired and hits scored.

In reality, to anyone interested in Argo it is fascinating to find how each new phase of the battle exemplifies one or other of the difficulties which Pollen had foreseen and which Dreyer had dismissed as being either of no consequence or beyond his capacity. More significantly, we shall find that at the decisive moments it was the known limitations of his gunnery that restricted Jellicoe's tactics, thus exemplifying Pollen's basic teaching as to the interdependence of gunnery and tactics.

As a first step to understanding the nature and importance of helm-free gunnery in battle, let us pause and consider the reasons for the failure of the Navy to discharge the relatively simple assignment of silencing the Turkish forts at the Dardanelles in 1915. In Naval gunnery there is no more elementary task than to hit a stationary target from a stationary ship. But while at anchor, the ships presented an easy target to the enemy howitzers, and were soon forced to get under way and keep moving. They circled round only to find that while doing so they were incapable of hitting their target.

The story of their failure is well told in Winston Churchill's *World Crisis* Vol.II; but needless to say he omits to point out that things might have been very different had he sought the best technical advice three years earlier. In a letter dated 8th November 1923 to 'Dear Mr Churchill', delightful in its irony, Arthur Pollen repaired the omission.

> Your Dardanelles story adds so many facts, and corrects so many misapprehensions, that it supersedes every other account of that well-conceived but ill-fated venture.
>
> For the first time, too, you have made the tragic consequences of this failure very clear, and you have brought out its causes with complete technical detail. And, finally, your own share in the undertaking is now seen to be very different from what previous, and not impartial, accounts had hitherto described.
>
> For my own sake, therefore, I intend, as soon as I get the opportunity, to recall and correct certain harsh criticisms that seemed justified when they were written, but now appear to be both erroneous and unjust.
>
> It was not, however, to make this confession that I am writing, but to put a specific question to you.

In Chapter XI, you show that, after a month's operations – culminating in a great combined attack – during which
between 7000 and 8000 shells were fired from over 120 guns
of a power vastly superior to those of our opponents, the forts
above the Narrows, the mine fields, and the batteries protecting
them from the sweepers, were all, on the evening of 18th
March practically intact. In Chapter XIII, you show why this
was so, and the remainder of your book demonstrates how this
failure was fatal to the venture as a whole.

It seems to me a summary of your argument to say that our
ships could not steam past the mine fields unless they were
swept, the mine fields could not be swept until the protecting
batteries were crushed; the batteries could not be put out of
business until the fortress guns were dismantled at long range,
and the mobile eight and six inch howitzers had compelled the
battle-ships to 'wheel and manoeuvre' which 'destroyed' the
accuracy of their long range fire.

Thus, forts, batteries and mine fields, were, at the end of it
all, as effective obstacles as they were when we began – a failure
so complete and disconcerting that the attempt was never
renewed, with the result you rightly and eloquently deplore.

Is it not obvious that, had 'wheeling and manoeuvring' not
been fatal to hitting at ranges from between 6000 and 14,000
yards, the remaining operations, the sequence of which appears
from the analysis I have just quoted, would have presented no
difficulty? The causa causans of the disaster, then, was the inability to keep the range under helm.

Pollen next reminds Churchill of the offer he made to him in
October 1912 of 'the whole of my work at your own price, if
only the opportunity of demonstrating what I could do was
afforded me . . . In that letter too I draw your attention to what
we had just done with our Clock in the Orion.'

The reader will recall that the demonstration carried out in
the *Orion* and described in detail in Chapter V was directed to
proving that the Argo Clock was capable of keeping the range
and bearing of a fixed marker while describing a large
quadrilateral figure without the aid of any range or bearing cor-
rections whatever. So effective was the Clock that at the end of
the run, which was made at high speed, it had the range to

within twenty-five yards and the bearing to within half a degree, thus demonstrating that they could have kept an invisible target under effective fire throughout the manoeuvre.

The parallel between that exercise and the task that faced the Navy at the Dardanelles three years later is exact: and it is obvious that had our ships been equipped with the Argo Clock, they would have experienced no difficulty in keeping the forts under effective fire while circling round for their own protection.

It might be objected that the ships employed at the Dardanelles were mostly old and outdated but among them was the *Queen Elizabeth*, the latest and finest battleship in the Service, whose low trajectory 15″ guns were thought to be ideal for the destruction of the high parapets of the forts. Yet she too was similarly handicapped when forced to circle around.

Not content with proving what might and should have happened at Gallipoli, Pollen next cited, in his 1923 letter to Churchill, as a further example of missed opportunities, a remarkable proposition which he had submitted to the Secretary of the Admiralty at the end of 1914, nothing less than a 'reasoned proposal' for a night bombardment of Heligoland by a ship of the *Queen Elizabeth* class,

> manoeuvring freely and at top speed without showing lights. I showed how the initial range and bearing could be found by day – the starting point of the run being fixed by a buoy that would burn a light at a chosen hour, and how the ship could steam at full speed past the buoy, starting the Clock and opening fire simultaneously.
>
> During such a run, of course, the ship could not have been hit by the fortress guns, and every shell must have hit the island somewhere. This proposal, I was afterwards informed, was referred to Sir Arthur Wilson, and never got past him.

The letter concludes, with bitter irony,

> In view of what you wanted to attempt at the Dardanelles, I cannot suppose, after reading of your fruitless efforts to make your insight and foresight prevail as to smoke-screens, tanks,

and shields, that either the facts of our 'ORION' experiment or their extraordinary significance, can ever have been brought to your attention.

I wonder if you will correct me if I am wrong?

Needless to say no answer to this letter was forthcoming.

With these two clear examples before us of the significance of the helm-free function we are now in a position to assess the more complex problems that were to arise at Jutland when the target was not a stationary fort but a fast moving fleet.

In brief the two unique attributes[3] of the Argo System were first the capacity to find and hold the target while the two fleets were converging rapidly (technically known as a high rate of change of range) and secondly the capacity to do so while our own ship was making large turns (helm-free fire control). These were the two functions of which Pollen had written to Churchill, in October 1912, that the Service System was 'not designed to attempt to perform them' although, in Pollen's view, 'their military value was incalculable'.

In addition, although this was only a matter of relative efficiency and not a case of total impotence of the Service gear, he claimed, and in this he had the strong support of Admiral Peirse, that his gear could find the range and bearing of the target very much more quickly than Dreyer's.

The Admiralty had rejected Argo on the grounds that the circumstances Argo was designed to meet would never arise. Actions would not be opened with the opposing Fleets racing at each other at top speed nor would our Commanders be so reckless as to change course while engaging the enemy.

Jutland was to prove them wrong.

At Jutland there were three separate encounters between the opposing Fleets – first Beatty and Hipper at 3.48 p.m. in the afternoon, next Jellicoe and Scheer at 6.00 p.m. and finally Jellicoe and Scheer once again at 7.10 p.m.

It is a remarkable fact and the key to the riddle of our failure at Jutland, that on each of these three occasions the rate of approach was in the neighbourhood of forty miles an hour and on each occasion the British Fleet, for differing reasons, was compelled to make a wide turn within minutes of opening fire – in other words compelled to fight in precisely the conditions which the Admiralty had supposed would never arise and for which they had refused to make provision.

To investigate the matter more fully a brief outline of the course of the battle is essential.

It will be recalled that prompted by reports of unusual activity in enemy bases, Jellicoe and Beatty had set out, late in the evening of the 30th May 1916, Jellicoe from Scapa with sixteen of his great fleet of twenty-four battleships, later to be joined by eight from Cromarty, and Beatty from Rosyth with his fleet of six battle-cruisers, supported by the four ships of the 5th Battle Squadron under Admiral Evan-Thomas, the latter the fastest and most heavily-gunned squadron in the fleet.

The plan was for the two forces to proceed on parallel easterly courses until 2 p.m. the following afternoon, by which time they were to have reached a position 260 miles from the Forth. In the absence of news of the enemy, Beatty was then to turn and head north to join the Commander-in-Chief off Horns Riff.

In the event it was 2.30 p.m. before the first news of the enemy was received, and by then Beatty had already turned northwards. The enemy force, later identified as five battle-cruisers of the Second Scouting Group under Admiral von Hipper, had been spotted some fifty miles to the east, heading north. Beatty, foreseeing that Hipper would at once turn and run for home, set off at top speed on an easterly course to cut off his retreat, leaving Jellicoe some seventy miles to the north with no chance of joining in the action, and Evan-Thomas with some nine miles of leeway to make up. An hour later, as Beatty had foreseen, Hipper's squadron was sighted some fourteen miles away to the north-east racing for home on a southerly course. To cut off his retreat and bring him to action Beatty was now left with no option but to make what was virtually a head-on attack against the enemy's broadside before swinging round to a parallel southerly course. At this point reference to the sketch plan headed 'Battle-Cruiser Action' will help the reader to follow the course of events.

Never was a prophecy more exactly fulfilled. For here we have precisely the circumstances foreshadowed by Pollen when in October 1912 he wrote to Churchill 'We maintain that range, speed and course *finding* must be available however high the relative speed, so as to enable a *Lion* at top speed to fight another *Lion* at top speed if she wished: and next that to be ready for war the *Lion* must be able to get the data for doing this while she is on a steady course or under helm. The proposed Service methods cannot do either of these things because they are not designed to attempt to do them. Yet their military value is incalculable.'

In place of such a system Beatty had at his disposal instruments of observation so ineffective that he believed and reported in his despatch that at 3.48 p.m. both sides had opened fire at 18,500 yards whereas the actual range had been only 15,000. The magnitude of this error confirms without any possibility of doubt that the Service System was not designed to attempt to deal with such a rate of approach.

In these unequal conditions the Germans within fifteen minutes, had scored[4] fourteen hits and sunk the *Indefatigable*, while the British had only three hits to their credit. Twenty minutes later the *Queen Mary* suffered the same fate and blew up. The loss of the *Queen Mary* was a particularly grievous blow for she alone of all the battle-cruisers was fitted with an Argo Clock (although not of course with the Argo plotter) and had been shooting particularly well. N. J. M. Campbell in his admirable book *Battle-Cruisers* (Conway Maritime Press), working from German sources, gives her credit for four hits on the *Seydlitz* which in the adverse conditions prevailing in the early stages of the battle was a better performance than any other ship in the Squadron.

To Beatty's critics these disasters served as evidence of the inefficiency of Battle-Cruiser marksmanship. In reality the loss

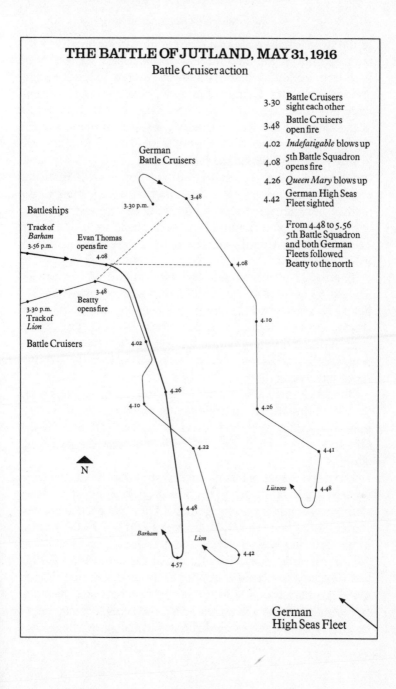

THE BATTLE OF JUTLAND, MAY 31, 1916
Battle Cruiser action

3.30	Battle Cruisers sight each other
3.48	Battle Cruisers open fire
4.02	*Indefatigable* blows up
4.08	5th Battle Squadron opens fire
4.26	*Queen Mary* blows up
4.42	German High Seas Fleet sighted

From 4.48 to 5.56
5th Battle Squadron
and both German
Fleets followed
Beatty to the north

German
Battle Cruisers

3.48

3.30 p.m.

4.08

Battleships

Track of
Barham
3.56 p.m.

Evan Thomas
opens fire
4.08

3.48

Beatty
opens fire

3.30 p.m.
Track of
Lion

Battle Cruisers

4.02

4.10

4.26

4.22

4.10

4.26

4.41

Lützow   4.48

4.48

Barham

Lion

4.42

4.57

N

German
High Seas Fleet

of the two British battle-cruisers was due, in each case, to the faulty design of the ammunition hoists which permitted the flash from exploding enemy shells to penetrate to the magazine and explode the charges. Strangely enough the German designers had made the identical mistake, which at the Battle of the Dogger Bank had very nearly resulted in the loss of the *Seydlitz*. She escaped at the cost of a tremendous fire that cost 200 lives. Thus warned the Germans, by the time of Jutland, had taken steps to lessen the risk of fire. The British had received no such warning and in addition were subject to the further disadvantage that the igniters attached to their charges, of which four were required for each shell, were filled with black powder, a volatile substance, which exploded instead of merely burning.

Meanwhile from our side the total failure of the Service System to cope with the conditions made it impossible for Beatty to respond effectively in the opening stages. Whether Beatty 'learned to do without' before or after his experience at Jutland is not material; in either case he would have been cruelly handicapped by the lack of data as to the enemy's speed and course.

On the German side the good shooting is explained first by the light being entirely in their favour and secondly by the fact that they could hold their straight course and were firing broadside not straight ahead, which is always the more difficult.

The next episode of significance to our enquiry was the coming into action of the 5th Battle Squadron some fifteen minutes after the opening of the engagement. They had opened fire and started hitting with their 15″ guns at a range of 19,000 yards. Their shooting was excellent and the impact of their 1900 pound projectile quite devastating. All the authorities, British and German, have paid tribute to their good shooting. Yet to the Argo man the vital factor in their success was that they came into action on a straight course, and being virtually out of range of Hipper's somewhat lighter guns had been able to hold that straight course without deviating and, what was no less important, without having to zig zag for their own protection. To be precise they started shooting while turning from East to South but only started hitting after getting on to a straight course at 4.10. On page seventeen of the official *Narrative of the Battle of Jutland*, we find

> Shortly after four o'clock their guns were beginning to range on the rear of the enemy line. The *Barham* opened fire at 19,000 yards and made a signal to concentrate in pairs on the rear ships. It was some minutes however before their fire became effective for the light was difficult and the targets constantly obscured.

True enough, no doubt, but there is no suggestion that visibility suddenly improved. All that happened was that by 4.10 when they started to hit they had got onto a straight course. As regards enemy fire, Captain Woollcombe of the *Valiant* records 'Although the ship was straddled many times the splashes appeared to be small and did not rise much above the hull of the ship . . . Due to this the control officers experienced no additional difficulties when the ship was being heavily fired at than when receiving no fire'.

A further point is that by the time they opened fire they were virtually on a course parallel to the enemy with a very low rate of change of range. Thus they alone of all the British Squadrons had the great good fortune to go into battle in conditions for which their fire-control was designed.

There is no need to tell yet again the story of the fierce battle that ensued between Beatty and Hipper on the run to the south, nor of the abrupt turn about to the north on the sudden appearance of Scheer coming up to meet them with the full strength of the High Seas (Battle) Fleet, nor yet of the subsequent rather straggling engagement as Beatty and Evan-Thomas in adverse visibility skilfully kept the Germans in play to lead them into the arms of Jellicoe's Grand Fleet.

Shortly before 6.00 p.m. Beatty coming up from the south was greeted by the welcome sight of Jellicoe's twenty-four battleships bearing down on a south-easterly course. For an hour and more the two great battle fleets had been on collision course, Jellicoe with the advantage of knowing of Scheer's approach, Scheer not even aware that Jellicoe was at sea. Still in cruising formation, six columns, each of four battleships, Jellicoe's problem at 6.00 p.m. was to decide how to deploy his great fleet into the single Line of Battle in which he intended to fight. It was at once apparent that Beatty was actively engaged against the enemy battle-cruisers, but Jellicoe elected to wait until 6.15 p.m. in order to be quite sure of the position of the enemy battle fleet before deciding the pattern of his deployment. The attached sketch map will assist the reader to picture the scene. In the event he chose to deploy 'on the port wing'; that is to say, the first division on the port wing, led by the *King George V*, took the lead and the other divisions turned first to port then to starboard on a follow-my-leader principle to form a single line.

The alternatives before him had been either to perform a similar manoeuvre on the starboard wing with the sixth divison in the lead, or else, for one of the two centre divisions to take the lead with the others doubling back in a more complicated manoeuvre to get into line. A glance at the map will show that deployment on the starboard wing at this late stage would have brought the Grand Fleet much closer, probably too close, to the enemy; whereas deployment on the port wing, Jellicoe's choice, in fact left them too far away in the poor conditions of visibility, to enable them to keep the enemy under fire or even under observation. Deployment on the centre although tactically ideal was regarded by Jellicoe as too complicated a manoeuvre for execution in such close proximity to the enemy. We shall revert again later to the latter possibility.

From the standpoint of our enquiry the essential fact is that whichever pattern of deployment he chose to adopt he would be faced with the inevitability of having to engage the enemy with a high rate of approach and while making large turns. With our knowledge of how the Argo gear could have handled

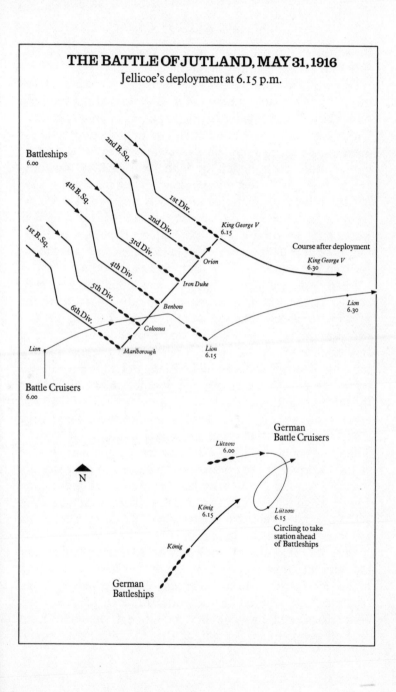

THE BATTLE OF JUTLAND, MAY 31, 1916
Jellicoe's deployment at 6.15 p.m.

Battleships
6.00

2nd B. Sq.

4th B. Sq.

1st B. Sq.

1st Div.

2nd Div.

3rd Div.

4th Div.

5th Div.

6th Div.

King George V
6.15

Orion

Iron Duke

Benbow

Colossus

Marlborough

Lion
6.15

Course after deployment

King George V
6.30

Lion
6.30

Lion

Battle Cruisers
6.00

N

German
Battle Cruisers

Lützow
6.00

König
6.15

König

Lützow
6.15

Circling to take
station ahead
of Battleships

German
Battleships

the situation, it is pathetic to read Jellicoe's account of the considerations on which his decision was based.

On page 350 of his *Grand Fleet* we find the revealing statement 'The German gunnery was always good at the start and their ships invariably found the range with great rapidity.' 'Great Rapidity' is a relative term and in any discussion of a contest between two individuals a statement to the effect that one or other does something 'with great rapidity' can only mean 'more rapidly than his opponent'. Thus the Commander-in-Chief is here telling us that in deciding his method of deployment he had to take into account the fact that the Germans would find the opening range more rapidly than we would; furthermore he is telling us that that knowledge contributed to his decision to choose the more cautious form of deployment.

Then again, on page 349, in the passage in which Jellicoe defends his choice of deployment he tells us that among the principal considerations in his mind at the time was the fact that deployment on either wing would result in 'an interval of at least four minutes elapsing between each division coming into line astern of the leading division, and a further interval before the guns could be directed onto the ships selected and the fire become effective'. On Chart II the point is repeated and expressed more concisely, 'Our own gunfire owing to the large alterations of course would be correspondingly ineffective'. These statements by Jellicoe are extremely important because of the tendency of Dreyer and his supporters to deny the fact that they were unable to maintain effective fire while changing course. Here we have a clear and unqualified statement from Jellicoe to the effect that their inability to do so was a vital factor in his choice of deployment.

With the Argo clock there would have been no need to wait for new data; alterations of course, however large, would have been continuously and automatically compensated: a simple repetition of the *Orion* exercise of 1912. Had Jellicoe's fleet been so equipped, he would have been free to choose his form of deployment in the knowledge that in neither case would

there have been any interruption in the efficiency of his gunfire: a perfect example of what Pollen in his long years of
advocacy always referred to as 'the emancipation of the tactician'.

An unusual and significant consequence of Jellicoe's deployment was that it was the tail-end of the line, the fifth and
sixth divisions, led respectively by the *Colossus* and the
Marlborough, that saw most of the fighting, and the leading
division led by the *King George V* that saw the least. This was
unfortunate, particularly from the standpoint of an Argo supporter, in that, for reasons that we can only guess, it was the
five ships mounting Argo Clocks that had been placed at the
head of the line, namely, *King George V*, *Ajax*, *Centurion* and
Erin of the First Division and the *Orion* the leader of the
second.

During the hour and a quarter that the two fleets were
within gun range there were only two, very short, spells of
general firing by the British battleships. At 6.30 the mist lifted
for a few minutes to give the British a clear view of their
counterparts, but not sufficiently for them to be visible to the
Germans. Dreyer, as Captain of the *Iron Duke*, Jellicoe's
flagship, whose experience was typical of others in the centre of
the line, reported as follows:

6.30½ p.m.   Opened fire on a Battleship of Konig Class. Bear-
               ing 70 Green – Range 12,000. The 2nd, 3rd
               and 4th salvoes hitting with a total of at least 6
               hits. Enemy steaming in the same direction on a
               slightly converging course.

6.33   The enemy was lit up by the sun, whereas 'Iron
               Duke' was probably invisible to them in the
               mist. However that may be, the Konig battle-
               ship did not return Iron Duke's fire, although
               heavily hit. 9 salvoes in 4 minutes 50 seconds.

Good shooting, but from the standpoint of our enquiry the
essential factors were first that in the absence of return fire,

Iron Duke was able to hold a steady course, and secondly, that the enemy was on an only 'slightly converging' course. Thus, no question of firing under helm and only a negligible change of range. In a word, what Pollen would have called 'Kindergarten' shooting conditions.

These conditions lasted for only a few minutes as the Germans were soon lost to sight again in the mist. At 6.35 Scheer, realizing that he was hopelessly outgunned, ordered his entire fleet to do an about turn, every ship turning simultaneously; a difficult manoeuvre, but one which the Germans, knowing that they would probably be outnumbered and outgunned, had practised assiduously. In the poor light they made good their escape to the west without Jellicoe realising what had happened.

Jellicoe, having lost sight of the enemy, held his course for a further twenty minutes without attempting to regain contact. At 6.55 he ordered his fleet to turn southwards by divisions: at the very same moment Scheer, too, had a change of mind, and ordered a second turn about to the east. Whether, as he subsequently claimed, he was seeking to reopen the engagement or whether, as seems much more likely, he was hoping to get home by passing behind and to the north of the Grand Fleet, has never been satisfactorily determined. However, as will be seen from the diagram, 'The Battle Fleet Action', the result of these movements, Jellicoe to the south and Scheer to the east, was to bring the two great battle fleets together in conditions that should have been fatal to Scheer. For Scheer, whether by accident or design had in fact charged plumb and almost perpendicularly into the centre of the vast mass of the British Battle Fleet, which now faced him in echeloned squadrons, a huge crescent of battleships with all broadsides bearing.

At 7.12, the *Marlborough* and the *Colossus*, respectively the leaders of the two nearest divisions, at the north-western end of the crescent, at once opened fire at ranges between 10,000 and 11,000 yards, shortly afterwards followed by the

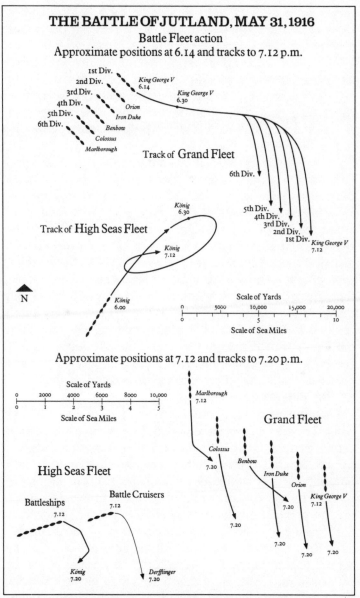

THE BATTLE OF JUTLAND, MAY 31, 1916

Battle Fleet action
Approximate positions at 6.14 and tracks to 7.12 p.m.

1st Div.
2nd Div.
3rd Div.
4th Div.
5th Div.
6th Div.

King George V
6.14

King George V
6.30

Orion
Iron Duke
Benbow
Colossus
Marlborough

Track of Grand Fleet

6th Div.

5th Div.
4th Div.
3rd Div.
2nd Div.
1st Div.

King George V
7.12

König
6.30

Track of High Seas Fleet

König
7.12

N

König
6.00

Scale of Yards

0   5000   10,000   15,000   20,000

0   5   10
Scale of Sea Miles

Approximate positions at 7.12 and tracks to 7.20 p.m.

Scale of Yards

0   2000   4000   6000   8000   10,000

0   1   2   3   4   5
Scale of Sea Miles

Marlborough
7.12

Grand Fleet

Colossus

7.20

Benbow

Iron Duke

Orion

King George V
7.12

High Seas Fleet

Battleships
7.12

Battle Cruisers
7.12

7.20

7.20

7.20

7.20

7.20

König
7.20

Derfflinger
7.20

The lower diagram is taken from the *Narrative of the Battle of Jutland* Plate 29 remainder of the fleet. So favourable was the light that the First Division at the south-eastern end of the crescent had a clear view of the enemy battleships at ranges between 18,000 and 19,000 – and once again found themselves invisible to the Germans. Scheer, faced with a force of more than double his own gun power had no alternative but to order yet another about turn 'together', while at the same time ordering his destroyers to make an all out torpedo attack to cover his retreat.

For five, perhaps ten, glorious minutes the British had it all their own way. Once again they were under no need to change course, and once again, while the Germans were making their about turn, no problem of rapid change of range, and in addition the light in their favour. In these unbelievably favourable conditions they scored a number of hits variously estimated at twenty-four to twenty-seven, of which two thirds were on the ill-fated battle-cruisers, who had reached a point some three thousand yards ahead of their Battle Fleet and were therefore the easier target. Among the British ships jointly credited by Campbell with five hits from 18,000 yards were the *Orion* with her Argo Clock and the *Monarch*. Admiral Jerram in his despatch mentions that at 7.20 *Orion* had just got a fresh battleship in her sights when ordered (by the C-in-C) to turn away.

With the approach of the destroyers Jellicoe found himself obliged to take an urgent and vital decision as to whether to turn towards or away from the attack. A battleship end-on to torpedo attack (whether advancing or retreating) presents only one fifth of a broadside target and the risk can be further reduced by half by turning in sub-divisions of two. In pondering this problem a major consideration in Jellicoe's mind, as at 6.15, would have been the knowledge that by making such a large turn he would be putting all his guns out of action for several critical minutes. Furthermore, he realised, as he explained in his *Grand Fleet* that if he passed through the first wave unscathed there would be further attacks necessitating further turns and further periods when the guns would be out of action.

In the account of the battle that he gives in *The Grand Fleet* Jellicoe admits that while Scheer's manoeuvre of retreating under cover of a torpedo attack had long been 'foreseen, expected and studied' no answer had been found: the difficulty was 'to a certain extent insuperable': or, as he had it in his despatch, 'There was no real counter'.

In all the circumstances and with the limitations of his system of fire control prominently in mind, it is perhaps not surprising that Jellicoe should have felt unable to do better than turn his whole line away from the attack even though it entailed allowing the Germans to escape, never to be seen again 'save' as Pollen later wrote', 'as looming shadows in the semi-darkness of the night, while Scheer, some hours later, crashed his way through our light craft, a few miles astern of Lord Jellicoe's command.'

The irony of the situation lies in the fact that in the pamphlet *The Gun in Battle* which Pollen had circulated in February 1913, in a last desperate attempt to convince the Admiralty of the need for his gear, he had actually chosen the inevitability of torpedo attack as the simplest and most convincing argument against the tactics and the system of fire-control on which the Admiralty had chosen to rely.

The pamphlet opens with the challenging statement that 'This pamphlet has been written to explain why a complete revolution in the preconceived notions of naval tactics is now certain.' He tactfully refrains from mentioning that a number of statements to the same effect could be found in his *Jupiter Letters* of 1905. Yet the point at issue was still the same. As evidence of contemporary support for the traditional doctrine he cites Admiral Sir Reginald Custance who 'in his exceedingly important work' *The Ship of the Line in Battle* had been 'quite uncompromising in his insistence that decisive action always means fleets drawn up on parallel lines, steering in the same direction and closing to ranges sufficiently short to make fire decisive.'

And again, Rear Admiral Fiske of America, 'a veteran in the cause of fire-control and a well known inventor of ingenious fire-control appliances', who, in a recent publication, had spoken of a change of range of 160 yards a minute as a rate 'far higher than would be met with in battle.' And, to come nearer home, he records that 'in a recent discussion with an officer highly distinguished for his gunnery services, I was informed that any captain who changed course to keep station, while within fighting range of the enemy, would deserve to be hung at his own yard arm, and that any Admiral ordering such a manoeuvre was unfit to command.'

To Pollen, writing in 1913, it seemed that of all the objections to the traditional concept of the rigid Line of Battle, the one most likely to influence the ruling clique was its vulnerability to torpedo attack.

In a paragraph aptly entitled *The Torpedo Menace* he developed his argument as follows:

> The question of the tactical employment of fleets has, of course, recently been complicated by the facts that the range of torpedoes is more than doubled; that their speed is very greatly increased and their efficiency (that is the extent to which they can be relied on to run well) has increased almost as much as their range and speed . . .
>
> The torpedo menace has undoubtedly confused the problem of fleet action in a most bewildering manner. . . . It is, of course, quite truly an element in fighting and a most serious element . . . but I find it hard to believe that the essential character of fleet actions or of naval war generally can be affected by them . . .
>
> It seems indisputable that the future must lie with the means of offence that has the longest reach, can deliver its blow with the greatest rapidity and above all that is capable of being employed with the utmost precision. In these respects the gun is and must remain unrivalled . . .
>
> The two directions in which fleet fighting seems likely to be most noticeably affected by the new weapon, are in the formation of fleets and the maintenance of steady courses.

I think there are other reasons why the tactical ideals set out above, viz that of using long lines of ships on parallel courses at equal speed in the same direction, will be questioned, but even if there were not, the fact that a mobile mine field can be made to traverse the line of our oncoming squadron, and that ships formed in line ahead offer between five and six times more favourable a target than a line of ships abreast, will make it certain that sooner or later there will be a tendency in favour of smaller squadrons, and, even with them, of large and frequent changes of course to lessen the torpedo menace.

To all of which, so he had argued, the only logical answer was to adopt his A.C. System of Fire Control, which by January 1913 had already proved its capacity to keep hitting the target while the firing ship was changing course.

Underlying the attitude of the Establishment was the basic fallacy first voiced by John Fisher in 1904, and repeated again in the memoirs[6] he published in 1919, that 'tactics dictate weapons', which in practice meant that weapons were chosen to meet the *currently accepted* tactical doctrines. Arthur Pollen, from the earliest days, had preached the exact contrary, that weapons dictate tactics; in other words that new weapons inevitably generate new tactics. It was his failure to convince the Admiralty of this elementary truth that stultified development and led to Jellicoe's frustration at Jutland.

CHAPTER XI

The Lessons of War

Parallel with his efforts to revive Jellicoe's interest in Argo after Jutland, Pollen had renewed his approach to the Americans. On their first introduction to his system in 1914, the experts of the Navy Department in Washington had been greatly impressed and it was confidently expected that an order would follow. However the outbreak of war interrupted negotiations, other ideas intervened and negotiations petered out.

Happily Pollen and E. C. Tobey, their representative in London, had much in common and remained in close touch all through the war. Jutland, as we have seen, brought Argo once more into contention and Tobey urged Pollen to go at once to Washington. However with Naval affairs at home in such turmoil and the submarine war on our shipping growing daily more serious, it was out of the question for Pollen to leave London. Progress on Argo was in consequence negligible until the beginning of February 1917 when the Department decided it was time to put their cards on the table. They accordingly sent Tobey a communication couched in the most appreciative and cordial language, explaining the Department's decision 'to try and work out their own solution'. The Department's letter[1] which was duly passed on to Pollen, ran as follows.

> As you probably know, Mr Pollen was in Washington in the early summer of 1914 and the various officers who went into Fire Control matters with him at that time formed a very high opinion of him and have the greatest respect for his ability as a

Naval critic in general, and on matters pertaining to Fire Control in particular. The Bureau was much impressed by what he had to say in this matter and was seriously considering the purchase of a set of his gear. The negotiations finally terminated without result partly on account of the cost of the outfit. A number of officers thought that results could be obtained in a simpler manner. As it stands now we are trying to work out our own salvation. Meanwhile, it has developed that the Fleet is not wholly in sympathy with the idea of abandoning the old system which they claim is so simple and not easily deranged.

To Pollen these were familiar arguments. Washington had evidently now reached the same state of uncertainty and in-decision as Whitehall in 1912, and for the same reasons. For Pollen there was this difference, that whereas his struggle with the Admiralty had had to be conducted in the rarefied atmos-phere of prophecy, it was now possible, in 1917, to point to the actual experience of war. In his reply to his friend Tobey he made the most of his opportunity. The letter, dated the 13th February 1917, is remarkable for the lucid, non-technical and convincing language in which he sets out the now familiar arguments as to the requirements of battle, to which he adds an interesting commentary on the performance of our gunnery in action.

At the Battle of the Falkland Islands, he writes, Admiral Sturdee had it all his own way. His gun power was to the enemy's roughly as eight to one, and he had a three if not four knot superiority in speed. He chose to fight at long range so as to reduce the risk of his ships being hit. As a result it took five hours to sink two armoured cruisers, either of which could be sunk by less than twenty hits. The rate[2] of hitting was certainly not greater than one hit per gun per two hours. At Jutland, he continues, the rate of hitting was certainly less than one hit per gun per three hours. Yet in battle practice the same guns, at a range of 14,000 yards, regularly achieved a rate of hitting of one hit per four or five minutes. And all because the Admiralty had failed, before the war, to appreciate the need to be able to keep the enemy under effective fire while the firing ship was changing course and changing speed.

'My system of instruments' he concludes 'is only to be justified because the conditions for which they are designed are inevitable, and their complexity is explained solely by the fact that the conditions are infinitely complex.'

In a postscript to the letter he writes 'if your friends will look at the enclosed scheme of trials they will perceive that the methods of Fire Control now in use could not undertake demonstrations of this kind at all. It was one drawn for a certain belligerent navy which adopted my system after its capacity to fulfil these tests was proved.

Arthur Pollen knew the Americans better than most Englishmen, and the tone of this letter, whatever its effect might have been at Whitehall, was well calculated to produce the desired reaction in Washington. In his acknowledgement Admiral Earle, Chief of the Bureau of Ordnance, describes it as a 'remarkably fine essay', and goes on to say,

> I was very anxious to have Mr Pollen come to Washington in order to consult him both on his Rangefinder and the general system for Fire Control for I fully intend to purchase one complete system at least in order to see whether ours is as good.

The papers relating to the ensuing negotiations are unfortunately missing from the Pollen archives but there is a letter on the file, dated 8th May 1918, from Admiral Sims accepting 'My dear Mr Pollen's' kind invitation to send an officer to the works in York to see the instruments in use before despatch to Washington. It is also known that the Navy Department later obtained a licence to build for their own requirements in America. The acquisition of the American rights came too late to be of any value in the war and it is beyond the scope of this volume to attempt to trace the post-war developments in American Naval gunnery.

The Americans owed a great deal to the genius of Hannibal Ford the inventor of the Ford Clock, who is not to be confused with the great Ford Motor organisation. On the other hand there is a letter on the file, dated January 1918, addressed to Tobey in London, from Headquarters in Washington, which suggests that they may owe even more to Arthur Pollen.

Pollen had spent the last six months of 1917 in the United States, on a visit with the two-fold purpose, first of talking to the Navy Department about his gear, and secondly on a propaganda mission at the personal request of John Buchan, the Director of Propaganda. His talks with the Navy Department evidently went well, and shortly after his return, Tobey in their London office, received a remarkable communication from a colleague in Washington which reads as follows:

You may be interested in two passages in official reports which have just reached us here. The first from Bingham says: 'I believe we have learned much from Mr Pollen concerning Fire Control. Until our interview with him in Washington, we had no idea in this Fleet that any so complete solution of the problem had ever been attempted. Results of the very greatest importance may be expected from the forthcoming trial of his instruments, if they function as described by him, and as, apparently, they should from their design'. The next passage is in a report from one of our men on your side; after describing the Fire Control System in use in British battleships and battle-cruisers, he concludes as follows: – 'Apart from the Director System, we can learn of nothing, in British Fire Control, which is superior to, or even as good as that which we have in the Atlantic Fleet now. When we are supplied with Ford Clocks, we shall be in better shape than any ship in the British Navy, except the three or four that have Argo Clocks now. We have reason to think that, in the majority of ships always, and in many cases, in all ships, the Dreyer System of instruments is not, in fact, employed in action. We heard no satisfactory explanation why this system, and not the Pollen System, is employed. In theory, the Pollen System is not only more scientific, but simpler. It seems capable, that is, of a high degree of accuracy which the Dreyer System can, seemingly, never attain. There is nothing in the Dreyer System equal to the Ford Clock and, if the Pollen Clock can keep the range of an invisible target while the firing ship is manoeuvring, it should be greatly superior to the Ford, assuming its accuracy in all respects to be equal to that of the Ford.

We learnt that the Pollen Plotting System has not been tried. It was, therefore, useless for us to ask for any official report on the Pollen Fire Control System as a whole. We have met but few officers who knew any details about the final form of Mr Pollen's instrument; though all are familiar with the fact of his being the pioneer of Fire Control in the British Navy. We were given to understand, however, that there was some personal quarrel between Mr Pollen and the Gunnery Authorities at the Admiralty, five years ago, and that the Department had decided to have no further dealings with him at all. It is said that this quarrel took place just as his system was completed, and that this explains why it has never been tried. It is a very extraordinary situation because, at the time of this quarrel, Mr Pollen was just realising the results of fourteen years' continuous labour, and experiments carried out, year after year, at the British Navy's expense. And it seems clear that the whole of these results had successfully been kept secret until it was suddenly decided not to give the system a trial, and to allow Mr Pollen to publish it to the world. It is supposed, in the British Service, that Mr Pollen will not publish his story till the war is over'.

To the historian this report from Washington, while valuable as evidence of the superiority of the Pollen system, is even more significant for what it tells us of the attitude of the Royal Navy towards the Dreyer system adopted in 1912. The statement, 'We have reason to think that, in the majority of ships always, and in many cases in all ships, the Dreyer system of instruments is not in fact employed in action', may be weak in syntax, but as a condemnation of the Dreyer system it is crushing. Read in conjunction with Beatty's personal letter to Pollen in which he laments the necessity of having to 'learn to do without their rangefinders', it is final.

If, to the lay mind, it should appear that too much emphasis has been placed on the details of Jellicoe's admissions regarding Jutland, let it not be forgotten that the investigation carried out by the U.S. Navy Department, following their country's entry into the war, was the only independent contemporary enquiry ever permitted into the relative merits of the Pollen and the Dreyer systems of fire control. The Americans had no reason to favour Pollen or belittle Dreyer, yet their report says of Pollen's system that prior to the enquiry they had no idea that any such complete solution of the problem had ever been attempted and that results of the greatest importance were to be expected from a trial of his instruments. Of Dreyer's system they state categorically that it offered nothing (apart from Percy Scott's Director) as good as what they already had in their Atlantic Fleet; and furthermore, that the British Navy preferred for the most part not to make use of it in action.

All of which makes it extremely difficult to understand how Jellicoe could have felt justified in asserting, first to Pollen in August 1916, and again in February 1919 in *The Grand Fleet*, that his gunnery instruments had fully met his requirements. Was he merely covering up in order to uphold the bad decision to which he and his fellow Lords of Admiralty had been persuaded in December 1912 by Moore and Dreyer? In his favour it could be argued that had he retained any recollection of the helm-free debate of 1912, and of the proved capacity of the *Orion* clock to keep the target under fire while manoeuvring at high speed, he would not have volunteered such revealing statements as to the inability of his chosen system to hold the target while making large turns.

On the other hand, we can now say with virtual certainty that if, by the end of 1917, he still believed Dreyer's system to be adequate, he must have been almost alone among officers of the Grand Fleet in that belief.

In support of this rather severe judgement we have, first, the American account which we have just been considering, and secondly a 'secret document[3]', entitled *Reports of the Grand Fleet Dreyer Table Committee* dated 5th September 1919. The occasion for the reports had been a formal three-line letter addressed to the Commander-in-Chief by the Admiralty, a year earlier, asking for 'proposals as to the type of consorts gun pencil recommended for fitting in the Mark V table of HMS *Hood*, observing that several types are understood to be fitted in the various ships of the Fleet.'

This seemingly minor enquiry, whether intentionally or not, unleashed a torrent of technical criticism of the Table, together with detailed particulars of the remedial measures introduced during the war by different ships. The three interim reports in which the criticisms and modifications are discussed, fill eight printed pages of foolscap and leave us in no doubt as to the dissatisfaction within the Service with the Dreyer Table, with which they went to war.

Amid this mass of technical detail, there occurs on page six a statement of principle, casually inserted, which takes us right back to the controversy of 1912. It will be recalled that what Pollen then called 'the real obstacle to the adoption of his gear', was the refusal of the Board, on the advice of Moore and Jellicoe, to admit that it might ever be necessary, or even desirable, to change course while in action and moving at high speed. Here, in the third interim report dated 18th October 1918, we find an allusion to 'the frequent alterations of course at high speed which are now the accepted conditions in action. . .' The very circumstances which Pollen had foreseen, but which had been discarded as figments of the landsman's imagination were now 'the accepted conditions of action'.

The three interim reports, all forwarded together by Beatty on 7th February 1919, dealt only with the existing Dreyer Table and the war-time modifications thereto. These were followed at an unspecified date[4] by a final report in which the four gunnery Commanders called for an entirely new design. In his covering letter (also undated) Beatty emphasized the importance of the subject and the need to ensure that 'the highest engineering skill available be brought to bear on the problem, without regard to financial considerations.' He proposed that a Committee of Experts be set up 'to study the question and to evolve the design', and went so far as to recommend that the Committee include Keith Elphinstone, of Elliotts, Dreyer's designer,

Harold Isherwood, Pollen's designer, and Hugh Clausen RNVR the gunnery lieutenant of the *Benbow*, who was later to join the civilian staff of the Admiralty as a Principal Scientific Adviser.

Nobody reading these papers and knowing the prejudice that prevailed at Whitehall at that time against Pollen, could fail to appreciate that Beatty, responding to the pleas of his gunnery commanders, was doing his best to ensure, in the most tactful possible manner, that the Argo designers be brought into consultation. In the event, as noted earlier, it was not until Beatty had himself gone to Whitehall as First Sea Lord, in 1920, that the proposed Admiralty Fire Control Committee was actually set up. Elphinstone, Isherwood and Clausen were all brought in, together with Isherwood's former assistant at Argo, D. H. Landstad the Swede who, at Isherwood's request, was named as designer.

When on 5th September 1919, Oswyn Murray the Secretary of the Admiralty found himself instructed by their Lordships to issue the reports and the relative correspondence to 'all Commanders of H.M. Ships and Vessels', great stress was laid on the care that should be taken not to discuss the instruments 'with any but officers on the active list'. Attention was called to 'the penalties attaching to any infraction of the '*Official Secrets Act*', (aptly dubbed by Arthur Leveson the *Deadly Secrets Act*,'). As with the Colville Report in 1910, any admission that Pollen had been right and their Lordships mistaken was a top secret to be protected by all the rigours of the law.

To conclude this chapter the reader will be introduced to yet another Pollen invention of which little mention has yet been made – the Pollen-Cooke rangefinder. The reader will recall that after six years research, the year 1906 had seen a double break-through in the quest for the perfect instrument of observation. For it was in that year that Barr & Stroud produced their 9′ rangefinder, the first to be capable of dealing with the long ranges which Pollen had set out to master; and in that year too, that Pollen had produced the perpetual running gyroscope which he needed to overcome the problem of yaw, and for which he had been waiting since 1901.

Throughout the three years from 1909 to 1912, these two instruments, the Barr & Stroud 9′ rangefinder and the Pollen gyro mounting, were virtually standard equipment for all new capital ships.

Meanwhile, however, Pollen in 1910 had hit upon an entirely new idea for the improvement of the light-gathering capacity of range finders and for the first time ventured into competition with Barr & Stroud, employing for the purpose the firm of Thomas Cooke & Son of York, of which he had recently bought control.

That this new and ambitious venture proved an immediate success is clear from a letter that Pollen wrote on the 20th March (1911) and sent to a number of friends in the Service, notably Jellicoe, Prince Louis, Peirse and Leveson. The letter reads as follows:

> I must intrude on your time for a minute to tell you what seems to me an interesting piece of news.
>
> Messrs. Cooke, of York, have for some months now been developing a Rangefinder built according to certain ideas which I have put before them.
>
> The principal object sought for is high light gathering capacity, the hope being that it will be possible to use the Rangefinder with effect as a Rangefinder in conditions under which all existing Rangefinders are useless.
>
> In the three very prolonged trials that I have made myself with Barr & Stroud Rangefinders in connection with my gear, I have found that as a rule the Rangefinder ceases to be usable about an hour before sundown. This, of course, varies with the clearness of the atmosphere, the time of year, etc., but my experience has always been to this effect, that the mast and yards of a ship, say between five and ten thousand yards off, were generally visible for an hour to an hour and a half after they had ceased to be visible on the Rangefinder.
>
> Last week I tried the new Rangefinder for the first time. It is not yet in perfect adjustment and there were slight errors in the ranges due to this cause, but it was interesting to note that all

the errors, such as they were, were constant. The object on which we ranged was a water tower, three and a half miles off (6200 yards) which had rising from it a couple of pipes. The tower and pipes stood out for a height, I should imagine, of about fifty feet against the skyline, say twenty-five feet of tower and twenty-five feet of pipes. The evening was an exceedingly stormy one and the light consequently very bad.

We began ranging at about twenty minutes to six. The Rangefinder has two powers, forty and twenty diameters. By ten minutes past six it had become impossible to take a range with the high power, and a little before this the pipes had become invisible to the naked eye. We continued to range, however, with the low power until between twenty minutes and a quarter to seven, the object having been invisible then for over forty-five minutes.

This seems to me to open up great possibilities, especially in the way of anti-torpedo attack control; while its importance in lengthening the period, both before and after sundown, in which great guns can be used at their longest ranges, cannot, it seems, be exaggerated.

I will write you again when further experiments have been made. The instrument is to be examined on Thursday next by the Admiralty experts at York.

P.S.   I ought perhaps, to add that the tests of the new Rangefinder so far have been limited to what I say, namely, its light gathering capacity. It is quite premature to say whether it can stand Service conditions; but, at any rate, it is a very promising beginning to have succeeded so completely in our main object.

Jellicoe replied at once, in a handwritten note:

My Dear Pollen, I am much interested to hear of your R.F. results which seem most promising indeed, so far as they have gone. I wish you every success.

But alas, by 1913, when the perfected instrument became available, the prejudice that had developed against Pollen and his company blinded the Admiralty to its possibilities and they refused even to inspect it. On the other hand, the fact that they had never seen any but the first admittedly faulty experimental model, did not prevent them, five years later, telling the Russians that they had tested the Pollen-Cooke rangefinder and found it in no way superior to the Barr and Stroud; and furthermore that they saw no justification for charging double the price. It was on these grounds that in February 1916, the Admiralty refused to allow the manufacture of the eight instruments ordered by the Russians following the successful performance of the two previous batches bought before the war.

Fortunately, Pollen at this date was in close touch with Arthur Balfour, the First Lord, and in a position to write a personal letter setting out the facts and pointing out 'the essential absurdity' of Admiralty officials with no knowledge of the instruments seeking to vary the order of the Russian experts who, with a large number of instruments at their disposal, had had two years in which to appraise their performance at sea in all weathers. By return of post came a letter from Balfour, regretting the misunderstanding and confirming that 'so far as this office is concerned the order can be placed at once with T. Cooke & Son.'

It would be interesting to know the names of the Russian ships in which the Pollen gear was installed. We know that one complete set of instruments was tried in the *Peter Velicky* (Peter the Great) and that following the trial five complete sets were ordered. We know too that a substantial number of the Pollen-Cooke rangefinders were delivered. But we have no other names and no definite information as to deliveries of the Clocks other than to the *Peter Velicky*. This is unfortunate because the Germans, during the war, were very meticulous in keeping and recording particulars of shell splinters picked up after an engagement, and this together with the evidence of observers, often enabled them to name both the ships and the weight of shell that had hit them. N. J. M. Campbell in his *Battle-Cruisers*, gives particulars of three engagements between the German battle-cruiser *Goeben* and the Russian Black Sea Fleet. In the second of these on 5th May 1915, at ranges of 17,500 to 16,000 yards the Russian pre-Dreadnought *Estafi* scored three 12″ hits and the *Goeben* none. On the 8th January 1916 the *Goeben* had her only action against a Russian Dreadnought, *Imperatritsa Ekaterina*. They engaged at 21,500 yards but the range was too great for the *Goeben* and she withdrew. She was pursued for 30 minutes by *Ekaterina* which was capable of ranging up to 28,000 yards. The final range was 25,000 yards and neither side scored a hit. It seems fair to assume that this was achieved with the Pollen-Cooke rangefinder, for it is extremely improbable that they would have been so interested in Pollen instruments had they had another that was capable of such unprecedented ranging.

But alas, despite the strong evidence as to the success of the telescope in the hands of the Russians, the Admiralty still declined to consider trying it out or even inspecting it for the possible adoption by the British Navy. For this Pollen had to wait until after Jutland.

In a letter dated 12 October 1916 from Pollen to Masterton-Smith, the First Lord's private secretary, we find:

> The Jutland despatch told us that the German fleet escaped comparatively unpunished on the 31st May last, partly because our rangefinders could not deal with the bad light and the low visibility. As the Cooke-Pollen instrument was designed to work precisely in these conditions I saw Sir Henry Jackson (the First Sea Lord) on the subject and, at his suggestion, wrote to the Commander-in-Chief. It is now six weeks since Sir John Jellicoe informed me that he had urged the Admiralty to try a Cooke-Pollen rangefinder.

He then goes on to say that if the usual procedure were followed of buying first one instrument and testing it and then ordering more 'there must be a very great delay in equipping the fleet.' He therefore offers to build a dozen 15 feet instruments which the Admiralty can purchase or not after trying the first. In other words he was offering to carry the whole financial responsibility himself provided the Admiralty would authorise Cookes to purchase the necessary materials and put the order in hand.

However the proposal was altogether too simple and too unorthodox for Whitehall and from the rather scanty records[5] still available in the Pollen files it is clear that by March 1918 no deliveries had been made although by this time Pollen had a firm order for thirty instruments. No change in design had been made since 1913 and there is little doubt that they could have had these thirty instruments before the outbreak of war, or at any rate shortly after, had they been willing to test them. Thus rangefinders must be added to the list of admittedly second-choice instruments on which, thanks to the incompetence and prejudices of Whitehall, the Navy was forced to rely throughout the 1914 war.

CHAPTER XII

The End of an Era

The month of April 1917 saw the climax of Arthur Pollen's wartime career as journalist and propagandist. At the same time, the revival of interest by the Americans in his system of fire control raised hopes that a decisive break-through might be imminent.

As the leading naval critic of the day it fell to him to report and comment, week by week, upon the terrifying acceleration in the rate of sinkings of our merchant shipping. From the already dangerous level of 250,000 tons a month, at the end of 1916, the total for March had risen to 600,000 tons, and the trend was still upward. (Of the figures here quoted about three quarters related to British shipping, the balance to Allied and Neutrals.)

Pollen's task was rendered the more difficult, indeed, virtually impossible by the fact that Jellicoe and Duff, the Admiral in charge of anti-submarine operations, were both resolutely opposed to the introduction of convoy, the age-old practice of gathering merchant ships together into large groups which are then given the protection of a warship as escort. So hostile were they to the idea of convoy that no mention of it was permitted by the censor. Yet to Pollen it was the only possible answer.

In protest against the censorship Pollen sought an interview with Jellicoe, but met determined opposition. Herbert Richmond, an active critic of Jellicoe's administration throughout his term as First Sea Lord, recorded the result of that interview, in a diary entry that read as follows:

> Pollen's account of his interviews with Jellicoe and Duff in
> March 1917 threw some light on the Admiralty's views about
> convoy. Jellicoe said convoy was impossible. Merchant ships
> could not keep station and unless convoys kept good order they
> were simply gifts to the enemy. He had no other valid reason.
> Duff shrieked when the word convoy was mentioned and said
> he would not listen to any suggestion or give any reason for not
> adopting it. Beatty was then urging convoy, as he told me. It
> was partially adopted in April and is now (March 1918) a going
> concern, and their Lordships pat themselves on the chest and
> say 'Look how clever we are and what good work we do to
> defeat the submarine.' It seems as if every measure has to be
> forced on them from the outside.

Pollen and his friends were convinced that the trouble all
stemmed from the fatal combination of a leadership that lacked
the spirit of attack, coupled with a nonsensical pattern of
administration under which the First Sea Lord was buried in
matters of administrative detail which ought never to come to
his notice, and this at a time when his energies should have
been devoted exclusively to the purely military function of
fighting the submarines.

For two years and more, while by no means uncritical,
Pollen had steadfastly defended the Establishment and become
recognized by the men in authority at Whitehall, such as
Arthur Balfour, Masterton-Smith and Reginald Hall, as their
ablest and most loyal P.R.O. Yet by the end of March it had
begun to look as if nothing but a full scale assault on Jellicoe,
his team and their methods could bring about the changes
which would save us from defeat.

To Pollen such an attack on a man who had once been a
good friend, and with whom until recently he had remained on
good terms, was distasteful in the extreme; the more so as his
fight was not so much against Jellicoe personally as against the
whole autocratic regime, dominated by Jackie Fisher and his
group, from whose misguided and ill-informed judgements he
had suffered for so long. To succeed he would have to attack

the whole regime, spare nobody's feelings and demand a clean sweep, regardless of consequences to himself. Yet to initiate such an attack and fail would be to undermine public confidence and do irreparable harm.

Was he strong enough to carry such an assault to a successful conclusion? Could it be done with *The Times* and virtually the whole national press backing Jellicoe and urging their readers not to lose confidence? It was a tremendous decision with which to be faced, but by mid-April he could see no alternative.

On the 19th April there appeared in *Land and Water* an article in which for the first time he told his readers what he really thought of the way the Navy had been led since the outbreak of war. There had been a Pilgrim's dinner the week before at which Lloyd George in the presence of Admiral Sims, the Commander-in-Chief of the United States Forces in Europe, had made the principal speech.

Pollen picked up the Prime Minister's theme and built his indictment around it. In summary, the article ran as follows:

> Now, what is it we need most? The Prime Minister has supplied the answer. Ships. The supply of new ships, the protection of the old.
>
> We have in other words to admit that without American help our sea supplies are in such danger as to jeopardise the whole campaign. It is of course an admission that our shipbuilding resources, for three years monopolised by the Admiralty, have not been put to the best use. It is an admission that the German warning of December 1914 was not taken seriously. It is an admission that Whitehall did not learn the lesson of the U-boat campaign of February to September 1915 in home waters – nor of the autumn campaign in the Mediterranean, nor of the preliminary campaign of 1916 that was checked not by our counter-measures but by the American ultimatum. Now it is not particularly pleasant for the government of Great Britain to say that the chiefs of the greatest navy in the world have simply failed in so crucial yet elementary a duty as protecting the sea-borne commerce of a sea-girt people.

The collapse of the naval effort at the Dardanelles put an end to the Fisher-Churchill regime – a system of administration which may be said to have combined the maximum of civilian interference with the minimum of expert naval co-operation.

The Balfour-Jackson regime which followed lasted for nineteen months. The naval men could do as they liked but in the absence of a Staff System the individual Directors carried on unillumined by the experience the Service was gaining. In November a change of personnel was made but no change in system. Carson was substituted for Balfour, Jellicoe for Jackson, but we are no nearer running the Navy on scientific lines.

I believe the chief reason why the Admiralty has broken down in the war is first that we have jumbled all the functions, civilian and military, together and shoved them on to a single Board, and next, that we have taken no steps to ensure that a single member of the Board shall be guided by the impersonal and concerted opinion of the Naval Service.

The following week Pollen stood aside for Admiral Custance to take up the cudgels. In a long three-page letter to the editor of *Land and Water*, over the signature 'Flag-Officer', he opened the case with an elegant bow to Mr Pollen:

In common, I am sure, with all your readers, I have been following Mr Pollen's articles with the greatest possible interest. Your correspondent is almost the only exponent in the press of what most of us consider enlightened naval views. During the last six months, especially, we have been hoping against hope that the doctrines which he has been setting out with such assured authority might soon be reflected in the policy of the Government. In this we have been disappointed.

With typical clarity and precision, Custance then proceeded to spell out, in eight numbered paragraphs, the unbroken series of blunders in doctrine and in policy which, by 1914, had resulted in the Navy finding itself totally unprepared for war. 'This,' wrote Custance, 'is the indictment your correspondent has brought against the military direction of the Navy.' To this already formidable list he added, by way of example, a long and detailed account of Pollen's contribution to fire control, of the time and money spent over the years by the Admiralty in developing and testing Pollen's ideas and instruments and, finally, of the inexplicable rejection without trial of the 'only possible solution' when presented.

All these disasters he attributes to the failure of the Admiralty to separate the functions of Supply and Command. He ends by aligning himself whole-heartedly behind Pollen's demand for the reorganization of the Command on scientific principles. The letter is notable, on the one hand for the clarity and force of his argument and, in contrast, for the modesty with which he adopts and maintains, throughout, the role of seconder of Pollen's indictment, and of his demand for the separation of the functions of Supply and Command.

'Flag-Officer's' letter, based as it was on Pollen's campaign of the previous weeks, was extensively quoted in the press and led to a lively controversy in *The Times*, in which the Admiral joined, this time in his own name, replying decisively to the arguments of Winston Churchill, Lord George Hamilton, Professor Pollard, Gerard Fiennes and others who sought to defend or excuse Jellicoe's tactics and policies.

Meanwhile, the Editor of that illustrious journal, who throughout April had backed the administration, began suddenly to realize that something big was on the way, and on the 4th May, started to prepare for a change in editorial policy. This time his chosen spokesman was Sir Spenser Wilkinson, the historian, to whom he allowed a full column for the statement of his case. In his letter the Professor developed, with acknowledgement and with much historical argument, 'Flag-Officer's' demand for the separation of the military from the supply functions of the Board of Admiralty.

As a sign of the times it is interesting to find that during that week, in every paper in the country, there appeared in heavy black print, a summary of the King's Proclamation to 'Our Loving subjects, the men and women of Our realm' urging the abstention 'from all unnecessary consumption of grain as the surest means of defeating the devices of the King's enemies'.

Arthur Pollen's next contribution to the debate took the form of an article intended for *Land and Water* of the 3rd May. In this, he came out with the bald statement that we had lost command of the sea, together with an unqualified demand for the removal of the ruling clique who had led us into such trouble. This was too much for the Censor who refused to allow publication. Such action against a reputable journal such as *Land and Water* brought matters to a head and evoked an outcry from both Press and Parliament.

Besieged on all sides for interviews, we find, all within this critical week, statements in the *Telegraph*, the *Westminster*, the *Daily Sketch* and the *Star*, and full scale articles in *Truth*, the *New Statesman* and the *Sunday Times*, all publicising his demand for a change of leadership and of policies. Of these, the cleverest and most effective was that published by the *Star* who under a cloak of light-hearted flippancy managed to convey the full gravity of Pollen's indictment. The interview was introduced by a leading article in which they complained:

> It is almost impossible for an editor to discover what it is permissible to think in public. Mr Pollen is beyond all question the best and ablest writer on naval matters not only in this country but in all the allied countries. His reputation is hardly second to that of the late Admiral Mahan. Throughout the war he has consistently expounded the views of the Senior Service. He has, in our view, gone too far in his fidelity to the official hierarchy, and in his efforts to represent everything that has been done, or left undone in the most favourable light.

The interview itself ran as follows:

> a *Star* man found Mr Pollen today at his Headquarters in Buckingham Street. He stood facing the thunderbolts of the censor under a portrait of Nelson and a print of the Battle of Trafalgar.
>
> The *Star* man asked him: 'Do you know the censor?'
>
> 'Well,' said Mr Pollen. 'He is a very gallant naval officer. He is the servant of the Board of Admiralty. He is bound to defend it to the last moment. Being a true Briton, he does not know when he is beaten.'

'Are you not hurt by the demolition of your article?'

'It is a choice between two demolitions. Either the article ought to be demolished or the Board. I object very strongly to the demolition of the Board on the strength of an article in *Land and Water*. It ought to be demolished by the Government. When it is demolished we shall know that the Government knows its business, and the Government ought to know its business without being told by the press, even by the most distinguished writer for the press.'

'Do you think the Germans know what you are not allowed to tell the British public?'

'Admiral Capelle said very clumsily in the Reichstag the same thing a week ago. I think it is highly probable that the Germans understand the situation.'

'Do you consider Sir Edward Carson is a better First Lord than Mr Balfour?'

'I shall know when I see his new Board.'

'Do you think the existing Board is a failure?'

'As to that, consult the last two returns of losses. The naval members of the Board command the Fleet. The function of the Fleet is to protect trade. Its success can be measured by the weekly list.'

'How long do you think we can stand these losses?'

'At the present rate, all our ships will be gone by July, 1918.'

'How long do you think our food supplies will last?'

'It depends upon whether we attempt to defend them or not.'

'How?'

'By organising the powers of the Fleet.'

'Have you a plan?'

'Yes.'

'What is it?'

'Put the Navy under people who will fight.'

'Is this not a rash proposal?'

'It may seem so after our experience of the last three years, but the idea is not original. It has been acted on by our ancestors.'

'Do you refer to Nelson?'

'Yes, but he is not the only exponent of a perfectly sound creed.'

'Do you think the situation is grave?'

'Very grave. It has been thus summed up by a very
distinguished general: "Can the Army win the war before the
Navy loses it?" We have lost the command of the sea for the
time being. We must have a Board that will regain it.'

Thus, as so often happens, the intervention of the censor
resulted in his message receiving maximum publicity.

Meanwhile, parallel with his public activities, Pollen had
been busy lobbying friends in the Press and in Parliament. In a
letter dated 28th April, addressed to Admiral Sir William
Henderson, the honorary editor of the influential Service
journal, *The Naval Review*, we find

I suppose you noted the leaders in the *Daily Chronicle* and
Daily News of yesterday and in the *Westminster Gazette* of
Thursday. I have seen a great number of people and the good
seed is, I think, springing up everywhere. Last night one of the
Prime Minister's private secretaries dined with me and told me
that he had been repeating Flag-Officer's arguments to the
Prime Minister. I am very satisfied with the progress that has
been made.

The Private Secretary referred to was Philip Kerr, an old
friend who, as the Marquess of Lothian, later served with
distinction as Ambassador in Washington in the early days of
Hitler's war. The following morning Pollen set out his views
in the form of a personal letter to Kerr. No reference is made to
their talk the previous evening but it had obviously been
agreed that a note should be prepared for the P.M. in antici-
pation of his forthcoming meeting on the 30th with Jellicoe. It
is reproduced here both for the significance of the timing and
for its value as a summary of his indictment of the whole Fisher
group.

Mr dear Philip,
    I have read the Prime Minister's speech carefully and need
say nothing about its general merits, which are obvious and at
this juncture priceless. But I draw your attention to two things.
The only practical measures he proposes in consequence of the
submarine war are better use of shipping and public discipline in

consumption and the speeding up of ship building. None of these is any remedy. They can only prolong the period during which we can stand the strain. Obviously there is a limit to this period. With all these measures put to the utmost we may be able to last six, nine, twelve months etc., according to the resources we have, the resources we can foresee, the lowness of the scale on which we can live.

But when it comes to the main point, viz. an active defence against the submarine, he can only express the pious hope that, with the assistance of French and American ingenuity we shall devise a method of dealing with them. It is, I believe, a complete fallacy to suppose that the solution of the submarine problem depends upon the perfection of any one form of device or trick. The real solution lies in having all the means we possess now, or ever may possess, directed with courage, understanding of the problem and energy. Without right direction no new devices will help us at all. With right direction the means already at our disposal could do incalculably more than is achieved under the present system, which is hopelessly inefficient.

I have a very strong feeling that the Prime Minister would do well to acquaint himself with the judgement and opinions of naval officers who have been studying war all their lives, but have been excluded from high command and from any share in Admiralty administration during the last thirteen years, because their opinions about war are diametrically opposed to the group headed by Lord Fisher. This group has exercised autocratic sway at the Admiralty, either through its chief until 1910 and then through his subordinates until he returned in the middle of the war, and since by his subordinates again. The facts speak for themselves as to the fallacies on which the naval policy of this group was founded. They have produced a navy which under the command of its members has been unable to win a victory over the main fleet of the enemy and now, after nearly three years warning, is unable to protect our commerce. The explanation of both failures is the same. They never contemplated fighting as the main business of the Fleet, and thought that material and mass would do the trick. They are the same people who are now shouting for some new invention for solving the submarine problem; but the only solution of all war problems is concentrated and continuous thought on the art of fighting. This is a subject they never approach with the consequences that we see.

That letter was delivered by hand on the 28th, two days before the Prime Minister's meeting with Jellicoe at which the vital decisions for the reorganization of the Admiralty were taken.

Meanwhile the campaign had been having an electrifying effect on our leaders at Whitehall and on Lloyd George in particular. We now know that as late as the 22nd April Lloyd George had flatly rejected Hankey's[1] recommendations and insisted that 'the shipping situation is not as serious as you think it is'. Yet three days later, on the 25th April, when invited at a Cabinet meeting to take the exceptional step of going to call on Jellicoe at the Admiralty, he at once agreed, and allowed an appointment to be made there and then for the 30th.

The following day, the 26th, a similar total reversal of attitude was registered at the Admiralty, when Admiral Duff, hitherto so fanatically opposed to convoy, suddenly submitted a memorandum in favour of it, to which, no less surprisingly, Jellicoe at once appended his approval.

No-one was more surprised than Hankey who recorded in his diary, on the 29th, 'a few days ago they scouted the idea of convoy, now they are undertaking it on their own initiative'.

The only technical reason for this sudden reversal of policy was the discovery by Commander R. G. H. Henderson, a nephew of the Admiral referred to above, that the Admiralty had for long misunderstood the statistics covering the number of ships entering and leaving the country and, had in consequence, exaggerated the magnitude of the task of providing convoy for overseas trade. The point was of some consequence, but there is no reason to imagine that it would have been sufficient to overcome Jellicoe's conviction that convoys of merchant ships would be 'sitting ducks' to the submarines, had it not been for the prospect of the forthcoming visit from the Prime Minister; thus we are driven back to the conclusion, voiced by Richmond in his diary note, that the change of policy was forced upon the Admiralty from outside.

As to the timing of Lloyd George's unorthodox decision to call upon Jellicoe, it is sufficient to recall that Lloyd George was first and foremost a politician with an ear keenly attuned to public opinion, who would certainly not have been deaf to the quality and strength of the criticism in the Press.

On balance there seems to be no reason to question the verdict given by E. C. Tobey, in the letter he addressed to a colleague in Washington late in May:

> Mr Arthur Pollen, who is just leaving England on a short visit to the United States, has for the last six weeks held the attention of his countrymen in a way that no other war writer has ever done. He may be said single-handed, to have revolutionised the Administration of the Admiralty . . . If the anti-submarine campaign is revitalised and made effective, if the naval strategy of the Allies is galvanised into active offence, these things will largely be Pollen's work.

In the event, the Prime Minister's meeting with Jellicoe passed off very peacefully with convoy accepted in principle and Hankey invited to formulate his plan for the reorganisation of the Admiralty with a civilian in charge of supply. Two weeks later Carson was able to announce the appointment of Sir Eric Geddes as Controller, a post formerly held by an Admiral with the title of Third Sea Lord. The acceptance of convoy and the appointment of Geddes met to perfection two out of Pollen's three demands. On the no less important issue of changes in personnel at the top, nothing whatever was done – with the result that the incompetence and inefficiency of the military command persisted for a further six months, to the unconcealed indignation[2] and fury of David Beatty, who had succeeded Jellicoe as Commander-in-Chief.

In July Geddes took Carson's place as First Lord but Jellicoe, whose downfall was to mark the end of the Fisher era, was allowed to remain in office as First Sea Lord until December.

Looking back on the events of April and May we can see that

in more ways than one Pollen's handling of the crisis marked the high point of his career as war-time writer and critic.

In the first place it drew from Admiral Custance, a former Director of Intelligence and a recognised authority on gunnery and naval warfare, the only contemporary public acknowledgement ever made of the nature and value of Pollen's work. The award of the Royal commission on Awards to Inventors, in 1925, was admittedly more authoritative and, as we have seen, equally definite in its rejection of Dreyer's claims and in its recognition of Pollen's, but it received no publicity. Custance's 'Flag-Officer' letter thus remains to this day the only[3] public acknowledgement ever made of Pollen's achievements as inventor.

To the reader of these pages the essential facts of the Argo story are already familiar but it is interesting to read, coming from such a source, that despite the rejection of Pollen's instruments, the long series of experiments and research which he initiated had already, in the Admiral's judgement, 'revolutionised the art of naval warfare the world over'. To Pollen the publication of this authoritative tribute was a landmark in his career as an inventor, not to be matched until eight years later when the Royal Commission decided in his favour.

Similarly, if for different reasons, it can be said that the success of the campaign marked a climax in his career as a critic. That 'Flag-Officer's' letter played a big part in its success is not to be denied but the modesty with which Custance, throughout that letter, assumed the secondary role of supporter of Pollen's indictment, reflects his determination to avoid responsibility and ensure that it be known that Pollen was the author and prime mover in the attack. Behind the success of Pollen's initiative is the fact that his influence as critic was founded on a long record of restraint and responsibility. To a man in his circumstances, who had suffered so much at the hands of the ruling clique, what finer tribute could there be to his integrity as a critic than to be accused by the editor[4] of a prominent journal, of having habitually 'gone too far in his fidelity to the official hierarchy'?

Yet it is no less true to say that his greatest service to his country was his readiness to put that reputation at stake in the hour of need.

One interesting and gratifying reaction to the role he had played was that of John Buchan, the Director of Propaganda, who, on hearing of Pollen's intention to go to America before the end of the year, begged him to go at once to publicise the work of the Navy. For the head of an important department of the Foreign Office to issue such an invitation to the Admiralty's leading critic showed not only imagination on his part, but also recognition in the upper echelons of government of the value of his recent activities.

A letter to Lady Beatty, dated the 25th May, enlarges on the circumstances of his going and incidentally gives us his private opinion as to what had been achieved and what remained to be done. Lady Beatty had made no secret of her Admiral's anxieties, and Pollen had to admit that the reshuffle did not reflect any real change in the mental outlook of the men at the top.

> Thank you very much for your letter which only confirms what I hear from other quarters. The real trouble of the situation is that the men at the top have no clear and definite idea of what they want to do. They have taken on the job just in the spirit and with the mental outlook that prevailed in times of peace. And no amount of reshuffling and no addition of younger and abler men can possibly change their mental outlook and, consequently, the essential character of what is done. The idea that a genuine division has been made between civil and military functions is all rubbish. The First Sea Lord still has to devote at least four-fifths of his time to dealing with questions that ought never to come before the Admiralty at all. . . . The despairing element of the situation is that a man who finds himself in the centre of this turmoil of nonsense, should know so little of what war means as not only to submit to this incredible dispersal of his attention over trifles, but actually to insist that the area of his

interference should not be limited. Since America has come into the war, it has become necessary that I should, at some time or other, go over to see the Navy Department on certain business on which they wish to consult with me. I had intended going in September and combining my business with a certain amount of lecturing on the sea war. Colonel Buchan, who is at the head of our Propaganda Department at the Foreign Office, heard of this intention of mine, asked to see me and urged me to go as soon as possible, as he had reason to believe that the months of June, July and August will be rather critical and because he thinks if I can manage to deliver a course of lectures there, they might arouse an enthusiasm for the war in quarters that cannot be reached by professed propagandist lecturers. This request, coming from this quarter, has decided me and I leave for America on Saturday week. I do not suppose I shall be back till the middle or end of August. I am, of course, sorry for all I miss by going – my visit to Aberdour, for instance and my periodical writing. I hope you will ask me again when I come back, so that the first I regard only as a pleasure postponed. As to the second matter I think I have done all I can usefully do for the moment. There are many evidences that the Government know that they have got the wrong lot at Whitehall, and I cannot help thinking that, before long, a change will take place. At least, we shall be in a bad way if it doesn't; at any rate, I have done all that I can to bring it about. As far as my own authority and influence go, I think they will gain and not lose by my going.

John Buchan, the future Lord Tweedsmuir and Governor General of Canada, had started life as one of the band of brilliant young men on Lord Milner's staff in South Africa; by 1916 as perhaps again today, he was better known to the public as the writer of the best-selling thrillers of the day. It was an imaginative choice to put him in charge of propaganda in 1917, when things were going so badly, and the appointment was an outstanding success.

From Arthur Pollen's point of view, Buchan's intervention was well-timed. The changes at Whitehall fell far short of what he knew to be necessary and there were good reasons for thinking that he could achieve more in America than would be possible at home.

In Washington he was assured of personal contacts with the Navy Department with whom he was looking forward to discussing his system of fire control. At an even higher level, he could count on a welcome from Colonel House, President Wilson's personal assistant, with whom he had established a friendly relationship during the Colonel's recent visit to England. In addition he had friends in many walks of life. It was twenty-five years since his first shooting expedition to the Rocky Mountains and his more recent business visits, on behalf of the Linotype Company, had enabled him to keep in touch with old friends, among others Teddy Roosevelt, the former President.

As a journalist he was already well known to the American public. Even prior to Jutland, a number of articles had appeared over his signature in American journals, and more recently the story of his campaign against Whitehall had been much publicised in the daily press.

At home, while primarily concerned with Naval affairs, his *Land and Water* mandate had included the handling of all problems affecting Anglo-American relations. The modern generation tend to forget the twenty-three months that elapsed between the sinking of the *Lusitania* in May 1915, and the entry of America into the war in April 1917; nearly two years of misunderstanding and diplomatic strain during which the exercise of our claim to intercept and search neutral shipping caused intense resentment in America.

One consequence of Britain's policy of blockade had been a recommendation from the General Board of the Navy to the effect that, ultimately, America should have a Navy as big and as strong as any other Navy, meaning of course the British Navy. Unlike the British Board of Admiralty, the American General Board was a purely advisory body whose recommendations were thrown open to debate in Committees of Congress and in the Press. It was inevitable that a proposal so revol-

utionary as the 'Big Navy' plan, formally submitted in 1915
by Josephus Daniels, should give rise to a major controversy;
nor is it surprising to find that early in 1916 Arthur Pollen
had been invited by the *North American Review* to make an
appraisal of the scheme. This he did in the issue of March
1916, examining in some detail the balance of the scheme as
between the different classes of ships, battleships, battle-
cruisers, destroyers and submarines. Nor did he shrink from
the delicate task of discussing the scale of the scheme as a
whole; all the more delicate for the fact that Britain was at war
and the Americans still neutral.

> The military power which a nation needs, either on land or on
> sea is settled by its circumstances and its policy. If Great Britain
> lost command of the sea – that is the certainty of being able to
> use it as the high road of supplies – the country holding an
> adverse command could impose its own terms of surrender on
> us in about six weeks time. For practical purposes we should be
> starving . . .
>
> To every Englishman, then, the answer to the question 'How
> strong a Navy does Great Britain need' has for some years been
> comparatively simple and plain. We look round the world, we
> calculate the naval strength of those likely to be opposed to us in
> war, and we provide a fleet adequate to engage the navies that
> might combine against us . . .
>
> Has America in this matter any guide as unmistakable as was
> ours? Mr Daniels's statement is quite silent on the subject. It is
> not a matter on which the foreigner gets very much enlighten-
> ment from such American writings, official or unofficial, as
> reach us on this side. And it is obviously not for him to suggest
> what the standard of American naval strength should be. And
> yet it looks like putting the cart before the horse to discuss the
> character and composition of the new navy without knowing
> first what it is for!
>
> The most powerful navy is the British. It has maintained its
> standard of strength for purely defensive purposes. It has been
> built to prevent being altered, to Great Britain's disadvantage,
> the existing balance of power in the world. It stands today for
> the sanctity of international contract, for the liberty of small

nations, for the right of Christendom to resist unscrupulous aggression and the public denial of justice, humanity and law. All these are fine things. The United States stands for them also. It would be to the world's benefit if they put themselves in a position to stand for them with effect.

In a private memorandum that he had given Colonel House in London, only a month before, he had enlarged on this theme of American leadership:

> If America is to gain the world position and do the world duty that her great economic position and the high character of her citizens entitles her to assume and discharge, she should, it would seem, adopt a platform in this matter that is wider, more consistent, and above all more far reaching.

The attitude adopted by Arthur Pollen at this early date is of particular interest when we realize the extent to which rivalry between the American and British Navies was to bedevil the relations between our two countries throughout the 1920's. The story is well told in Stephen Roskill's *Naval Policy between the Wars*. In his Introduction he speaks of the tendency of historians to underplay if not ignore the serious differences of opinion and the rivalry in many fields which arose between the two nations during the inter-war period and concludes:

> It was the rise of the dictatorships in the 1930's that gradually produced the realisation that Britain and America had common interests, traditions and outlook which transcended the issue of which country should possess the more powerful navy.

Yet as early as 1916 we find Pollen openly welcoming the United States as equal partners in the role of world policeman; once again, so it would seem, some twenty years ahead both of public opinion and of Service opinion at home.

Even Custance, more far seeing than most of his contemporaries, failed to see the point. In a letter of the 28 March 1917 we find,

> I am quite satisfied that it is not to the interest of this country to

teach the art of war at sea to the people of the United States, but
to the peoples of the British Empire. Nor is it advisable to stir
up the enthusiasm of Americans for maritime power. I am well
aware that it is almost impossible to get clear ideas about such a
subject into the minds even of the ablest and still less into those
of the masses. Hence it may be that I am rather exaggerating
the effect of your proposed tour. Nevertheless I am clearly of the
opinion that you will not be wise to undertake the job. You are
doing more good on this side I think. Please remember that we
have not yet got our own Navy to think correctly.

Custance and Pollen remained on good terms, corresponding in short and frequent little notes, but it is clear from
Pollen's letter of the 31st May, written immediately before his
departure that the difference was by no means resolved. After
thanking Custance for an introduction to Admiral Goodrich he
concludes 'I wish I were not going . . . but the Foreign Office
has asked me to go and I am glad to be persuaded that I am
doing something for my country.'

In the event, Pollen's 1917 visit lasted from mid-June to the
end of the year. Immediately on arrival he was invited to a
discussion on policy with Admiral W. S. Benson, Chief of
Naval Operations and Mr Daniels. The meeting must have
gone well if we are to judge from the fact that only a few weeks
later he was called into consultation again to help to iron out a
whole series of petty disputes with Whitehall.

It would be out of place here to attempt a full account of
Pollen's activities during the critical six months of his visit. We
have already seen in an earlier chapter that his discussions with
the Navy Department on fire control met with unqualified success, resulting in an immediate order for one set of his instruments and, later, a licence to construct to meet their own
requirements. As to his public activities, we are fortunate in
that shortly before his return to this country he thought it
advisable to send Lord Reading, our Ambassador in
Washington, a brief outline of the objectives he had set himself
and of the difficulties he had encountered. His letter[5] ran as
follows:

My first stay in Washington, the last three weeks of June, was all private talks, conferences with small groups, confidential lectures to the naval staff in Washington and neighbourhood, the officers of the Fleet, on board the Flagship, at Annapolis, etc. Many I met were old friends, many more, of course, strangers. Everyone seemed familiar with the course of professional controversy in England, and a very large majority took what I may call the Custance, Henderson, Sydenham, *Land and Water* view of naval policy, North Sea strategy, and Jutland tactics. I was not surprised to find a very generous admiration expressed for the valour, fighting spirit, vigilance, etc. of British confreres. But I was surprised when I realised the result which disapproval of Whitehall's past policy and the present distrust of the Board had engendered. It came to this. The Admiralty is responsible for the failure of the British Fleet to blockade, to win at Jutland, to prepare adequately for the threatened submarine war, to adopt so obvious a measure as convoy to protect ships. Naval failure to win decisively has been complete, and explains why the Central Powers are still so strong, why, in fact, the war still continues. It threatens to ham-string America in coming to the Allies help, and, by the loss of supplies, to force political disintegration on Russia, Italy, and even France, before a military victory can be won. The Admiralty is answerable for prolongation of the war, and may be responsible for its inconclusive ending. . . . As I saw the situation there were only two courses possible. The First was to identify the American Navy with the British in a joint responsibility for the war. This would at least stop the evil at its then stage. It would flatter and please the American people; and it would make a quarrel less likely. The second would be a really large propaganda describing the actual effective work the Navy has done.

To achieve the second I arranged a lecture tour with the Navy League. But the League quarrelled with Mr Daniels, and this and other causes made the thing impossible. The second part of my programme, then, has been limited to a few public lectures, and a great number of private addresses to the Navy Consulting Board, the Chambers of Commerce, the Rotary Clubs, and business, newspaper and other associations, etc., and to occasional writings and interviews.

Throughout his visit, the fact that he was known to be a

leading critic of the current administration at the British Admiralty, assured him of a ready hearing. On the other hand, the role of a 'Leader of the Opposition' who ventures abroad is never easy, and he was not without his critics, prominent among whom was Vice-Admiral Sir Montague Browning, formerly a close personal friend and supporter, now Commander-in-Chief, North America and West Indies. To Browning it was disloyal for Pollen to speak disparagingly, while in America, of Jellicoe or of his administration and he reported both to Jellicoe and to Beatty that he thought Pollen was being unwise and causing trouble: a misguided and unfair comment that has found its way into more than one recent biography.

Who can doubt that Pollen would have made himself ridiculous and ceased to have any influence, had he suddenly changed his attitude and posed as a supporter and admirer of an administration against which he had conducted so public a campaign? By December, when he left to return home, it was generally recognised that his mission had been a tremendous success and he was warmly thanked from both sides. Colonel House wrote:

> I am sorry to know that you are to leave America even for a short stay and I hope your Government will think well to ask you to return.
> You have worked assiduously and successfully and, I have been told, gratuitously. I hope some arrangement can be made which will bring you back to us again within the very near future.

Gareth Garrett, the editor of the *New York Tribune*, in a note of rare perception and sensitivity, was equally appreciative:

> It is a pity you could not stay. Your understanding of the American mind and heart is very rare and at this time we can hardly afford to spare you. Like minded as we are, your people and mine, there are yet many points at which we seem to miss sympathetic comprehension of each other's moods. We look askance at each other for the most ludicrous reasons. Wherein

we are alike, it is fundamental; and wherein we are not alike it is superficial. More is the pity.

I trust we shall have you back soon.

Eric Geddes, backed by John Buchan, pressed him to return. By way of inducement he was offered a good salary, liberal expenses and a knighthood. In a letter to his wife he laments the failure of the authorities to understand the underlying reason for his success, and their refusal to give formal recognition to his services to gunnery by the grant of money and a title, and so make it possible for him to return and resume the good work.

I have just had a talk with the First Lord, who sent me a telephone message by Masterton-Smith this morning that he wanted to see me. What do you suppose it was for? Nothing less than that I should go back to America and resume my propaganda work of last year. Gaunt[6] & Co. have apparently been vocal about my success. You remember Reggie Hall's compliment about my reply to Kerensky. Nobody else, it seems, could have got the English answer into fifteen thousand daily papers. I gather that the military and political attachés have been at work too, and House as good as his word. His letter was evidently quite sincere, and the Washington powers think me much the most useful of the pro-Ally team.

E.G.'s offer was handsome enough – reasonable pay, liberal expenses, and the authority of the Prime Minister for a knighthood before or after as I might think best. But of course I could not accept it. It would have been obtaining money and honours under false pretences. The secret of my success was my independence. So long as I was there as a critic the Admiralty had silenced, a volunteer paying my own expenses, I had authority, and was better 'copy' than even Alfred (Northcliffe) or Reading; the papers everywhere printing me at length, and the Chicago Dinner doubling in numbers when I took Reading's place. Of course I knew what Geddes did not know, namely, that to label me as an official apologist would be to make my mission futile. If I could afford it I would go again like a shot, but I had to say that I could not. If it had been possible for me to prove my rights to proper royalties on the alleged Dreyer Fire Control, I would cheerfully have spent it all on such a mission, but E.G. would not force this issue on the Admiralty now, so the whole scheme falls to the ground. I don't suppose you will be sorry. My only regret is that I know they are right. What I did do and can do is unique. It is curious that neither the people on the spot or here know why.

To this modest explanation of the success of his mission, it is fair to add first that Pollen's good understanding of the American political scene stemmed from a genuine and deep-rooted affection and respect for America and Americans; and secondly that his imagination, self-confidence and, as we might say today, his somewhat extrovert manner, made a strong appeal to Americans, to whom the reserve and understatement of the typical Englishman was both suspect and boring.

It might be thought that in refusing to go back again on the Admiralty's terms after the turn of the year, he was being over sensitive. Having already made his name in America as a critic of the Admiralty, was it likely that the American public would notice whether the knighthood had been granted for his services to gunnery or for his work on Public Relations? Would they have known whether he was drawing a salary or working on his own? The answer no doubt lay in his statement 'the secret of my success was my independence'.

For he realised that apart from any question of being 'labelled' an official apologist, the mere fact of accepting a place on the government pay-roll would make him subject to direction from London. Such criticisms as Browning's would carry more weight, questions would be asked in the House, and instructions issued through the Embassy in Washington. What he wanted and felt entitled to demand, was formal recognition of his services to gunnery, coupled with his former freedom to speak his own mind and choose his own tactics. But Geddes had enough trouble handling the Admirals and could hardly be expected to challenge the Establishment on this delicate issue.

CHAPTER XIII

'The Navy in Battle'

Arthur Pollen returned from America on Christmas Eve to be greeted with the news that Jellicoe had been superseded as First Sea Lord by Sir Rosslyn Wemyss, his Deputy. To Pollen it was an immense relief to know that he could now resume his duties as Naval critic without further reference to the very distasteful campaign in which he had been engaged when he departed for America at the end of May.

With Wemyss at Whitehall, Beatty Commander-in-Chief and the Navy well on the way to mastering the submarine menace, Pollen soon found himself reverting to his former role of supporter and apologist for the administration. Welcome as this was on personal grounds, it was something of an anti-climax professionally and coming as it did after six months absence in America, such an attitude might well have resulted in his losing his public. Yet the contrary was the case, and his book, *The Navy in Battle*, when eventually it was allowed to appear, was an immediate and unqualified success. Much of it dated from 1916, when it was refused publication by the censor. 1918 saw the addition of the chapters on Jutland, but once again permission to publish was refused. In the end it was released for publication somewhat hastily, by Chatto and Windus, on the 30th November 1918 without any attempt to bring it up to date after the Armistice. Indeed, such was the sense of urgency that it was thought inadvisable even to await the production of an index. Of the factors that influenced the decision, the most important was the knowledge that Jellicoe's own account of his stewardship was about to appear and the belief that if Pollen failed to take the initiative the more controversial chapters might have to be recast and appear as comment on Jellicoe's account, thus perhaps changing the whole character of the book.

In the event, and despite its superficial defects, *The Navy in Battle*, attractively produced in black cloth with a frieze of battleships in gold, was at once a best seller, appearing not infrequently at the head of Selfridges 'Books of the Week'. Even the third edition, which came out in July, won him top place, ranking ahead of such well-known works as, *The Undying Fire* by H. G. Wells, *Mr Standfast* by John Buchan, with seventh place accorded to Daisy Ashford's *The Young Visiters*.

Of the few journals who dared to take sides on the basic issues he had raised, the *Spectator* supported him with a clear statement that 'The doctrine which was fashionable among many of our leading naval thinkers before the war was a negation of the Nelson spirit'. And again, 'Mr Pollen's statement of the rival naval doctrines is by far the ablest we have read. The answer to the questions he has raised will determine the manner in which the doctrines of the Navy will be framed in future'.

The New Statesman, in their issue of 25 January 1919, drew attention to the identity of doctrine that lay behind Pollen's *The Navy in Battle* and Marshal Foch's *The Principles of War*, of which the English translation by Hilaire Belloc had just appeared. They showed that like Mr Pollen, the Foch lectures 'proceed from a definite attitude of mind, from belief in the value of attack and in the necessity to seek out the enemy's forces and destroy them'. The review concludes 'The lay reader can derive (from Foch's lectures) some notion of the spirit which should animate a staff and an army, and a notion of what it is that Mr Pollen advocates'.

This was fair comment, for Pollen's underlying theme was condemnation of the doctrines of Fisher and his followers, who had dominated Naval policy for the ten years preceding the outbreak of war and indeed until the end of 1917. True to form, Pollen opened his indictment with a chapter entitled, 'A Plea for First Principles', immediately followed by 'Some Root Doctrines'. The argument may be briefly summarized as follows.

In war it is the primary duty of the armed forces, whether on land or at sea, to defeat the armed forces of the enemy in battle 'and so disintegrate and destroy them'. If either side retreats to a stronghold the other will pass on to siege. The purpose of siege is to compel the defenders or their rescuers to come out and fight, alternatively to induce surrender by hardship.

This basic principle was never understood by Fisher and his group. They espoused the false doctrine that the fleet existed to seize and control communications, not realising that control of sea communications is the result of, not the prelude to, victory. When, in the early months of the war, we quickly established control of the surface of the sea they believed their objective had been realised and failed to see the need to force the enemy to battle. In 1914, thanks to our gallant support of Belgium, we had world opinion on our side; we could have and should have at once enforced a strict blockade to stop vital raw materials reaching Germany through neutral countries. Instead, we waited until 'gigantic exporting interests had been created in America, which, once vested, made the restriction of them wear the appearance of intolerable hardship', with the result that the rigid blockade to which we were entitled under international law was actually never attempted until the United States themselves became belligerents. He concludes 'It is this which explains perhaps the greatest paradox in history, viz. that Germany imposed a strict blockade on Great Britain before Great Britain imposed such a blockade on Germany'.

The failure of the group to formulate their strategical aim was matched by an even less excusable failure to determine their tactical doctrine. 'I direct attention' wrote Pollen 'to the singular fact that the British Fleet on the 31st May fought as two separate units until six o'clock, and that the leaders of the two units were animated by conflicting theories of war. One Admiral represents the fighting fervour of the fleet, the other the caution, perhaps the wise caution, of the Higher Command.'

'There is no getting out of this dilemma. If Admiral Jellicoe was right in refusing to face the risks inseparable from a resolute effort to make the battle decisive, then Sir David Beatty must have been wrong to have fought in a way which cannot be intelligently explained except on the basis that from first to last he had decisive victory as his object. If the tender care that brought the Grand Fleet through the action with hardly a man killed and only two ships touched was right and wise, then the clear vision, all the more luminous for seeing and counting the cost, which exposed *Indefatigable, Queen Mary* and *Invincible* to destruction, was woefully wrong. Now it seems extraordinary, if the strategy of waiting till the Germans attacked was right – if this was the Admiralty doctrine – that it was not communicated to Sir David Beatty as well as to Sir John Jellicoe.'

The third piece of neglect for which Pollen held Whitehall responsible was their failure, the failure of the so-called materialists, to get their material right. For this Pollen is ruthless in his attack upon Churchill. Taking his theme from Churchill's famous article in *The London Magazine* of October 1916, he reminds us that Churchill ended that article with a plea for greater generosity to be shown to Admirals 'to whom Naval warfare is almost entirely novel. Scarcely one had ever had any experience of sea fighting. All had to learn *the strange new, unmeasured and in times of peace largely immeasurable conditions*' (Pollen's italics).

On this, Pollen comments 'Whence arose this theory that naval warfare consisted of unfathomable mysteries?' 'Any rightly organised system of enquiry, investigation and experiment would have dissipated this atmosphere of mystery at once. When new inventions are made that affect the processes of industry, it is not the men who go about talking of their untold possibilities, and their incalculable effects and their immeasurable results that get the commercial advantage of their development. It is those who take immediate steps to investigate the limits of their action and the precise scope of their operations who turn new discoveries to account. To talk as if the performance of guns, torpedoes, submarines and aircraft were beyond human calculation was really a confession of incompetence.

It was want of preparation in these matters that was undoubtedly one of the deciding factors in tying us down both to defensive strategy and defensive tactics'.

After the war, Pollen wrote only one serious study of the Fisher era, namely the essay entitled *The Tragedy of Lord Fisher of Kilverstone* which we considered in Chapter III: and that was written for the strictly limited and professional circle of the readers of the *Naval Review*.

There was good reason for this reticence. First the fact that to discourage controversy, most of the documents relative to Jutland, notably the Battle Orders of Jellicoe and Beatty, were classified as Secret and all reference to them consequently forbidden. The refusal to publish these vital documents made serious discussion of the principles at stake virtually impossible. Richmond, writing as late as 4th August 1927, said 'I have written and intend to write nothing in this matter until it becomes possible to discuss the fighting instructions, and I candidly believe that all discussion which omits them is Hamlet without the Prince of Denmark'.

Pollen and his friends were rightly confident that the orders would exemplify, and thus enable them to explain, without any appearance of prejudice, the fundamental difference in outlook and temperament between the two commanders; a difference crystallised by Richmond in a letter[1] to Pollen in the phrase 'none of the recent writers have recognised what to me is the essential fact, that a man goes into battle (having prepared himself for battle) in either one or the other of two frames of mind – to beat the enemy or avoid being beaten. Custance, a few years later (1933), was more explicit. 'The real causes of the indecision at Jutland were the character of the Admiral and the decision not to fight at decisive ranges. All other things are secondary and only confuse the issue.'

Yet the prohibition on any reference to the evidence of the Battle Orders meant that any mention of these fundamental, and not necessarily derogatory differences, could be dismissed as personal bias. To this day it is not difficult to find among the writings of modern historians statements attributing Pollen's criticism of Jellicoe to the fact that before the war Jellicoe had turned down his inventions.

For these and other reasons Pollen's published writings between the wars were limited almost exclusively to reviews and criticisms of the biographies and memoirs that appeared in a steady flow, almost to the outbreak of war in 1939.

In reality the so-called controversy was very one-sided, for the simple reason that Jellicoe had been the Commander-in-Chief and that for an officer to write a eulogy of his one time chief, or in defence of his tactics, was an act of loyalty in the best tradition of the Service. But such were the known differences between the tactics and methods of Jellicoe and Beatty, that it was virtually impossible to write a fair appreciation of Beatty's tactics without an implied criticism of Jellicoe. As a result we find among the war books of the period no less than eight by Admiral Sir Reginald Bacon, Pollen's one time adversary, three by Admiral Mark Kerr, another faithful friend and admirer of Jellicoe's, one by Frederic Dreyer, Pollen's former rival who had been Jellicoe's Flag-Captain at Jutland, and no less than three by Jellicoe himself.

In contrast the first life[2] of Beatty, by Admiral Chalmers, was not published until 1951. Of the leading Service critics of the Establishment only Captain Kenneth Dewar and Commander Filson Young dared to write what they thought. Arthur Pollen, inhibited from writing his own history of the war, was yet able in his review of the Fisherite volumes to strike some telling blows in Beatty's defence, as will be seen from the extracts given below. But book reviews are ephemeral stuff, with very limited circulation, and the general effect of the one-sided nature of the published material was to indoctrinate the general public very strongly in favour of the pre-war Establishment and against Beatty's Battle-Cruiser group.

Of the standard criticisms of Beatty, the commonest was, (and remains), that he should have kept Admiral Evan-Thomas, with his powerful Fifth Battle Squadron, in close support instead of stationing him five miles to the north of the Battle-Cruisers. To Pollen this criticism was but a reflection of the defensive thinking of the critics. If it was right for Jellicoe to station his two fleets sixty miles apart why was it wrong for Beatty to station Evan-Thomas five miles nearer to Jellicoe? The criticism overlooks the essential purpose of Jellicoe's sweep to the east, which was to seek out the enemy and attack him. If you are searching for the enemy you spread your forces and only concentrate after locating him. Clearly the underlying hope was that the Germans would be found in a latitude between Jellicoe's two prongs; and but for the fortuitous circumstance of the rival Battle-Cruiser commanders each sending a destroyer to identify a neutral steamer, Hipper might well have been trapped. Had he not received this early warning of a British presence he might have been many miles further north at the moment of discovery and both Jellicoe's and Beatty's dispositions would have been hailed as brilliant examples of their genius.

Disregarding the might-have-beens, it was Pollen's contention that Beatty's disposition of Evan-Thomas's slower but more powerful squadron, between himself and Jellicoe, was wholly consistent with the offensive nature of Jellicoe's plan. Nor, for that matter, was there a remote possibility of his being caught unawares by a superior force.

Another no less common criticism is that revived by Admiral Harper in his book *The Truth about Jutland*, to the effect that Beatty had failed to keep the C-in-C properly informed as to the enemy's position and movements. To this Pollen retorted that the theory that ships zig-zagging and manoeuvring at twenty-five knots would ever know their right position had been exploded long before the battle, so that reliance should not have been placed on distances and bearings from alleged points at any given moment. He concludes, 'what the Admiral does not tell us is that Lord Jellicoe could have established visual touch, by at least 5 p.m., had he chosen – when he first heard that the High Sea Fleet was at sea and went at full speed to meet them – to send his fast, instead of his slow, cruisers forward. But he was tied by his original diagram. As his armoured cruisers were little if at all faster than the battle-ships he actually drove into the oncoming ships – British and German – without any screen at all.'

We see here a good example of how Pollen was frequently driven to criticism of Jellicoe, not on his own initiative but as the only answer to foolish and prejudiced criticism of Beatty. In reality, while Pollen did have to make a strong personal attack on Jellicoe in May 1917, for his failure as First Sea Lord to deal adequately with the very grave menace of the sub-marine war against our shipping, his criticism of Jellicoe's conduct as Commander-in-Chief was nearly always tempered by a clear indication that it was official doctrine and not lack of initiative in action that was at fault. The following extract, taken from an article in the *Nineteenth Century*, published in August 1927, is a fair example of how he would rally to Jellicoe's defence when unfairly attacked.

It is one of the strange features of the present position that Mr Churchill should not yet understand that the reason why Lord Jellicoe could not take the initiative and keep it at Jutland is the same reason why the battleships at the Dardanelles could not attack the Turkish forts except while at anchor. The decision that sent the Grand Fleet hamstrung to its task, was the same decision that caused the initial failure of the Gallipoli adventure. The mystery of Jutland is not that there was an unforeseen factor that robbed us of victory. It was simply that a factor that was foreseen and provided for was not understood by those to whom the nation had entrusted its security. And finally, the villain of the piece is not the brave but unfortunate man who was forced into commanding a fleet unequipped to fight, but the whole group, of which indeed he was one, that held the Navy in pawn from 1905 till their final fiasco, and whose greatest triumph was the capture and enthralment of Mr Churchill himself.

The sincerity of Pollen's resentment of the injustice of Churchill's criticism is clearly brought out in a private letter, written six months earlier, dated 18th March, to fellow-historian Professor Spenser Wilkinson.

> I love your letter – the few of us who both can and do think sanely on public affairs, are right in cheering each other on when we get the chance, but I doubt if it does much good . . .
>
> Look at Churchill's book; he ends by jeering at Jellicoe for running away when, five pages before, he has shown triumphantly that it was to do this and nothing else – if the Germans refused an annihilating action – that he was chosen, equipped and instructed by the Admiralty. They knew he would not fight – unless the Germans accepted a knock-out – and they put him there for that and for no other reason. Those who said that the whole damned lot were wrong in the beginning, have a right to say that the whole damned lot were wrong at the end. But for one of the damned lot to pick out the man who had the least influence on their policy, and all the odium of being faithful to it, as a target for his sarcasm, well, it is a bit thick.

Looking back it is something of a shock to realise how consistently wrong Churchill had been at all his points of contact with Pollen. First in backing the wrong side in the 1913 gunnery dispute, later in his handling of the Dardanelles expedition and again in his first pronouncement in October 1916, on the consequences of Jutland. Yet, fundamentally, in his conception both of tactics and leadership, Pollen was far closer to Churchill than to Jellicoe. In 1927 it was only the injustice of the criticism voiced by Churchill, the politician turned historian, that brought Pollen to Jellicoe's defence. We have seen how in June 1915, Pollen had been quick to note and applaud the 'lofty moral bravery' of his fighting speech to his Dundee constituents following the collapse of his Dardanelles venture. Twenty years later, in what proved to be the present writer's last serious talk on these matters with his father, he epitomized his continuing faith in the Churchill potential in the phrase 'The greatest miss of the century'.

At this date in 1936 Churchill was fighting what appeared to be a losing battle for rearmament and, as regards naval warfare, the failure of the authorities to recognise the principles at stake had become a source of increasing anxiety to Pollen and his friends. This is well brought out in a letter from Richmond to Pollen written as late as the 11th November 1936. Pollen had written to Admiral Sir Herbert Richmond, as he had then become, to congratulate him on his appointment as Master of Downing College, Cambridge. In reply Richmond expressed the hope that it would give him time to produce 'something in the way of a book or books'. First, an outline of British Strategy from Elizabeth to 1918, and later 'if still time',

> I would like to add one more to the pestilential books on the war, for we really learned very little from it. Bacon's latest book on Jellicoe will now be read by the rising generation of sea officers who will learn from it that 'Safety First' is the Navy's slogan.
> It's damnable.

'It's damnable!' In those two words we see bursting out, twenty years after the battle, all the bitterness of feeling of those who, like Pollen, believed that the morale of the Service was being undermined and felt obliged, despite their hatred of all the publicity and of the 'pestilential' books to which it gave rise, to go on fighting.

By way of postscript to this commentary on the Navy's performance at Jutland, it is relevant to recall Arthur Pollen's long involvement both with its development prior to 1914, and later with its leaders during the war. There is a tendency among modern historians to discount his views on the grounds that in 1919, and indeed until the release some ten years ago of the relevant documents under the fifty-year rule, so little was known of the detail of the battle. In reality it is probably true to say that the Battle Orders which he was never privileged to see, were more true to form than he would ever have imagined; that the contrast between Jellicoe's defensive use of destroyers and Beatty's insistence that their primary duty was 'to pour in a long-ranged torpedo fire at the enemy's leading battleships' was spelt out more clearly than he would have thought possible.

As compared with the deprivation of these official documents what would today's historians not have given for Pollen's contacts with Jellicoe and Beatty? For, following his official visit as a naval journalist to both fleets on the eve of the battle, he received from Jellicoe within the ten days following the battle no less than three hand-written letters. Of the first of these, nothing is known except that Pollen was too good a friend to preserve a private note, written in a moment of weakness and despondency, and promptly destroyed it.

The second, dated the 4th June, gave a long account of the battle – 'His Battle Fleet turned away every time we got at him and disappeared in the mist. We slated them hard for the short time we got at them. . . . Our Battle-cruisers showed up their terribly weak point viz want of protection as compared with the Germans. The public should know how poorly they compare in this respect. Perhaps you will tell them . . .

'I am very unhappy about the fight. We should have finished them off without a doubt on a clear day even although there was only two hours of daylight left.' In the third letter he expresses regret that he cannot give Pollen any information for publication. 'I fully appreciate your object and know how much you have done to keep the head of the public straight. . . . I might easily lay myself open to the imputation, so often hurled at other senior officers, of using the press for my own ends, than which nothing could be more repugnant to me. . . . I thought your article excellent but it was of course incorrect as regards the Battle Fleet. My despatch will clear that up, but of course only a portion will be published. They /the Germans/ won't publish anything, you will see . . . but alas this country is not built that way.'

As regards Beatty, Pollen had the remarkable experience, despite his being at the time a working journalist, of being entrusted by him immediately after the battle with a frank statement, supported by a signed sketch, of his intentions at the most critical moment of the battle.

It is well-known that Beatty's loyalty to his Commander-in-Chief was such that to the end of his life he never said in public, or published, one word in criticism of his Chief's conduct of the battle. It may, therefore, well be asked why he should have entrusted to Pollen, a working journalist at the time, so confidential a statement. Yet there is an interesting parallel in the account given by Lord Chatfield in *The Navy and Defence* of how, early in 1917, while he was serving as Flag Captain, Beatty had sent for him to show him a letter in his own handwriting that he was sending to his bank, to be opened only in the event of his death, which conveyed to posterity the truth about our so called armour-piercing shell, which exploded on impact instead of first penetrating the enemy armour and bursting on the inside. 'If I am killed' he said to Chatfield, 'so also will you be, probably. This letter, if the Fleet ever fails to do all that is expected of it in action, will place the blame where it should lie and not on the shoulders of the officers and men of the Fleet when I am unable to defend them.'

In drawing his sketch for Pollen, Beatty would have been actuated by precisely the same motive. Although willing to keep silent, indefinitely if need be, as to what he regarded as his Commander-in-Chief's fatal choice of deployment, he was determined that the truth as to his own plan of battle should not die with him. Moreover, one can well imagine that he would have seen in Pollen the one man with the knowledge, the standing and the ability to tell the story effectively should occasion arise: or, alternatively, with the integrity to hold his peace should he himself survive the war.

The circumstances in which the sketch was drawn are explained in the following letter dated the 19th May 1936, written by Arthur Pollen to Admiral Sir Reginald Hall shortly after Beatty's death:

Put on your thinking cap and answer this conundrum! I have framed here a pencil sketch, signed 'D.B.' that Beatty made for me when I asked him exactly what he expected Jellicoe to do, explaining his going straight across the front of the Grand Fleet before deployment had begun. Beatty's answer was that Jellicoe had a definite battle formation and one only. His general orders were if the enemy were encountered to get to his station at the head of the battle line as rapidly as possible. On 31st May it seemed to him obvious that as his four battle-cruisers were in action, with their guns trained forward, the course he was steering was an obvious indication to Jellicoe that he was going to his battle station, and that that fact prescribed the deployment J.J. should have ordered to complete the picture. I then pointed out that Jellicoe's fleet, six ships abreast, pointed a long way ahead of the point to which he, D.B. was steering. He then drew the diagram showing how Jellicoe should have held back his right and advanced his left, he himself in the centre advancing at full speed so as to lead the battle-ship line in behind the battle-cruisers, the squadrons on his left following him, two right-hand squadrons circling and falling in behind them on the left. He said he could not believe his eyes when he was told that the battle fleet was deploying away from him. I asked him if I was at liberty to publish this. He said – 'Not while I am alive without my permission. When I am dead you can do as you like'. The fact that I have the signed plan is, of course, complete confirmation of my story.

Hall's reply read as follows:

I have really thought a good deal on the subject matter of your letter. My own feeling is that it would be a pity to waste such valuable ammunition at a single shot: remember that Bacon is writing Jellicoe's life and is pretty sure to have a fling at Beatty (vide his *Jutland Scandal*). Then, I think, would be the time to take up the cudgels. Many times at the I.D. I had good stuff which I kept many months before using, just to bide the proper moment, and I feel that your sketch and information comes under this head. The controversy is not actively alive today; when it revives, as of course it will, we could make an unanswerable case.

Pollen accepted Hall's advice, but, alas, died suddenly in the following January, with the result that the story was never made public.

The tactical technicalities of the argument, that is to say the rights and wrongs of the tactical manoeuvre here described, are beyond the scope of this personal biography; but if the reader will look back to Chapter X and to the plan facing p. 181 he will recall that of the three alternative methods of deployment open to Jellicoe, we dismissed deployment on the centre as being, in Jellicoe's judgement, too complicated a manoeuvre on which to embark in such close proximity to the enemy.

Against this it is well known that the Dewar brothers[3], generally regarded as spokesmen for the 'Battle-Cruiser' group, later argued that deployment on the centre would have been the correct answer, with the implication that this had been Beatty's intention. Modern historians tend to reject that view and to believe that that solution was only worked out by the Dewars long after the battle. To those who have always given Beatty credit for the bold plan, the sketch and Pollen's account will be welcome as unique and conclusive evidence in his favour. They will note, too, that in the Pollen-Hall exchange there is not one word in either letter to suggest that there was any novelty in the suggestion that this was Beatty's intention. In their circle it was common knowledge. Their interest in the sketch lay wholly in its value as 'ammunition' and in the fact that in Hall's words, properly used, the sketch would give *them* an unanswerable case.

To Pollen's biographer the story has the further fascination that it explains a major inaccuracy in the account that appears in *The Navy in Battle*; the inaccuracy that led Professor Marder to cite Pollen's account as evidence of how little was

THE BATTLE OF JUTLAND, MAY 31, 1916

The method of deployment on the centre
advocated by the Dewars
in the *Naval Staff Appreciation*[3]

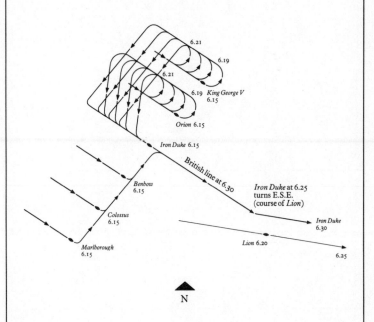

Based on Diagram 23 of the *Naval Staff Appreciation*

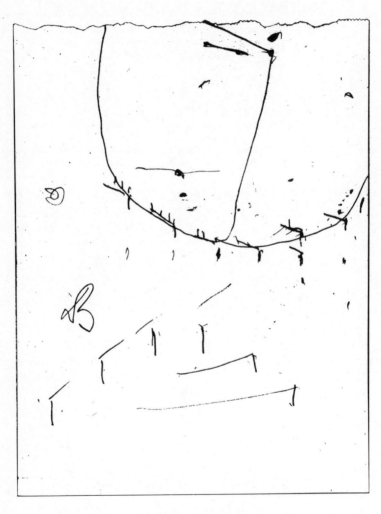

The Beatty Sketch

known of the battle at that time, and which led Professor Temple Patterson, Jellicoe's latest biographer to speak, less politely, of Pollen's 'ridiculous mistakes'. For the simple fact is that Beatty, when talking to Pollen, was under the impression that Jellicoe had deployed his fleet to the north east when, in reality, the course after deployment was South East.

As to the possibility of Beatty's being so mistaken, we must bear in mind Jellicoe's own evidence as to the conditions prevailing at the time. In the *Grand Fleet*, he tells us on page 344, that at 5.40 Dreyer had reported that 'the visibility appeared to be best to the southward'; on the following page we learn that 'shortly after 6 p.m.', 'owing to the mist, it was not possible to make out[4] the number of ships that were following the *Lion*.' At 6.15, the *King George V*, the nearest ship of the First Division, was approximately twice as far from the *Lion* as Jellicoe's *Iron Duke* and moreover due north in which direction the visibility was worst. From this it seems certain that Beatty and his observers would have been unable to see any ship in that division. All they would have known was that every battleship in sight was turning away to the north east.

Beatty's natural conclusion was that the Fleet was deploying to the North East and it is clear both from Pollen's letter to Hall, and from the diagrams, that their talk was based on that assumption. To the layman, Beatty's diagrams, here reproduced, are not easy to follow. To get their meaning we must first appreciate that they represent alternatives and not consecutive movements: secondly, that they are drawn without reference to the points of the compass but from the standpoint of the Commander-in-Chief whose fleet, still in cruising formation is moving up the paper in six columns of four battleships. The upper of the two diagrams with which we are here concerned depicts Jellicoe's actual deployment, *as it appeared to Beatty at the time*, the lower the deployment for which Beatty was hoping. In the former it will be seen that all six divisions are shown turning to port, implying that the whole Fleet was

THE BATTLE OF JUTLAND, MAY 31, 1916
Grand Fleet deployment at 6.15 p.m.

Diagram A

→——— Jellicoe's line of deployment

--------- Deployment expected by Beatty

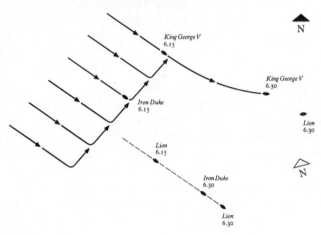

Diagram B

→——— Start of Jellicoe's deployment as seen by Beatty at 6.15 p.m.

--------- Track of Grand Fleet as depicted in *The Navy in Battle*

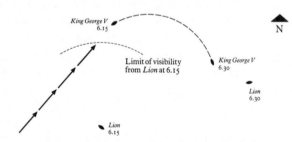

Allowance has been made for the fact that *The Navy in Battle* was written in the belief that the bearings given in the Despatches were true bearings whereas they were in fact magnetic, a difference of 13 degrees heading to the north east. In reality the First Division, which was not visible to Beatty held its course and led the Fleet to the south east.

To clarify the situation the reader is offered two conventional diagrams, in the first of which is shown Jellicoe's actual deployment together with the alternative expected by Beatty, and in the second Jellicoe's deployment as it appeared to Beatty, together with that depicted by Pollen in *The Navy in Battle*.

To Pollen, as a writer, it was a singular misfortune to have been given an inaccurate account, from such an unassailable source, the more so as it was given in the strictest confidence, so that it could only appear as his own unsupported conjecture. For the next eighteen months no fresh information was published but fortunately he knew that Jellicoe had returned to join Beatty by 6.35 and was therefore able to show the battleships in their correct position at that time in the sketch plan that appears in *The Navy in Battle*.

To anyone concerned about the significance of Beatty's sketch as evidence of his intention at the time, the error in the story given to Pollen is invaluable as proof of the date when the meeting took place. For it is inconceivable, if we bear in mind Beatty's serious purpose in giving Pollen the story, that he would deliberately have misled him or failed to make his meaning clear. The account that Pollen gave to Hall must therefore reflect Beatty's belief at the time; yet Beatty could not have remained under such a misapprehension on such a major point for more than a very few days. We are thus forced to the conclusion that the meeting could only have taken place during the weekend immediately following the battle, when it is known that Pollen was in Edinburgh, having dashed up on the Friday night to see his wounded brother.

Thus the sketch assumes a unique place in the history of the battle as the only firm evidence of the fact that deployment on the centre really was at the heart of Beatty's battle plan at Jutland, and not just a clever after-thought of his supporters.

To the present writer, it is a great pleasure to conclude this account of his father's contribution to Naval thought and to the achievements of the Royal Navy, by making known in discharge of the obligation imposed on his father by David Beatty, the message entrusted to him by the Admiral at the saddest moment of that great man's life.

EPILOGUE

On the conclusion of the war Arthur Pollen found himself at the age of fifty-two, with no visible means of support and two sons ready for Oxford. It was at about this time that he made the casual observation to the present writer that, while he had earned his living ever since he came down from Oxford, his principal source of income had never been the same for more than four years at a stretch. The war had killed his Argo business and now peace had brought to an end his brief but successful career as a journalist. Yet without any hint of anxiety he talked of the possibilities before him.

The owners of *Land and Water* who had so brilliantly weathered the change from peace to war in 1914, now lacked the initiative to find a new role in the post-war world. Pollen, in any case, saw no future in writing professionally, and realized that only by going back into business would he be able to live as he wished. He had kept his part-time directorship of Linotype; he had a short-term assignment to act for the Guaranty Trust of New York in Europe and in addition was shortly to be offered a seat on the Board of the Birmingham Small Arms Company. Among other activities, B.S.A. owned the Daimler Company and Pollen, as can be imagined, was full of ideas for the improvement and popularizing of Daimler cars. Unfortunately the Managing Director, Percy Martin, who with his wife became close friends, although a brilliant engineer, was altogether too conservative and complacent to be moved by Pollen's enthusiasms and the company never developed as it should have done.

Nevertheless he found much else to interest him among B.S.A.'s varied activities; in particular, his directorship gave him a place on the Council of the Federation of British Industries, where he was soon taking a prominent part in the great political and economic controversies of the day. The war and the unemployment that followed the short-lived boom of 1919, had proved a ready breeding ground for socialist doctrine and relations between management and labour were at a low ebb.

Prior to the war the case for private enterprise had never been properly stated. Characteristically, Pollen urged the need to take the initiative and attack, and deplored the negative approach implied in such titles as the Anti-Socialist or the Anti-Communist Associations.

Elected Chairman of the British Commonwealth Union and Vice-President of the F.B.I., it fell to him to co-ordinate the activities of the leading industrialists, both in and out of Parliament, in the preparation of a case in a form that would be understood and accepted by the public. His opening move was the preparation of a pamphlet, *The Vital Principle of Business*, in which he set out in simple everyday language the vital role of the entrepreneur, first in the choice and design of the product and secondly in risking his capital throughout the lengthy and expensive processes of development, manufacture and, most important of all, selling.

His next move was to tackle R. H. Tawney, the Balliol Don, the brains behind the Fabian Society's campaign and the archapostle of nationalization. His first approach, a letter dated the 12th April 1921, reveals a delicate balance of courtesy and thrust, and is a good example of his style in controversy:

> I am taking the liberty of sending you a report of a speech delivered by Sir Halliwell Rogers at the Annual Meeting of the Birmingham Small Arms Company on Monday last. My reason for sending it to you is that for two years I have had on my desk an article of yours that appeared in the Hibbert Journal

in 1919, which has interested me so greatly that I have referred to it again and again, and have often wished that I had both the courage and the ability to reply to it point by point. But the lack of both these qualifications, plus occupations so engrossing that I should have had no time even for the task for which I was unfitted, have prevented my attempting it.

The views put forward by Sir Halliwell Rogers seem to me both novel from an economic point of view, and certainly destructive of the case you set out so eloquently two years ago, and I cannot help hoping that next time you have occasion to write you will point out where, and how, Sir Halliwell is wrong, if after examining the speech his principles seem to you untenable.

Pollen, at the time, was a member of the Board and there can be little doubt that the passage in the Chairman's speech, of which he writes, was largely his own work.

By the end of the year, Pollen and Tawney were in active discussion, dining together at Brooks's and corresponding at length. It is interesting, and a tribute to the intellectual integrity of both men, that they should have continued their discussions for so long, on such a friendly basis, while remaining so far apart in their views. Pollen was sometimes accused of having been dictatorial and tactless in his dealings with the Admiralty, but his friendship and correspondence with Tawney is one of many examples of his patience and modesty when faced with intelligent argument. In reality it was only when opposed by stupidity and insincerity, as happened all too often at the Admiralty, that he at times gave way and allowed the sudden crushing retort to escape and mar the presentation of his case.

Behind the scenes, and unknown even to his closest friends, Pollen's long-drawn-out struggle to clear his reputation with the Admiralty and establish his Argo rights, remained, as ever, a constant preoccupation. In 1916, having gained Balfour's confidence, he had had hopes of winning from him at least a withdrawal of the unfair charges that had led to his being insulted and struck off the list of Admiralty contractors: in 1918 a very similar situation had arisen through his good relations with Geddes: in 1922 after Beatty had gone to the Admiralty he tried yet again, preferring a private settlement to a battle before the Royal Commission. But even Beatty had had to say, with obvious justification, that there was no-one at the Admiralty who could fairly be asked to sit in judgement on all that had happened since 1906. There remained no alternative but to take his claim to the Royal Commission, and by the end of the year we find him heavily engaged on the formidable task of assembling the evidence. In the end it was not until 1925 that the Commission made known its recommendation, and not until much later that he abandoned the struggle over its interpretation. All in all, the case remained a constant worry and occupied much of his time and thought from 1918 until well into 1929.

In 1926 at about the time when the Royal Commission case was drawing to a close, Pollen's old job as Managing Director of Linotype again fell vacant. In 1904 while remaining a Director, he had felt obliged to resign his executive position in order to concentrate on his naval work, and it was a great stroke of luck that it should again be offered to him at so opportune a moment some twenty years later. With characteristic enthusiasm he at once engaged the help of T. Gerald Rose, a pioneer in the role of consultant. Today the Management Consultant is a well-known and fashionable profession; in those days it was a novel idea and it is typical of Pollen's thorough and scientific approach to any new problem that he should have been one of the first industrialists in this country to appreciate and make use of this new breed of professional.

Pollen's success with Linotype led to his being invited four years later to reorganize B.S.A. as Chairman. Unfortunately it proved impossible to double the B.S.A. and Linotype jobs, and nothing came of the offer. In later years he accepted a number of other directorships but Linotype was the only one where he took control and was able to prove his undoubted talent for organization and management.

Appropriately enough, Pollen's last major undertaking was to assist in the revival of the *Tablet*, the leading Catholic weekly.

The *Tablet* had fallen into low water when, in 1936, a group of influential Catholic laymen got together to acquire control. By an inspired choice Douglas Woodruff, then a leader-writer on *The Times*, and still in his thirties, was appointed editor and Arthur Pollen chairman. Despite the difference in age, the partnership was an outstanding success. Pollen's prestige and experience gave Woodruff precisely the support that he needed, and the paper made rapid progress.

After his death, less than a year later, Douglas Woodruff in a leading article in his paper paid eloquent tribute to the quality of his mind and the breadth of his interests.

If the essence of civilized living is the power to discriminate, to appreciate fine distinctions over a wide field, no man met the test better. His intellectual and aesthetic interests were extremely widespread, and he brought his judgement and taste to all the finer points in the arts of living. It was not accidental, but of his very nature, that he was a first-rate host, and his conversation was the conversation of a man who could not only talk from a full mind, but who appreciated in others, and had perfected in himself, the art of talking, of conveying new impressions and ideas, in an easy and friendly way which concealed a feeling for the essential forms of spoken sentences and a classic presentation. It is characteristic that the last piece of writing which he had hoped to do for the *Tablet* was a study of the art of public speaking. It remained unfinished, and writing, indeed, had ceased to be the easy thing it once had been, but it had been his intention to trace the needless eclipse of standards of oratory. In field after field his acute eye had noted through a lifetime the gradual, and latterly the rapid, decline in English civilization, in its standards and in the power of critical appraisement. But while in so many ways he belonged naturally to an earlier day, to the day when the life of clubs and the meetings of learned men held a more central place, there was another side to him: the inventor, restless, looking to the future, eager to experiment, to reform, to sweep away. The American company which made him for so long its representative in London showed much discernment, for he blended in a unique way a feeling for the past and for the future.

In the presentation of the story of the great controversies in which Arthur Pollen became involved, both as inventor and as writer, the qualities that came to the fore were, inevitably, the fighting qualities: the uncompromising clarity of his thinking, his powers of advocacy, his tenacity and self-confidence. Douglas Woodruff's study has shown us something of the finer qualities of his mind and of his intellectual and aesthetic sensitivity. Yet to the present writer, the characteristic that he associates most vividly with his father was the invariable gaiety and good spirits with which he greeted and entertained his family and his friends.

We see it reflected in his correspondence; whether writing to Claude Phillips to report that following the removal of his appendix he is once again 'as fit as a Stradivarius', or sending an instruction to a colleague on an everyday affair, the buoyancy of spirit is always peeping through. For example, to Gerald Rose, his adviser on management methods at Linotype, he wrote in October 1936, barely three months before his death.

> Thank you for the suggestion about *The Times* letter. Why should we not continue our old parts, you doing all the work and I getting all the credit? The play, after all, has a very simple plot, or I suppose I should say graph, so write a letter bringing in all the points and I will abbreviate and polish and boldly claim authorship.

To complete the picture, let us turn to the human and personal message contributed by Lord Russell of Killowen. As befits an old friend of sixty years' standing, and a judge, he speaks directly of Arthur Pollen, the man:

> Worldly-wise, and stocked with knowledge on unsuspected subjects, he was ever ready to help with sound advice. A model host, an entertaining talker, stating his views with a confidence almost dogmatic, but willing also to listen, though critically, to the differing views of others. He was, I think, most charming in his contacts with young people. No dogmatism then; but a sympathetic attitude, amounting almost to deference. A handsome

member of a handsome family, I can see him now on the Walton Heath golf links, striding along the fairway, looking every inch a conqueror even in the moment of defeat. For he played his games as he lived his life; taking any buffets of misfortune with philosophic calm, but looking to the future with his head held high, and his heart full of hope.

APPENDIX

THE ROYAL COMMISSION ON AWARDS TO INVENTORS

CLAIM OF THE ARGO CO. LTD. and
ARTHUR HUNGERFORD POLLEN
IN RESPECT OF A SYSTEM OF
NAVAL FIRE CONTROL

CLAIM OF REAR ADMIRAL
FREDERIC CHARLES DREYER
IN RESPECT OF
THE DREYER FIRE CONTROL TABLES

CLAIM OF MAJOR R. G. F. DUMARESQ
IN RESPECT OF
THE DUMARESQ RATE OF CHANGE INDICATOR.

RECOMMENDATION

These three claims have been heard together and may be considered in the reverse order to that in which they are mentioned above.

I. Major Dumaresq's Claim

This claim is by the legal personal representative of the late Admiral Dumaresq and can be disposed of shortly. In 1902 Admiral Dumaresq invented an instrument of admitted utility relating to the obtaining of ranges and bearings and calculating the rates of change. The instrument has been in use in the Navy more or less since its invention.

In 1913 the Admiral received from the Admiralty an award of £1,500 in respect of it. He died in 1922 without having made any further claim. We are of opinion that this case is covered by the principle laid down by the Commission with reference to stale claims and that a claim for a further award cannot be entertained.

II. Rear Admiral Dreyer's Claim

This claim is for a mechanism called the Dreyer Table, the latest developments of which are known as Marks IV and V. It has been adopted by the Admiralty and is used in connexion with the Admiralty System of Fire Control. It has original features of considerable merit, the credit for which is due to Admiral Dreyer, even if in other respects it owes inspiration to other sources, or is the application of common knowledge. Having regard however, to the position and status of Admiral Dreyer and to the fact that he received from the Admiralty in 1916 an award of £5,000 in respect of it, we do not think proper to recommend any further award to him.

III. Argo Co. Ltd. and Mr Pollen's Claim

This claim falls into two parts.

First a claim in respect of a system of Naval Fire Control alleged to have been invented by Mr Pollen, and to have been used by the Admiralty and,

Secondly a claim in respect of an integrating machine and other elements which, or the principle of which, is alleged to be substantially reproduced in the Clock mechanism and other elements of the Dreyer Table. Both claims are made under Head 3 of the Royal Warrant though there exist secret patents in respect of the integrating machine which have been assigned to the Admiralty.

The first part of the claim (which on this occasion was

reheard at the special request of the Lords Commissioners of His Majesty's Treasury) is for a method of making observations and using for the purposes of naval fire control the data obtained from such observations. We are satisfied that the essential features of the method which Mr Pollen advocated were in his own view as follows:

(1) A method of taking or using observations of bearings corrected gyroscopically.
(2) Automatic transmission of data to plotting table.
(3) Speed and course plotting, and
(4) The use of an integrating machine of a special kind.

We are of opinion that this so called method or system claimed (as it is claimed) apart from any special mechanism for operating it cannot be regarded as an invention, design or process within the meaning of Head 3 of the Royal Warrant. Further, even if it could be so regarded we find that by reason of substantial differences in essential features, it is not the method employed by the Admiralty.

It may be observed that in 1908 Mr Pollen indicated the value which he put upon this method or system regarded apart from any particular mechanical devices employed in carrying it into effect and that though the Admiralty declined the method or system they paid to Mr Pollen, and he accepted a substantial sum (£11,500) not very far short of his estimate of the value of the system for his undoubted services in the matter.

After 1908 the Admiralty developed a system with another method of plotting, which Mr Pollen then regarded we think rightly as something different from the method or system which he himself advocated. We do not think the view he now presents is consistent with his earlier view or can be supported.

We think, therefore, the first part of the claim fails although in coming to that conclusion we do not omit to recognise that Mr Pollen's activities, were of great value to the Admiralty and the Country.

As to the second part of the claim we are satisfied that Mr Pollen and the Argo Co. Ltd. were the first to produce a mechanical integrator of the kind hereinbefore referred to, namely the Argo Clock, and that the clock mechanism of the Dreyer Tables Marks IV and V works substantially on the same principles although there are differences of mechanical detail.

Further we are satisfied upon the facts that the principle and details of the Argo Clock were communicated to the Admiralty and to those who were at work on the Dreyer Tables and directly contributed to the evolution of the clock mechanism of the Dreyer Tables Marks IV and V. The knowledge so acquired made plain the feasibility of converting the clock mechanism of the earlier types of Dreyer Table into a form which served the same function and was based upon the same principle as the Argo Clock and while we acquit all concerned of any intention or desire to copy or take unacknowledged the benefit of the claimants' work (and any suggestion of the kind was disclaimed at the hearing) we think it impossible to question the influence of that work upon the ultimate result.

There are also other elements in the Dreyer Tables which in our judgement owe their origin to communications by Mr Pollen to the Admiralty.

In our view upon the principles which have been applied hitherto by the Commission an award can properly be made to the Argo Co. Ltd. and Mr Pollen under this head of their claim.

We recommend that the amount of the award should be the sum of £30,000 (thirty thousand pounds) this sum to be in addition to the sums already paid to the claimants by the Admiralty and to be accepted in full satisfaction of all claims in respect of all user past, present or future by His Majesty's Government of the principles, details and elements in the Dreyer Tables or any future modification thereof which owe their origin to communications by the Claimants or either of them and whether the same or any of them are covered by Letters Patent or not.

30 October 1925   Signed T. J. C. TOMLIN
                                              Chairman

PRINCIPAL OFFICE HOLDERS
1900 – 1914

First Lord

Earl of Selborne	Nov. 1900 – March 1905
Earl Cawdor	March 1905 – Dec. 1905
Lord Tweedmouth	Dec. 1905 – April 1908
Reginald McKenna	April 1908 – Oct. 1911
Winston Churchill	Oct. 1911 – May 1915

First Sea Lord

Admiral Lord Walter Kerr	Sept. 1899 – Oct. 1904
Admiral Sir John Fisher	Oct. 1904 – Jan. 1910
Admiral of the Fleet Sir A. K. Wilson	Jan. 1910 – May 1911
Admiral Sir Francis Bridgeman	May 1911 – Dec. 1912
Admiral HSH Prince Louis of Battenberg	Dec. 1912 – Oct. 1914
Admiral of the Fleet Lord Fisher of Kilverstone	Oct. 1914 – May 1915

Third Sea Lord and Controller

Rear-Admiral A. K. Wilson	Aug. 1897 – April 1901
Rear-Admiral W. H. May	April 1901 – Feb. 1905
Captain H. B. Jackson	Feb. 1905 – Oct. 1908
Rear-Admiral Sir John Jellicoe	Oct. 1908 – Dec. 1910
Rear-Admiral C. J. Briggs	Dec. 1910 – May 1912

Rear-Admiral Sir Archibald
  Moore — May 1912 – Aug. 1914

Director of Naval Ordnance

Rear-Admiral E. F. Jeffreys	Sept. 1897 – Feb. 1901
Rear-Admiral W. H. May	Feb. 1901 – March 1901
Rear-Admiral Angus MacLeod	March 1901 – Oct. 1903
Captain H. D. Barry	Oct. 1903 – Feb. 1905
Captain J. R. Jellicoe	Feb. 1905 – Aug. 1907
Captain R. H. S. Bacon	Aug. 1907 – Nov. 1909
Captain A. G. H. W. Moore	Dec. 1909 – May 1912
Captain F. C. T. Tudor	June 1912 – Aug. 1914

Director of Naval Intelligence

Rear-Admiral Reginald N. Custance	Mar. 1899 – Dec. 1902
Captain HSH Prince Louis of Battenberg	Dec. 1902 – Feb. 1905
Captain Charles L. Ottley	Feb. 1905 – Nov. 1907
Captain Herbert G. King-Hall	Nov. 1907 – Dec. 1907
Captain Edmond J. W. Slade	Dec. 1907 – April 1909
Rear-Admiral Hon. A. E. Bethell	April 1909 – Feb. 1912
Captain Thomas Jackson	Feb. 1912 – Dec. 1913
Rear-Admiral H. F. Oliver	Dec. 1913 – Nov. 1914
Captain W. R. Hall	Nov. 1914 – Feb. 1919

Inspector of Target Practice

Rear-Admiral Sir Percy Scott	March 1905 – July 1907
Captain F. T. Hamilton	July 1907 – Feb. 1909
Rear-Admiral Sir Richard Peirse	Feb. 1909 – Jan. 1911
Captain Montague Browning	Jan. 1911 – mid-1913 when office abolished

NOTES

CHAPTER I
Note

1 p.19   Later Sir Joseph Lawrence. Born 1848.
Sheriff of City of London 1900/1901.
Represented Monmouth Boroughs as Conservative 1901-1906. A dedicated supporter of Joseph Chamberlain and Tariff Reform, he played an active part in holding the Conservative Party together after the rout of 1906 and again, in 1917, as the central figure in defeating an attempt by the abortive National Party to absorb the Tariff Reform League. Created Knight Bachelor in 1902 his name appeared in the New Years Honours List for 1918 among the recipients of a Baronetcy but he died in 1919 before the formalities necessary for enrolment had been completed.

2 p.20   Later Admiral Sir William Goodenough, G.C.B., M.V.O.; Professor Marder wrote of him, at Jutland,
'With intelligent and almost unique understanding of his duties as a Scouting Commander, he held on with great gallantry closing with the enemy's Battle Fleet in order to get the information he wanted about the speed, course and composition of the enemy force'.

3 p.22   Pollen addressed himself to Lord Walter Kerr the First Sea Lord on the 26th January 1901, to Lord Selborne the First Lord on the 4th February 1901, and to the Secretary of the Admiralty on the 25th February 1901.

4 p.26   Pollen called his system A.C., for Aim Correction, perhaps deliberately understating his objective.

CHAPTER II
Note

1 p.32   In his letter to Lord Walter Kerr in January 1901 Pollen spoke of 20,000 yards. In his memorandum of August 1904 he proposed to start plotting at 17,000 yards. In 1912 his instruments

were calibrated to 16,000 yards. In contrast, Jellicoe records in *The Grand Fleet* (p.38) that 'in pre-war days our Battle Practice had been carried out at a maximum range of about 9,500 yards, and only on one occasion when the *Colossus* fired at a target at 14,000 yards off Portland in 1912, had this range been exceeded.'

2 p.35   These inventions were based on the application of the technique of the ball, disc and cylinder differential integrator, invented by Kelvin's brother James Thomson and described by him in the *Proceedings of the Royal Society* in 1876.

3 p.35   In addition to Admiral Parr, the Commission was composed of Captain Oliver R.N., Cdr. Thomas Crease R.N., Captain E. W. Harding R.M.A., representing the Admiralty and Captain Locke, representing the Artillery.

4 p.36   The Service (Whitehead) gyro ran only for two or three minutes: furthermore it lacked the power to control the transmission of corrected bearings. During experiments conducted in the *Jupiter* it performed well enough during its brief working moments to impress the Commission with the potential of a continuous running instrument. The Argo continuous running gyro was designed in 1906, perfected in 1908 and 45 were delivered and paid for during the years 1910, 1911 and 1912.

     In 1911 Pollen learnt that a German of the name of Anschutz had produced one which not only ran continuously but was also an automatic North seeker and therefore available as a compass. He at once suggested to the Admiralty that the balance of the rangefinder mountings due for delivery should be supplied with Anschutz receivers in all ships in which the Anschutz compass was installed, and the Argo gyro dropped altogether. His action in doing so was consistent with his contention that his system was something far more important, and independent of, any individual instrument. (See brief prepared by Pollen for his Counsel in 1924. Part II p.34A)

5 p.42   *Fear God and Dread Nought*, Arthur J. Marder 1904-14 pp 87-88.

6 p.42   The Secretary of the Admiralty to Pollen, 21 Sept. 1906.

7 p.43   Captain Harding wrote under the name of Rapidan, notably *The Tactical Employment of Naval Artillery* published in 1903. He was also one of the small group of officers who founded the Naval Review in 1912.

8 p.45   Later Lord Greene, O.B.E., M.C., Master of the Rolls.

9 p.45   For particulars of the authorities consulted see A.H.P. brief for Counsel (1924). Part II p.22.

CHAPTER III
Note

1 p.47   Ruddock F. Mackay *Fisher of Kilverstone*.

2 p.49   Sir Winston Churchill *World Crisis*, Vol.I 1911-14 pp 73-4.

3 p.52   *Fear God and Dread Nought*, A. J. Marder 1904-14 p.351.

4 p.52   Sir Winston Churchill, *World Crisis* 1911-14, p.77.

5 p.53   Lord Fisher's *Memories* pp.246-7.

6 p.53   Sir Winston Churchill *World Crisis* 1911-14 p.92.

7 p.54   Pollen to Admiral Sir Edmund Slade 24 Jan. 1910.

8 p.60   *The Life of William Thomson, Baron Kelvin* by Sylvanus P. Thompson II, pp.734, 735.

9 p.61   *Fear God and Dread Nought*, A. J. Marder 1914-20 p.56 *note*.

10 p.62   *Fear God and Dread Nought*, A. J. Marder 1904-14 p.241 *note* 1.

11 p.62   Ibid. *note* 2.

12 p.63   Lieutenant George Gipps, Gunnery Officer in the *Ariadne*. In 1911 he was officially seconded to work with Pollen.

CHAPTER IV
Note

1 p.66   The Watkins two observer system had been in use for many years by sea forts as a position finder. In 1892 it was tried in the *Arethusa* as a means of finding ranges. When accused by Dreyer in 1908 of plagiarising Watkins Pollen retorted that he had in fact never even heard of it and knew nothing about it except that it was still, in 1908, a secret patent. In any event good ideas were of no more value than good intentions if not given practical form. As a means of finding ranges between two moving ships the Watkins System had failed and long since been abandoned before he started to develop A.C.

2 p.67   Hugh Clausen,the Senior Principal Scientific Officer who served on the Admiralty Fire Control Committee in the 1920's, explained to the author in 1970, that in the Royal Navy the term Clock was used for an integrator which did not embody the plotting function and the term Table if it did embody plotting.

3 p.72   '*Polyanthropy*'. In a letter to the D.N.O., Captain Bacon, dated 27 February 1908 Arthur Pollen informed him that Dreyer's competing method of reading off the information from the rangefinders and compasses, passing it orally, and plotting it manually, required nine men. Under the Pollen system which provided mechanisms for recording and plotting the information, one supervisor could produce the plot. This feature of

the Dreyer system was characterized by Pollen' as 'polyan-thropic'.

4 p.74   Pollen to Spender 12 April 1910.

5 p.75   In a letter dated 13 April 1910 to J. A. Spender, the Editor of the *Westminster Gazette*, Pollen spoke of Ogilvy having been designated by Lord Fisher as the next Captain of the *Excellent*.

6 p.78   In a letter dated 14 May 1973, the late Vice-Admiral Sir Francis Pridham, K.B.E., C.B., who had served in the *Natal* as assistant to Lieut. (later Admiral Sir William) James wrote to the present writer to say what a splendid team they had had in the *Natal* and recalled that 'out of the goodness of his heart, your father brought on board a special gift of oysters for Ogilvy. Alas one or two held typhoid germs. Ogilvy died in December and the torpedo lieutenant, Riley, was also stricken and remained a crock for the rest of his life.'

7 p.80   The names appear on a fragment, apparently prepared in 1924 for the use of Counsel, before the Royal Commission.

CHAPTER V
Note

1 p.82   See Admiral Colville's report to C-in-C Home Fleet 1 July 1910 Drax papers, Churchill College Cambridge.

2 p.82   Among the Pollen papers there is a copy of Plunkett's informal letter of 28 June to W.W. Fisher, frankly recording the history of A.C., also a copy of his formal report of 4 July 1910 on the trials.

3 p.84   The Argo Clock Mark I was that tried in the *Natal*. The first helm-free clock, for which designs were submitted in May 1911, was designated Mark II. Later, slightly modified, it was designated Mark IV and supplied to the *Orion* for trial in July 1912. On 26 October 1912 five further Mark IV Clocks were ordered. There are no records of the Mark III Clock. The Mark V in which a gyro was embodied, in addition to that in the plotter, was supplied only to the Russians. In December 1914 Pollen submitted to the Admiralty a plan for the bombardment of Heligoland by night, on the basis of observations taken and markers placed, by day, which in his belief could have been successfully undertaken with the Mark V. This plan, he later stated, never got past Admiral Wilson. See also Pollen to Churchill 8 November 1923, quoted in full on page 171.

4 p.85   In 1922 or thereabouts, when Pollen was seeking to have his claim settled out of Court, Hall, in a long personal letter to Beatty the First Sea Lord, paid high tribute to Pollen's pre-war

contribution to gunnery and also to his constructive and public-spirited work as naval correspondent during the war. An undated draft of that letter survives among the Pollen papers.

5 p.85   Ibid.

6 p.86   Draft letter, much amended, dated 23 August 1912.

7 p.86   Memorandum dated 6 December 1912.

8 p.88   Peirse to Pollen 25 August 1912.

9 p.89   Peirse to Prince Louis 7 Sept. 1917. Battenberg Papers.

10 p.92   See also Pollen to Beatty 28 June 1920. 'In battle practice, the *Orion* going full speed under large helm did what had hitherto been regarded as an absolute impossibility, firing salvo after salvo making hits every time.'
Pollen also recorded that Percy Scott on being told of the *Orion*'s performance commented that it was 'either a lie or a miracle.'

11 p.93   Pollen to Peirse 20 September 1912.

12 p.93   The story of the Pollen-Cooke rangefinder will be further discussed in Chapter XI.

13 p.95   Jellicoe to Pollen 14 November 1912.

14 p.95   Stephen Pollen, known to his friends as Peter, had served from 1890-99 as A.D.C. to two Viceroys in India, first to the Marquess of Lansdowne and next to the Earl of Elgin. In 1914 he rejoined the Army and served as Military Secretary to General Sir Ian Hamilton, throughout the Gallipoli campaign and later as Military Secretary to the C-in-C British Forces in Egypt, until July 1917.

15 p.99   Admiral Mark Kerr, although not among the reformers with whom Pollen worked, had other claims to distinction. While serving as C-in-C of the Greek Navy (1913-15) he took the Royal Aero Club's Pilots Certificate on a Sopwith Seaplane, and in 1914 made the longest sea flight on record, from Phaleros to Paros Island. On 10 October 1917, he submitted the memorandum which, so he claimed, persuaded the Cabinet to form the R.A.F., and later served as Deputy Chief of Air Staff with the rank of Major-General Air Force. Finally *Who Was Who* carries the laconic entry, 'Attempted Atlantic Flight 1919'.

16 p.102   Pollen to Scott, 19 November 1912.

CHAPTER VI
Note

1 p.106   'Financial Secretary' was a Political not a Permanent appointment.

2 p.107 Churchill to Walter 24 March 1913.

3 p.107 Pretyman to Pollen 5 February 1913.

4 p.108 Pollen to Peirse 14 January 1914.

5 p.108 Later Sir James E. Masterton-Smith (1878-1938), Private Secretary, successively, to McKenna, Churchill, Balfour, Carson and Geddes as First Lords 1910-17 and later Permanent Under-Secretary of State for the Colonies 1921-24.

6 p.109 See 'Admiralty and the Pollen System' Times 24 June 1913, and 'Naval and Military Intelligence: The Firing of the *Orion*' Times 27 June 1913. Also Churchill reply to question in the House of Commons below.

7 p.113 Pollen to Spender 22 April 1910.

8 p.113 Pollen to Hall 15 January 1914.

9 p.113 Pollen to Peirse 14 January 1914.

10 p.114 Battenberg Papers DS/MISC/20,174 microfilm copy in The Imperial War Museum. Among them are 'Extract from 3rd Lord's Minute dated 13.8.12, a letter from Peirse to Prince Louis dated 7 September 1912 and a letter from Admiral A. G. H. Moore, the Controller, to Prince Louis, dated 19.9.12.

11 p.115 Taken from Third Lord's Minute referred to in Note 10.

12 p.118 Copies of the three memoranda prepared for his supporters are in the Pollen files but not individually identified.

13 p.121 Marder, *Fear God and Dread Nought*, 1904-14, p.439.

14 p.125 Pages 34-35 of the Report.

15 p.126 Ibid. pages 61/62.

CHAPTER VII
Note

1 p.136 Proceedings on 6 August 1925 p.104.

2 p.142 See also Chapter XI p.

CHAPTER VIII
Note

1 p.147 Pollen to Spender 24 August 1914.

2 p.147 From Hall's (draft) letter to Beatty 1922.

3 p.149 *Jellicoe Papers* Vol II p.42 footnote 1 and p.192 footnote 1.

4 p.151 From Hall's (draft) letter to Beatty.

5 p.151 Jellicoe to Pollen 4 June 1916.

6 p.153 The Rev. Anthony H. Pollen of the Birmingham Oratory who, at the age of 62, was awarded the D.S.C. for the rescue of two

seamen from a fire in one of the 6″ batteries in the battleship *Warspite* at Jutland. See Stephen Roskill's *H.M.S. Warspite* (Collins 1957).

CHAPTER IX
Note

1 p.161　The October issue of the *London Magazine* had appeared on the 24th September.

2 p.165　Admiral Lord Charles Beresford K.C.B., G.C.V.O., was the second son of the Marquess of Waterford. He retired in 1911, and sat as Member of Parliament for Portsmouth from 1910 to 1916 when he was created a Baron and took the title of Lord Beresford.

3 p.165　*Land and Water*, 30 November 1916.

CHAPTER X
Note

1 p.169　Richmond to Pollen 7 August 1916.

2 p.170　Beatty to Pollen 10 August 1916.

3 p.174　The wording in the text is an oversimplification. To be precise the Service System was incapable of dealing with rapid variation in the rate of change of range and also far too slow in operation to deal effectively with a high rate of change even when the rate was constant.

4 p.176　A. J. Marder *From the Dreadnought to Scapa Flow* III p.58 N. J. M. Campbell's estimate for both figures is slightly higher.

5 p.187　*Jutland and the Unforeseen* in *The Nineteenth Century* August 1927.

6 p.189　Fisher. *Records* p.144.

CHAPTER XI
Note

1 p.190　n.d. but acknowledged by A.H.P. to Tobey 13 Feb 1917.

2 p.191　The figures for rate of hitting could be calculated more accurately today but the difference would not be sufficient to invalidate Pollen's argument.

3 p.195　Public Record Office. A.D.M. 186/241.

4 p.196　The interim and the final reports were all bound together in the document circulated on 5 Sept. 1919.

5 p.202　It appears from p.33 of Great Britain, Admiralty, Technical History Section, *Fire Control in H.M. Ships.* Series: *The Technical History and Index: A Serial History of Technical*

Problems Dealt with by Admiralty Departments, part 23 (December, 1919) Naval Library, that the order for thirty instruments was not placed until March 1918 and that after the Armistice the Admiralty was 'able to cancel' the order for twenty out of the thirty.

CHAPTER XII
Note

1 p.212   See Stephen Roskill, *Hankey, Man of Secrets* p.382 Lt. Col. Maurice Hankey (later 1st Baron Hankey) served during the war successively as Secretary to the Committee of Imperial Defence (C.I.D.), and Secretary to the War Cabinet (1916 onwards).

2 p.213   See A. J. Marder *From the Dreadnought to Scapa Flow* IV p.180 a Memorandum by Beatty, written in July 1917, outlining his very severe criticisms of the Admiralty.

3 p.214   This remained true until the publication in June 1979 of Jon Sumida's article in the *Journal of Modern History*. Chicago.

4 p.214   The editor of the *Star* quoted above.

5 p.220   Pollen had seen Reading on 1 November and had been asked to submit his views in writing. The report took the form of a 12-page letter to Col. Arthur Murray, assistant to the Naval attache in Washington, dated 10 November 1917.

6 p.223   Captain Gaunt R.N., Naval Attache in Washington.

CHAPTER XIII
Note

1 p.229   Richmond to Pollen 4 August 1927.

2 p.230   *The Life and Letters of David Beatty*, by W. S. Chalmers 1951.

3 p.238   Captain A.C. and R.Ad. K. G. B. Dewar were both gold medallists and both highly competent officers. Both, in particular Kenneth, were too critical of the Establishment to endear themselves to their colleagues. In 1920 they were invited by Beatty, the First Sea Lord, to write a 'purely factual account' of the Battle of Jutland. Their report entitled *Naval Staff Appreciation* was subsequently suppressed as too critical of Jellicoe for publication and replaced by *The Narrative of the Battle of Jutland*.

4 p.241   See also *Grand Fleet* p.328 footnote. 'I was not aware of the loss of the *Queen Mary* and the *Indefatigable* until the morning of June 1st.'

INDEX

Note: Ranks shown are generally the highest attained

writing, 19; marriage, 19; with Linotype, 19, 21, 35, 37, 60, 248, 250; sees naval gunnery trials, 20, 30; dedication to naval gunnery, 21-2, 25-6; relations with Admiralty, 24, 27, 57, 64, 68-9, 75, 247; on effect of AC system on naval warfare, 26-7, 39, 123-4, 183, 187-8; opposition to, 28-9; on naval range-finding, 30-35; and 1905 instrument trials, 37-8; negotiates monopoly terms with Admiralty, 39-44, 69, 71, 74, 86-7, 91, 97, 115; 1906 contract agreement, 42-4, 53-4, 64; claims right to award before Royal Commission, 45, 130-39, 144-5, 214, 247-8, 252-5; supported by Service gunnery experts, 45-6, 79-81, 105, 122, 169; on Fisher, 47-9, 51; gratitude to Beresford, 50; competition with Dreyer, 55; Wilson rejects system, 57-9, 64; Fisher declines to meet, 61; Dreyer attacks, 66; Dreyer plagiarises, 67; favours true-plot, 67; and Isherwood, 67-8; Admiralty pays settlement to, 69; re-submits system to Admiralty, 69-70; and *Natal* trials, 71-2, 79; 1909 Admiralty contract, 74, 78; buys Thomas Cooke and Sons, 78; and selling abroad, 78, 89; financial commitments, 78-9; and 1910 *Natal* trials, 82-3; system rejected by Admiralty, 83; and development of Clock, 84-7, 94-5; seeks support, 88-9; letter to Churchill, 90-92, 174, 176; and Argo Clock tender, 95-6; writes to Battenberg, 97-9, 103; and night fire control, 98; on Battenberg and war, 100; relations with

Scott, 100, 102-3; accepts rejection by Admiralty, 103; end of monopoly contract with Admiralty, 105; and dispute over secrecy of patents, 107-9, 116, 131-2; name raised in Commons and *Times*, 109-13; and AC system abroad, 113-14, 128-9; Moore's arguments against, 115-21; and reaction to war, 130, 146; learns of plagiarising of Clock, 136; correspondence with Admiralty on Royal Commission findings, 141-2; submission to Royal Commission on helm-free plotting, 143-4; voluntary war offer, 146; as wartime naval journalist, 147-9, 203, 217; lectures, 148-9; on Jutland, 149, 152-7, 161, 167, 231-42; defends Churchill, 158; argues against Churchill's wartime naval policy, 160-66; welcomes Jellicoe as First Sea Lord, 168; re-submits system to Jellicoe, 169-70; challenges Churchill on Dardanelles, 171-4; proposes Heligoland bombardment, 173, 261n3; on torpedo menace, 188-9; US interest in system, 190-94; visits USA, 193, 213, 215-17, 220-24; and high-speed course changes, 196; Pollen-Cooke rangefinder, 197-202; on shipping losses and convoy, 203-4; critical campaign against Admiralty administration, 204-10, 213-15; on US naval strength, 218-19; declines knighthood, 223-4; censored, 225; strategic aims and ideas, 226-9; post-war writings, 230-31 and post-war rearmament, 234; Beatty confides Jutland sketch to, 236-7, 242-4;